1

2

WILLIAM CULLEN BRYANT

COMPLETE POETICAL WORKS

The Library of Early
American Literature

William Cullen Bryant (1794-1878)

The Library of Early American Literature
William Thomas Sherman, series editor
1604 NW 70th St.
Seattle, WA 98117
wts@gunjones.com

NOTE ON THE TEXT.

Text taken from 1876 edition of *POETICAL WORKS William Cullen Bryant, Collected and Arranged by the Author.*

Footnotes and endnotes are presented here using the modern numbering approach, rather than the formal and more inconspicuous end-notes Bryant utilizes, in order to take advantage of word processing and Kindle formats and technologies.

TABLE OF CONTENTS

10

THIS edition contains several of the author's poems which have not appeared in any previous collection. These, as well as the others in the volume, have been made to follow each other in the order in which they were written, the author deeming this arrangement to be quite as satisfactory to the reader as any classification founded on the nature of the subjects or their mode of treatment.

New York, *August,* 1876.

~~~~~******~~~~~

WILLIAM CULLEN BRYANT [Introductory Biography]

THE ancestry of William Cullen Bryant might have been inferred from the character of his writings, which reflect whatever is best and noblest in the life and thought of New England. It was a tradition that the first Bryant of whom there is any account in the annals of the New World came over in the Mayflower, but the tradition is not authenticated. What is known of this gentleman, Mr. Stephen Bryant, is that he came over from England, and that he was at Plymouth, Mass., as early as 1632. He married Abigail Shaw, who had emigrated with her father, and who bore him several children between 1650 and 1665, it is to be presumed at Plymouth, of which town he was chosen constable in 1663. Stephen Bryant had a son named Ichabod, who was the father of Philip Bryant, who was born in 1732.Philip Bryant married Silence Howard, the daughter of Dr. Abiel Howard, of West Bridgewater, whose profession he adopted, being a practitioner in medicine in North Bridgewater. He was the father of nine children, one of whom, Peter Bryant, born in 1767, succeeded him in his profession. Young Dr. Bryant became enamored of Miss Sarah Snell, the daughter of Mr. Ebenezer Snell, of Bridgewater, who removed his family to Cummington, whither he was followed by his future son-in-law, who married the lady of his love in1792. Two years later, on the 3d of November, there was born to him a man-child, who was to win, and to leave,

> "One of the few immortal names
> That were not born to die."

Dr. Bryant was proud of his profession; and in the hope, no doubt, that his son would become a shining light therein, he perpetuated at his christening the name of a great medical authority who had departed this life four years before—William Cullen. Dr. Bryant was the last of his family to practise the healing art, for Nature, wiser than he, early determined the future course of Master William Cullen Bryant. He was not to be a doctor, but a poet. A poet, that is, if he lived to be anything; for the chances were against his living at all. The lad was exceedingly frail, and had a head the immensity of which troubled his anxious father. How to reduce it to the normal size was a puzzle which Dr. Bryant solved in a spring of clear, cold water, which burst out of the ground on or near his homestead, and into which the child was immersed every morning, head and all, by two of Dr. Bryant's students—kicking lustily, we may be sure, at this matutinal dose of hydropathy.

William Cullen Bryant came of Mayflower stock, his mother being a descendant of John Alden, and the characteristics of his family included some of the sterner qualities of the Puritans. Grandfather Snell was a magistrate, and, without doubt, a severe one, for the period was not one which favored leniency to criminals. The whipping-post was still extant in Massachusetts, and the poet remembered that it stood about a mile from his early home at Cummington, and that he once saw a young fellow of eighteen who had received forty lashes as a punishment for a theft he had committed. It was, he thought, the last example of corporal punishment inflicted by law in that neighborhood, though the whipping—post remained in its place for several years, a possible terror to future evil-doers. "Spare the rod, spoil the child," was the Draconian code then; and the rod, in the shape of a little bundle of birchen twigs, bound together with a small cord, was generally suspended on a nail against the wall in the kitchen, and was as much a part of the necessary furniture as the crane that hung in the fire-place, or the shovel and tongs.

Magistrate Snell was a disciplinarian of the stricter sort; and as he and his wife resided with Dr. Bryant and his family, the latter stood in awe of him, so much so that young William Cullen was prevented from feeling anything like affection for him. It was an age of repression, not to say oppression, for children, who had few rights that their elders were bound to respect. To the terrors of the secular arm were added the deeper terrors of the spiritual law, for the people of that primitive period were nothing if not religious. The Minister was the great man; and his bodily presence was a restraint upon the unruly, and the ruly too, for that matter. The lines of our ancestors did not fall in pleasant places as far as recreations were concerned; for they were few and far between, consisting, for the most part, of militia musters, "raisings," corn-huskings, and singing schools, diversified with the making of maple sugar and cider. Education was confined to the three R's, though the children of wealthy parents were sent to colleges as they are now. It was not a genial social condition, it must he confessed, to which William Cullen Bryant was born, though it might have been worse but for his good father, who was in many respects superior to his rustic neighbors. A broad-shouldered, muscular gentleman, proud of his strength, his manners were gentle and reserved, his disposition was serene, and he was fond of society. He was not without political distinction, for he was elected to the Massachusetts House of Representatives for several terms, and afterward to the State Senate, and he associated with the cultivated circles of Boston both as a legislator and as a physician.

William Cullen Bryant was fortunate in his father, who, if he was disappointed when he found that his son was born to be a follower of Apollo and not of AEsculapius, kept his disappointment to himself, and encouraged the lad in his poetical attempts. We have the authority of the poet himself that his father taught his youth the art of verse, and that he offered him to the Muses in the bud of life. His first efforts were several clever "Enigmas," in imitation of the Latin writers, a translation from Horace, and a copy of verses which were written in his twelfth year, to be recited at the close of the winter school, "in the presence of the Master, the Minister of the parish, and a number of private gentlemen." They were printed on the 18th of March, 1807, in the *Hampshire Gazette*, from which these particulars are derived, and which was favored with other contributions from the pen of "C. B."

The juvenile poems of William Cullen Bryant are as clever as those of Chatterton, Pope, and Cowley; but they are in no sense original, and it would have been strange if they had been. There was no original writing in America at the time they were written; and if there had been, it would hardly have commended itself to the old-fashioned taste of Dr. Bryant, to whom Pope was still a power in poetry, as Addison, no doubt, was in prose. It was natural, therefore, that he should offer his boy to the strait-laced Muses of Queen Anne's time; that the precocious boy should lisp in heroic couplets, and that he should endeavor to be satirical. Politics were running high in the first decade of the present century, and the favorite bugbear in New England was President Jefferson, who in 1807 had laid an embargo on American shipping, in consequence of the decrees of Napoleon, and the British orders in council in relation thereto. This act was denounced, and by no one more warmly than by Master Bryant, who made it the subject of a satire, which was published in Boston in 1808. It was entitled "The Embargo; or. Sketches of the Times," and was printed for the purchasers, who were found in sufficient numbers to exhaust the first edition. It is said to have been well received, but doubts were expressed as to whether the author was really a youth of thirteen. His friends came to his rescue in an "Advertisement," which was prefixed to a second edition of his little *brochure*, published in the following year, and certified to his age from their personal knowledge of himself and his family. They also certified to his extraordinary talents, though they should prefer to have him judged by his works, without favor or affection. They concluded by stating that the printer was authorized to disclose their names and places of residence.

The early poetical exercises of William Cullen Bryant, like those of all young poets, were colored by the books which he read. Among these were the works of Pope, as I have already intimated, and, no doubt, the works of Cowper and Thomson. The latter, if they were in the library of Dr. Bryant, do not appear to have impressed his son at this time; nor, indeed, does any English poet except Pope, so far as we can judge from his contributions to the *Hampshire Gazette*, which were continued from time to time. They were bookish and patriotic; one, which was written at Cummington on the 8th of January, 1810, being "The Genius of Columbia;" and another, "An Ode for the Fourth of July, 1812," to the tune of "Ye Gentlemen of England." These productions are undeniably clever, but they are not characteristic of their writer, nor of the nature which surrounded his birthplace, with which he was familiar, and of which he was a close observer as his poetry was soon to disclose.

He entered Williams College, in Williamstown, Mass., in his sixteenth year, and remained there until 1812, distinguishing himself for aptness and industry in classical learning and polite literature. At the end of two years he withdrew, and commenced the study of law, first with Judge Howe, of Worthington, and afterward with Mr. William Baylies, of Bridgewater. So far he had written nothing but clever amateur verse; but now, in his eighteenth year, he wrote an imperishable poem. The circumstances under which it was composed have been variously stated, but they agree in the main particulars, and are thus given in "The Bryant Homestead Book"(1870), apparently on authentic information: "It was here at Cumming-ton, while wandering in the primeval forests, over the floor of which were scattered the gigantic trunks of fallen trees, mouldering for long years, and suggesting an indefinitely remote antiquity, and where silent rivulets crept along through the carpet of dead leaves, the spoil of thousands of summers, that the poem entitled "Thanatopsis" was composed. The young poet had read the poems of Kirke White, which, edited by Southey, were published about that time, and a small volume of Southey's miscellaneous poems; and some lines of those authors had kindled his imagination, which, going forth over the face of the inhabitants of the globe, sought to bring under one broad and comprehensive view the destinies of the human race in the present life, and the perpetual rising and passing away of generation after generation who are nourished by the fruits of its soil, and find a resting place in its bosom." We should like to know what lines in Southey and Kirke White suggested "Thanatopsis," that they might be printed in letters of gold hereafter.

When the young poet quitted Cummington to begin his law studies, he left the manuscript of this incomparable poem among his papers in the house of his father, who found it after his departure. "Here are some lines that our William has been writing," he said to a lady to whom he showed them. She read them, and, raising her eyes to the face of Dr. Bryant, burst into tears—a tribute to the genius of his son in which he was not ashamed to join. Blackstone bade his Muse a long adieu before he turned to wrangling courts and stubborn law; and our young lawyer intended to do the same (for poetry was starvation in America seventy years ago), but habit and nature were too strong for him. There is no difficulty in tracing the succession of his poems, and in a few instances the places where they were written, or with which they concerned themselves. "Thanatopsis," for example, was followed by "The Yellow Violet," which was followed by the "Inscription for the Entrance to a Wood," and the song beginning " Soon as the glazed and gleaming snow." The exquisite lines "To a Waterfowl" were written at Bridgewater, in his twentieth year, where he was still pursuing the study of law, which appears to have been distasteful to him. The concluding stanza sank deeply into a heart that needed its pious lesson:

> "He who, from zone to zone,
> Guides through the boundless sky thy certain flight,
> *In the long way that I must tread alone*
> *Will lead my steps aright.*"

The lawyer-poet had a long way before him. but he did not tread it alone; for, after being admitted to the bar in Plymouth, and practising for a time in Plainfield, near Cummington, he removed to Great Barrington, in Berkshire, where he saw the dwelling of the Genevieve of his chilly little "Song," his Genevieve being Miss Frances Fairchild of that beautiful town, whom he married in his twenty-seventh year, and who was the light of his household for nearly half a century. It was to her, the reader may like to know, that he addressed the ideal poem beginning "O fairest of the rural maids" (circa1825), "The Future Life" (1837), and "The Life That Is" (1858); and her memory and her loss are tenderly embalmed in one of the most touching of his later poems, "October, 1866."

"Thanatopsis" was sent to the *North American Review* (whether by its author or his father we are not told), and with such a modest, not to say enigmatical, note of introduction, that its authorship was left in doubt. The *Review* was managed by a club of young literary gentlemen, who styled themselves "The North American Club," two of whose members, Mr. Richard Henry Dana and Mr. Edward Tyrrel Channing, were considered its editors. Mr. Dana read the poem carefully, and was so surprised at its excellence that he doubted whether it was the production of an American, an opinion in which his associates are understood to have concurred. While they were hesitating about its acceptance, he was told that the writer was a member of the Massachusetts Senate, and, the Senate being then in session, he started immediately from Cambridge for Boston. He reached the State House, and inquired for Senator Bryant. A tall, middle-aged man, with a business-like look, was pointed out to him. He was satisfied that he could not be the poet he sought, so he posted back to Cambridge without an introduction. The story ends here, and rather tamely; for the original narrator forgot, or perhaps never knew, that Dr. Bryant was a member of the Senate, and that it was among the possibilities that *he* was the Senator with a similar name. American Poetry may be said to have commenced in 1817 with the September number of the *North American Review*, which contained "Thanatopsis" and the "Inscription for the Entrance of a Wood," the last being printed as a "Fragment." Six months later, in March, 1818, the impression which "Thanatopsis "created was strengthened by the appearance of the lines "To a Waterfowl," and the "Version of a Fragment of Simonides."

Mr. Bryant's literary life may now be said to have begun, though he depended upon the practice of his profession for his daily bread. He continued his contributions to the *North American Review* in the shape of prose papers on literary topics, and maintained the most friendly relations with its conductors, notably so with Mr. Dana, who was seven years his elder, and who possessed, like himself, the accomplishment of verse. At the suggestion of this poetical and critical brother, he was invited to deliver a poem before the Phi Beta Kappa Society at Harvard College—an honor which is offered only to those who have already made a reputation, and are likely to reflect credit on the Society as well as on themselves. He accepted, and in 1821wrote his first poem of any length, "The Ages," which still remains the best poem of the kind that was ever recited before a college society either in this country or in England; grave, stately, thoughtful, presenting in animated, picturesque stanzas a compact summary of the history of mankind. A young Englishman of twenty-one—Thomas Babington Macaulay—delivered in the same year a poem on "Evening," before the students of Trinity College, Cambridge; and it is instructive to compare his conventional heroics with the spirited Spenserian stanzas of William Cullen Bryant. The lines "To a Waterfowl," which were written at Bridgewater in 1815, were followed by "Green River," "A Winter Piece," "The West Wind," "The Burial-Place," "Blessed are they that mourn," "No man knoweth his sepulchre," "A Walk at Sunset," and the "Hymn to Death."

These poems, which cover a period of six busy years, are interesting to the poetic student as examples of the different styles of their writer, and of the changing elements of his thoughts and feelings. "Green River," for example, is a momentary revealment of his shy temperament and his daily pursuits. Its glimpses of nature are charming, and his wish to be beside its waters is the most natural one in the world. The young lawyer is not complimentary to his clients, whom he styles "the dregs of men," while his pen, which does its best to serve them, becomes "a barbarous pen." He is dejected, but a visit to the river will restore his spirits; for, as he gazes upon its lonely and lovely stream,

"An image of that calm life appears
That won my heart in my greener years."

"A Winter Piece" is a gallery of woodland pictures which surpasses any-thing of the kind in the language. "A Walk at Sunset " is notable in that it is the first poem in which we see (faintly, it must be confessed) the aboriginal element, which was soon to become a prominent one in Mr. Bryant's poetry. It was inseparable from the primeval forests of the New World, but he was the first to perceive its poetic value. The "Hymn to Death"—stately, majestic, consolatory—concludes with a touching tribute to the worth of his good father, who died while he was writing it, at the age of fifty-four. The year 1821 was an important one to Mr. Bryant, for it witnessed the publication of his first collection of verse, his marriage, and the death of his father.

The next four years of Mr. Bryant's life were more productive than any that had preceded them, for he wrote upward of thirty poems during that time. The aboriginal element was creative in "The Indian Girl's Lament," An Indian Story," "An Indian at the Burial-Place of his Fathers," and, noblest of all, "Monument Mountain;" the Hellenic element predominated in "The Massacre at Scio " and "The Song of the Greek Amazon;" the Hebraic element touched him lightly in "Rizpah" and the "Song of the Stars;" and the pure poetic element was manifest in "March," "The Rivulet" (which, by the way, ran through the grounds of the old homestead at Cummington), "After a Tempest," "The Murdered Traveler," "Hymn to the North Star," "A Forest Hymn," "O fairest of the rural maids," and the exquisite and now most pathetic poem, "June." These poems and others not specified here, if read continuously and in the order in which they were composed, show a wide range of sympathies, a perfect acquaintance with many measures, and a clear, capacious, ever-growing intellect. They are all distinctive of the genius of their author, but neither exhibits the full measure of his powers. We can say of none of them, "The man who wrote this will never write any better."

The publication of Mr. Bryant's little volume of verse was indirectly the cause of his adopting literature as a profession. It was warmly commended, and by no one more so than by Mr. Gulian C. Verplanck, in the columns of the *New York American*. He was something of a literary authority at the time, a man of fortune and college-bred, known in a mild way as the author of an anniversary discourse delivered before the New York Historical Society in1818, of a political satire entitled "The Bucktail Bards," and later of an "Essay on the Doctrine of Contracts." Among his friends was Mr. Henry D. Sedgwick, a summer neighbor, so to speak, of Mr. Bryant's, having a country-house at Stockbridge, a few miles from Great Barrington, and a house in town, which was frequented by the *literati* of the day, such as Verplanck, Halleck, Percival, Cooper, and others of less note. An ardent admirer of Mr. Bryant, Mr. Sedgwick set to work, with the assistance of Mr. Verplanck, to procure him literary employment in New York, in order to enable him to escape his hated bondage to the law; and he was appoint-ed assistant editor of a projected periodical called the *New York Review and Athenaeum Magazine*. The at last enfranchised lawyer dropped his barbarous pen, closed his law-books, and in the winter or spring of 1825 re-moved with his household to New York. The projected periodical was started, as these sanguine ventures always are, with fair hopes of success. It was well edited, and its contributors were men of acknowledged ability. The June number contained two poems which ought to have made a great hit. One was "A Song of Pitcairn's Island; " the other was " Marco Bozzaris." There was no flourish of trumpets over them, as there would be now; the writers merely prefixed their initials, "B." and "H." The reading public of New York were not ready for the *Review*, which had been projected for their mental enlightenment; so, after about a year's struggle, it was merged in the *New York Literary Gazette*, which began its mission about four years before. This magazine shared the fate of its companion in a few months, when it was consolidated with the *United States Literary Gazelle*, which in two months was swallowed up in the *United States Review*. The honor of publishing and finishing the last was shared by Boston and New York. Profit in these publications there was none, though Bryant, Halleck, Willis, Dana, Bancroft, and Longfellow wrote for them. Too good. or not good enough, they lived and died prematurely. Mr. Bryant's success as a metropolitan man of letters was not brilliant so far; but there were other walks than those of pure literature open to him, as to others, and into one of the most bustling of these he entered in his thirty-second year. In other words. he became one of the editors of the *Evening Post*. Henceforth he was to live by journalism.

Journalism, though an exacting pursuit, leaves its skillful followers a little leisure in which to cultivate literature. It was the heyday of those ephemeral trifles, Annuals, and Mr. Bryant found time to edit one, with the assistance of his friend Mr. Verplanck, and his acquaintance Mr. Robert C. Sands (who, by the way, was one of the editors of the *Commercial Advertiser*),and a very creditable work it was. His contributions to "The Talisman" included some of his best poems. Poetry was the natural expression of his genius—a fact which he could never understand, for it always seemed to him that prose was the natural expression of all mankind. His prose was, and always continued to be, masterly. Its earliest examples, outside of his critical papers in the *North American Review* and other periodicals (and out-side of the *Evening Post*, of course), are two stories entitled "Medfield" and "The Skeleton's Cave," contributed by him to "Tales of the Glauber Spa "(1832)—a collection of original stories by Mr. James K. Paulding, Mr. Verplanck, Mr. Sands, Mr. 'William Leggett, and Miss Catharine Sedgwick. Three years before (1829) he had become the chief editor of the *Evening Post*. Associated with him was Mr. Leggett, who had shown some talent as a writer of sketches and stories, and who had failed, like himself, in con-ducting a critical publication, for which his countrymen were not ready. He made a second collection of his poems at this time (1832), a copy of which was sent by Mr. Verplanck to Mr. Washington Irving, who was then, what he had been for years, the idol of English readers, and not without weight with the Trade. Would he see if some English house would not reprint it? No leading publisher nibbled at it, not even Murray, who was Mr. Irving's publisher; but an obscure bookseller named Andrews finally agreed to undertake it, if Mr. Irving would put his valuable name on the title-page as the editor. He was not acquainted with Mr. Bryant, but he was a kind-hearted, large-souled gentleman, who knew good poetry when he saw it, and he consented to "edit" the book. He was not a success in the estimation of Andrews, who came to him one day, by no means a merry Andrew, and declared that the book would ruin him unless one or more changes were made in the text. What was amiss in it? He turned to the "Song of Marion's Men," and stumbled over an obnoxious couplet in the first stanza:

> "The British soldier trembles
> When Marion's name is told."

"That won't do at all, you know. The absurdity of the objection must have struck the humorist comically; but as he wanted the volume republished, he good-naturedly saved the proverbial valor of the British soldier by changing the first line to:

> "The foeman trembles in his camp,"

and the tempest in a teapot was over, as far as England was concerned. Not as far as the United States was concerned, however; for when the circum-stance became known to Mr. Leggett, he excoriated Mr. Irving for his sub-serviency to a bloated aristocracy, and so forth. Mr. John Wilson reviewed the book in *Blackwood's Magazine* in a half-hearted way, patronizing the writer with his praise.

The poems that Mr. Bryant wrote during the first seven years of his residence in New York (some forty in number, not including translations) exhibited the qualities which distinguished his genius from the beginning, and were marked by characteristics which were rather acquired than inherited. In other words, they were somewhat different from those which were written at Great Barrington. The Hellenic element was still visible in "The Greek Partisan" and "The Greek Boy," and the aboriginal element in "The Disinterred Warrior." The large imagination of "The Hymn to the North Star" was radiant in "The Firmament," and in "The Past." Ardent love of nature found expressive utterance in "Lines on Revisiting the Country," "The Gladness of Nature," "A Summer Ramble," "A Scene on the Banks of the Hudson," and "The Evening Wind." The little book of immortal dirges had a fresh leaf added to it in "The Death of the Flowers," which was at once a pastoral of autumn and a monody over a beloved sister. A new element appeared in "The Summer Wind," and was always present afterward in Mr. Bryant's meditative poetry— the association of humanity with nature—a calm but sympathetic recognition of the ways of man and his presence on the earth. The power of suggestion and of rapid generalization, which was the key-note of "The Ages," lived anew in every line of "The Prairies," in which a series of poems present themselves to the imagination as a series of pictures in a gallery—pictures in which breadth and vigor of treatment and exquisite delicacy of detail are everywhere harmoniously blended, and the unity of pure Art is attained. It was worth going to the ends of the world to be able to write "The Prairies."

Confiding in the discretion of his associate Mr. Leggett, and anxious to escape from his daily editorial labors, Mr. Bryant sailed for Europe with his family in the summer of 1834. It was his intention to perfect his literary studies while abroad, and to devote himself to the education of his children; but his intention was frustrated, after a short course of travel in France, Germany, and Italy, by the illness of Mr. Leggett, whose mistaken zeal in the advocacy of unpopular measures had seriously injured the *Evening Post*. He returned in haste early in 1836, and devoted his time and energies to restoring the prosperity of his paper. Nine years passed before he ventured to return to Europe, though he managed to visit certain portions of his own country. His readers tracked his journeys through the letters which he wrote to the *Evening Post*, and which were noticeable for justness of observation and clearness of expression. A selection from Mr. Bryant's foreign and home letters was published in 1852, under the title of "Letters of a Traveler."

The life of a man of letters is seldom eventful. There are, of course, exceptions to the rule: for literature, like other polite professions, is never without its disorderly followers. It is instructive to trace their careers, which are usually short ones; but the contemplation of the calm, well-regulated, self-respecting lives of the elder and wiser masters is much more satisfactory. We pity the Maginns, and Mangans, and Poes, whom we have always with us; but we admire and reverence such writers as Wordsworth, and Thackeray, and Bryant, who dignify their high calling. The last thirty years of the life of Mr. Bryant were devoid of incidents, though one of them (1866) was not without the supreme sorrow— death. He devoted himself to journalism as conscientiously as if he still had his spurs to win, discussing all public questions with independence and fearlessness; and from time to time, as the spirit moved him, he added to our treasures of song, contributing to the popular magazines of the period, and occasionally issuing these contributions in separate volumes. He published "The Fountain and Other Poems" in 1842; "The White-Footed Deer and Other Poems" in 1844; a collected edition of his poems, with illustrations by Leutze, in 1846; an edition in two volumes in 1855; "Thirty Poems" in 1866; and in 1876 the present illustrated and only complete edition of his poetical writings. To the honors which these volumes brought him he added fresh laurels in 1870 and 1871 by the publication of his translation of the "Iliad" and the "Odyssey"—a translation which was highly praised both at home and abroad, and which, if not the best that the English language is capable of, is, in many respects, the best which any English-writing poet has yet produced.

There comes a day in the intellectual lives of most poets when their powers cease to be progressive and productive, or are productive only in the forms to which they have accustomed themselves, and which have become mannerisms. It was not so with Mr. Bryant. He enjoyed the dangerous distinction of proving himself a great poet at an early age; he preserved this distinction to the last, for the sixty-four years which elapsed between the writing of "Thanatopsis" and the writing of "The Flood of Years" witnessed no decay of his poetic capacities, but rather the growth and development of trains of thought and forms of verse of which there was no evidence in his early writings. His sympathies were enlarged as the years went on, and the crystal clearness of his mind was colored with human emotions.

To Bryant, beyond all other modern poets, the earth was a theatre upon which the great drama of life was everlastingly played. The remembrance of this fact is his inspiration in "The Fountain," "An Evening Revery," "The Antiquity of Freedom," "The Crowded Street," "The Planting of the Apple-Tree," "The Night Journey of a River," "The Sower," and "The Flood of Years." The most poetical of Mr. Bryant's poems are, perhaps, "The Land of Dreams," "The Burial of Love," "The May sun sheds an amber light," and "The Voice of Autumn;" and they were written in a succession of happy hours, and in the order named. Next to these pieces, as examples of pure poetry, should be placed "Sella" and "The Little People of the Snow," which are exquisite fairy fantasies. The qualities by which Mr. Bryant's poetry are chiefly distinguished are serenity and gravity of thought; an intense though repressed recognition of the mortality of man-kind; an ardent love for human freedom; and unrivaled skill in painting the scenery of his native land. He had no superior in this walk of poetic art—it might almost be said no equal, for his descriptions of nature are never inaccurate or redundant. "The Excursion" is a tiresome poem, which contains several exquisite episodes. Mr. Bryant knew how to write exquisite episodes, and to omit the platitudes through which we reach them in other poets.

It is not given to many poets to possess as many residences as Mr. Bryant, for he had three—a town-house in New York, a country-house, called "Cedarmere," at Roslyn, Long Island, and the old homestead of the Bryant family at Cummington. He passed the winter months in New York, and the summer and early autumn months at his country-houses. No distinguished man in America was better known by sight than he.

"O good gray head that all men knew,"

rose unbidden to one's lips as he passed his fellow-pedestrians in the streets of the great city, active, alert, with a springing step and a buoyant gait. He was seen in all weathers, walking down to his office in the morning, and back to his house in the afternoon—an observant antiquity, with a majestic white beard, a pair of sharp eyes, and a face which, noticed closely, recalled the line of the poet,

"A million wrinkles carved his skin."

Mr. Bryant had a peculiar talent, in which the French excel—the talent of delivering discourses upon the lives and writings of eminent men; and he was always in request after the death of his contemporaries.

Beginning with a eulogy on his friend Cole, the painter, who died in 1848, he paid his well-considered tributes to the memory of Cooper and Irving, and assisted at the dedication in the Central Park of the Morse, Shakespeare, Scott, and Halleck monuments. His addresses on those occasions, and others that might be named, were models of justice of appreciation and felicity of expression. His last public appearance was at the Central Park, on the afternoon of May 29th, 1878, at the unveiling of a statue to Mazzini. It was an unusually hot day, and after delivering his address, which was remarkable for its eloquence, he accompanied General James Grant Wilson, an acquaintance of some years' standing, to his residence in East Seventy-fourth street. General Wilson reached his door with Mr. Bryant leaning on his arm; he took a step in advance to open the inner door, and while his back was turned the poet fell, striking his head on the stone platform of the front steps. It was his death-blow; for, though he recovered his consciousness sufficiently to converse a little, and was able to ride to his own house with General Wilson, his fate was sealed. He lingered until the morning of the 12th of June, when his capacious spirit passed out into the Unknown. Two days later all that was mortal of him was buried beside the grave of his wife at Roslyn.

Such was the life and such the life-work of William Cullen Bryant.

R. H. STODDARD.

~~~~~~~********~~~~~~~

POEMS

~**~

THE AGES. [1]

I.

WHEN to the common rest that crowns our days,
Called in the noon of life, the good man goes,
Or full of years, and ripe in wisdom, lays
His silver temples in their last repose;
When, o'er the buds of youth, the death-wind blows
And blights the fairest; when our bitter tears
Stream, as the eyes of those that love us close,
We think on what they were, with many fears
Lest goodness die with them, and leave the coming years.

II.

And therefore, to our hearts, the days gone by,
When lived the honored sage whose death we wept,
And the soft virtues beamed from many an eye,
And beat in many a heart that long has slept—
Like spots of earth where angel-feet have stepped,
Are holy; and high-dreaming bards have told
Of times when worth was crowned, and faith was kept,
Ere friendship grew a snare, or love waxed cold—
Those pure and happy times—the golden days of old.

III.

Peace to the just man's memory; let it grow
Greener with years, and blossom through the flight
Of ages; let the mimic canvas show
His calm benevolent features; let the light
Stream on his deeds of love, that shunned the sight
Of all but heaven, and in the book of fame
The glorious record of his virtues write
And hold it up to men. and bid them claim
A palm like his, and catch from him the hallowed flame.

IV.

But oh, despair not of their fate who rise
To dwell upon the earth when we withdraw!
Lo I the same shaft by which the righteous dies,
Strikes through the wretch that scoffed at mercy's law,
And trode his brethren down, and felt no awe

---

[1] [*This and subsequent footnotes come from the end-notes of the original edition of* Poetical Works.] In this poem, written and first printed in the year 1821, the author has endeavored, from a survey of the past ages of the world, and of the successive advances of mankind in knowledge, virtue, and happiness, to justify and confirm the hopes of the philanthropist for the future destinies of the human race.

Of Him who will avenge them. Stainless worth,
Such as the sternest age of virtue saw,
Ripens, meanwhile, till time shall call it forth
From the low modest shade, to light and bless the earth.

V.

Has Nature, in her calm, majestic march,
Faltered with age at last? does the bright sun
Grow dim in heaven? or, in their far blue arch,
Sparkle the crowd of stars, when day is done,
Less brightly? when the dew-lipped Spring comes on,
Breathes she with airs less soft, or scents the sky
With flowers less fair than when her reign begun?
Does prodigal Autumn, to our age, deny
The plenty that once swelled beneath his sober eye?

VI.

Look on this beautiful world, and read the truth
In her fair page; see, every season brings
New change, to her, of everlasting youth;
Still the green soil, with joyous living things,
Swarms, the wide air is full of joyous wings,
And myriads, still, are happy in the sleep
Of ocean's azure gulfs, and where he flings
The restless surge. Eternal love doth keep,
In his complacent arms, the earth, the air, the deep.

VII.

Will then the merciful One, who stamped our race
With his own image, and who gave them sway
O'er earth, and the glad dwellers on her face,
Now that our swarming nations far away
Are spread, where'er the moist earth drinks the day,
Forget the ancient care that taught and nursed
His latest offspring? will he quench the ray
Infused by his own forming smile at first,
And leave a work so fair all blighted and accursed?

VIII.

Oh, no! a thousand cheerful omens give
Hope of yet happier days, whose dawn is nigh.
He who has tamed the elements, shall not live
The slave of his own passions; he whose eye
Unwinds the eternal dances of the sky,
And in the abyss of brightness dares to span
The sun's broad circle, rising yet more high,
In God's magnificent works his will shall scan-
And love and peace shall make their paradise with man.

IX.

Sit at the feet of History—through the night

Of years the steps of virtue she shall trace.
And show the earlier ages, where her sight
Can pierce the eternal shadows o'er their face;—
When, from the genial cradle of our race,
Went forth tribes of men, their pleasant lot
To choose, where palm-groves cooled their dwelling-place,
Or freshening rivers ran; and there forgot
The truth of heaven, and kneeled to gods that heard them not.

X.

Then waited not the murderer for the night,
But smote his brother down in the bright day,
And he who felt the wrong, and had the might,
His own avenger, girt himself to slay;
Beside the path the unburied carcass lay;
The shepherd, by the fountains of the glen,
Fled, while the robber swept his flock away,
And slew his babes. The sick, untended then,
Languished in the damp shade, and died afar from men.

XI.

But misery brought in love; in passion's strife
Man gave his heart to mercy, pleading long,
And sought out gentle deeds to gladden life;
The weak, against the sons of spoil and wrong,
Banded, and watched their hamlets, and grew strong;
States rose, and, in the shadow of their might,
The timid rested. To the reverent throng,
Grave and time-wrinkled men, with locks all white,
Gave laws, and judged their strifes, and taught the way of right;

XII.

Till bolder spirits seized the rule, and nailed
On men the yoke that man should never bear,
And drove them forth to battle. Lo! unveiled
The scene of those stern ages! What is there!
A boundless sea of blood, and the wild air,
Moans with the crimson surges that entomb
Cities and bannered armies; forms that wear
The kingly circlet rise, amid the gloom,
O'er the dark wave, and straight are swallowed in its womb.

XIII.

Those ages have no memory, but they left
A record in the desert—columns strown
On the waste sands, and statues fallen and cleft,
Heaped like a host in battle overthrown;
Vast ruins, where the mountain's ribs of stone
Were hewn into a city; streets that spread
In the dark earth, where never breath has blown
Of heaven's sweet air, nor foot of man dares tread
The long and perilous ways—the Cities of the Dead!

21

XIV.

And tombs of monarchs to the clouds up-piled—
They perished, but the eternal tombs remain—
And the black precipice, abrupt and wild,
Pierced by long toil and hollowed to a fane;—
Huge piers and frowning forms of gods sustain
The everlasting arches, dark and wide,
Like the night-heaven, when clouds are black with rain,
But idly skill was tasked, and strength was plied,
All was the work of slaves to swell a despot's pride.

XV.

And virtue cannot dwell" with slaves, nor reign
O'er those who cower to take a tyrant's yoke;
She left the down-trod nations in disdain,
And flew to Greece, when Liberty awoke,
New-born, amid those glorious vales, and broke
Sceptre and chain with her fair youthful hands:
As rocks are shivered in the thunder-stroke.
And lo! in full-grown strength, an empire stands
Of leagued and rival states, the wonder of the lands.

XVI.

Oh, Greece! thy flourishing cities were a spoil
Unto each other; thy hard hand oppressed
And crushed the helpless; thou didst make thy soil
Drunk with the blood of those that loved thee best;
And thou didst drive, from thy unnatural breast,
Thy just and brave to die in distant climes;
Earth shuddered at thy deeds, and sighed for rest
From thine abominations; after-times,
That yet shall read thy tale, will tremble at thy crimes!

XVII.

Yet there was that within thee which has saved
Thy glory, and redeemed thy blotted name;
The story of thy better deeds, engraved
On fame's unmouldering pillar, puts to shame
Our chiller virtue; the high art to tame
The whirlwind of the passions was thine own;
And the pure ray, that from thy bosom came,
Far over many a land and age has shone,
And mingles with the light that beams from God's own throne.

XVIII.

And Rome—thy sterner, younger sister, she
Who awed the world with her imperial frown—
Rome drew the spirit of her race from thee,
The rival of thy shame and thy renown.
Yet her degenerate children sold the crown

Of earth's wide kingdoms to a line of slaves;
Guilt reigned, and woe with guilt, and plagues came down,
Till the North broke its floodgates, and the waves
Whelmed the degraded race, and weltered o'er their graves.

XIX.

Vainly that ray of brightness from above,
That shone around the Galilean lake,
The light of hope, the leading star of love,
Struggled, the darkness of that day to break;
Even its own faithless guardians strove to slake,
In fogs of earth, the pure ethereal flame;
And priestly hands, for Jesus' blessed sake,
Were red with blood, and charity became,
In that stern war of forms, a mockery and a name.

XX.

They triumphed, and less bloody rites were kept
Within the quiet of the convent-cell;
The well-fed inmates pattered prayer, and slept,
And sinned, and liked their easy penance well.
Where pleasant was the spot for men to dwell,
Amid its fair broad lands the abbey lay,
Sheltering dark orgies that were shame to tell,
And cowled and barefoot beggars swarmed the way,
All in their convent weeds, of black, and white, and gray.

XXI.

Oh, sweetly the returning muses' strain
Swelled over that famed stream, whose gentle tide
In their bright lap the Etrurian vales detain,
Sweet, as when winter storms have ceased to chide,
And all the new-leaved woods, resounding wide,
Send out wild hymns upon the scented air.
Lo! to the smiling Arno's classic side
The emulous nations of the West repair,
And kindle their quenched urns, and drink fresh spirit there.

XXII.

Still, heaven deferred the hour ordained to rend
From saintly rottenness the sacred stole;
And cowl and worshipped shrine could still defend
The wretch with felon stains upon his soul;
And crimes were set to sale, and hard his dole
Who could not bribe a passage to the skies:
And vice, beneath the mitre's kind control,
Sinned gayly on, and grew to giant size,
Shielded by priestly power, and watched by priestly eyes.

XXIII.

At last the earthquake came—the shock, that hurled

To dust, in many fragments dashed and strown,
The throne, whose roots were in another world,
And whose far-stretching shadow awed our own.
From many a proud monastic pile, o'erthrown,
Fear-struck, the hooded inmates rushed and fled;
The web, that for a thousand years had grown
O'er prostrate Europe, in that day of dread
Crumbled and fell, as fire dissolves the flaxen thread.

XXIV.

The spirit of that day is still awake,
And spreads himself, and shall not sleep again;
But through the idle mesh of power shall break
Like billows o'er the Asian monarch's chain;
Till men are filled with him, and feel how vain.
Instead of the pure heart and innocent hands,
Are all the proud and pompous modes to gain
The smile of Heaven;—till a new age expands
Its white and holy wings above the peaceful lands.

XXV.

For look again on the past years;—behold,
How like the nightmare's dreams have flown away
Horrible forms of worship, that, of old.
Held, o'er the shuddering realms, unquestioned sway:
See crimes, that feared not once the eye of day,
Rooted from men, without a name or place!
See nations blotted out from earth, to pay
The forfeit of deep guilt;—with glad embrace
The fair disburdened lands welcome a nobler race.

XXVI.

Thus error's monstrous shapes from earth are driven;
They fade, they fly—but Truth survives their flight;
Earth has no shades to quench that beam of heaven;
Each ray that shone, in early time, to light
The faltering footstep in the path of right,
Each gleam of clearer brightness shed to aid
In man's maturer day his bolder sight,
All blended, like the rainbow's radiant braid,
Pour yet, and still shall pour, the blaze that cannot fade.

XXVII.

Late, from this Western shore, that morning chased
The deep and ancient night, which threw its shroud
O'er the green land of groves, the beautiful waste.
Nurse of full streams, and lifter-up of proud
Sky-mingling mountains that o'erlook the cloud.
Erewhile, where yon gay spires their brightness rear,
Trees waved, and the brown hunter's shouts were loud
Amid the forest; and the bounding deer
Fled at the glancing plume, and the gaunt wolf yelled near.

XXVIII.

And where his willing waves yon bright blue bay
Sends up, to kiss his decorated brim,
And cradles, in his soft embrace, the gay
Young group of grassy islands born of him,
And crowding nigh, or in the distance dim,
Lifts the white throng of sails, that bear or bring
The commerce of the world;—with tawny limb,
And belt and beads in sunlight glistening,
The savage urged his skiff like wild bird on the wing.

XXIX.

Then all his youthful paradise around,
And all the broad and boundless mainland, lay
Cooled by the interminable wood, that frowned
O'er mount and vale, where never summer ray
Glanced, till the strong tornado broke his way
Through the gray giants of the sylvan wild;
Yet many a sheltered glade, with blossoms gay
Beneath the showery sky and sunshine mild,
Within the shaggy arms of that dark forest smiled.

XXX.

There stood the Indian hamlet, there the lake
Spread its blue sheet that flashed with many an oar,
Where the brown otter plunged him from the brake,
And the deer drank: as the light gale flew o'er.
The twinkling maize-field rustled on the shore:
And while that spot, so wild, and lone, and fair.
A look of glad and guiltless beauty wore,
And peace was on the earth and in the air,
The warrior lit the pile, and bound his captive there.

XXXI.

Not unavenged—the foeman, from the wood,
Beheld the deed. and when the midnight shade
Was stillest, gorged his battle-axe with blood:
All died—the wailing babe—the shrinking maid—
And in the flood of fire that scathed the glade,
The roofs went down; but deep the silence grew,
When on the dewy woods the day-beam played;
No more the cabin-smokes rose wreathed and blue,
And ever, by their lake, lay moored the bark canoe.

XXXII.

Look now abroad—another race has filled
These populous borders—wide the wood recedes,
And towns shoot up, and fertile realms are tilled:
The land is full of harvests and green meads;
Streams numberless, that many a fountain feeds,

Shine, disembowered, and give to sun and breeze
Their virgin waters; the full region leads
New colonies forth, that toward the western seas
Spread, like a rapid flame among the autumnal trees.

XXXIII.

Here the free spirit of mankind, at length,
Throws its last fetters off; and who shall place
A limit to the giants unchained strength,
Or curb his swiftness in the forward race?
On, like the comet's way through infinite space,
Stretches the long untravelled path of light,
Into the depths of ages; we may trace,
Afar, the brightening glory of its flight,
Till the receding rays are lost to human sight.

XXXIV.

Europe is given a prey to sterner fates,
And Writhes in shackles; strong the arms that chain
To earth her struggling multitude of states;
She too is strong, and might not chafe in vain
Against them, but might cast to earth the train
That trample her, and break their iron net.
Yes, she shall look on brighter days an(l gain
The meed of worthier deeds; the moment set
To rescue and raise up, draws near—but is not yet.

XXXV.

But thou, my country, thou shalt never fall,
Save with thy children—thy maternal care,
Thy lavish love, thy blessings showered on all—
These are thy fetters—seas and stormy air
Are the wide barrier of thy borders, where,
Among thy gallant sons who guard thee well,
Thou laugh'st at enemies: who shall then declare
The date of thy deep-founded strength, or tell
How happy, in thy lap, the sons of men shall dwell?

******

THANATOPSIS.

   To him who in the love of Nature holds
Communion with her visible forms, she speaks
A various language; for his gayer hours
She has a voice of gladness, and a smile
And eloquence of beauty, and she glides
Into his darker musings, with a mild
And healing sympathy, that steals away
Their sharpness, ere he is aware. When thoughts
Of the last bitter hour come like a blight
Over thy spirit, and sad images
Of the stern agony, and shroud, and pall,

And breathless darkness, and the narrow house,
Make thee to shudder, and grow sick at heart;—
Go forth, under the open sky, and list
To Nature's teachings, while from all around—
Earth and her waters, and the depths of air—
Comes a still voice—Yet a few days, and thee
The all-beholding sun shall see no more
In all his course; nor yet in the cold ground,
Where thy pale form was laid, with many tears,
Nor in the embrace of ocean, shall exist
Thy image. Earth, that nourished thee, shall claim
Thy growth, to be resolved to earth again,
And, lost each human trace, surrendering up
Thine individual being, shalt thou go
To mix for ever with the elements,
To be a brother to the insensible rock
And to the sluggish clod, which the rude swain
Turns with his share, and treads upon. The oak
Shall send his roots abroad, and pierce thy mould.

Yet not to thine eternal resting-place
Shalt thou retire alone, nor couldst thou wish
Couch more magnificent. Thou shalt lie down
With patriarchs of the infant world—with kings,
The powerful of the earth—the wise, the good,
Fair forms, and hoary seers of ages past,
All in one mighty sepulchre. The hills
Rock-ribbed and ancient as the sun,   the vales
Stretching in pensive quietness between;
The venerable woods—rivers that move
In majesty, and the complaining brooks
That make the meadows green; and, poured round all,
Old Ocean's gray and melancholy waste, —
Are but the solemn decorations all
Of the great tomb of man. The golden sun,
The planets, all the infinite host of heaven,
Are shining on the sad abodes of death,
Through the still lapse of ages. All that tread
The globe are but a handful to the tribes
That slumber in its bosom.—Take the wings
Of morning, pierce the Barcan wilderness,
Or lose thyself in the continuous woods
Where rolls the Oregon, and hears no sound,
Save his own dashings—yet the dead are there:
And millions in those solitudes, since first
The flight of years began, have laid them down
In their last sleep—the dead reign there alone.
So shalt thou rest, and what if thou withdraw
In silence from the living, and no friend
Take note of thy departure? All that breathe
Will share thy destiny. The gay will laugh
When thou art gone, the solemn brood of care
Plod on, and each one as before will chase
His favorite phantom; yet all these shall leave
Their mirth and their employments, and shall come
And make their bed with thee. As the long train

Of ages glide away, the sons of men,
The youth in life's green spring, and he who goes
In the full strength of years, matron and maid,
The speechless babe, and the gray-headed man—
Shall one by one be gathered to thy side,
By those, who in their turn shall follow them.

So live, that when thy summons comes to join
The innumerable caravan, which moves
To that mysterious realm, where each shall take
His chamber in the silent halls of death,
Thou go not, like the quarry-slave at night,
Scourged to his dungeon, but, sustained and soothed
By an unfaltering trust, approach thy grave,
Like one who wraps the drapery of his couch
About him, and lies down to pleasant dreams.

******

THE YELLOW VIOLET.

WHEN beechen buds begin to swell,
  And woods the blue-bird's warble know,
The yellow violet's modest bell
  Peeps from the last year's leaves below.

Ere russet fields their green resume,
  Sweet flower, I love, in forest bare,
To meet thee, when thy faint perfume
  Alone is in the Virgin air.

Of all her train, the hands of Spring
  First plant thee in the watery mould,
And I have seen thee blossoming
  Beside the snow-bank's edges cold.

Thy parent sun, who bade thee view
  Pale skies, and chilling moisture sip,
Has bathed thee in his own bright hue,
  And streaked with jet thy glowing lip.

Yet slight thy form, and low thy seat,
  And earthward bent thy gentle eye,
Unapt the passing view to meet
  When loftier flowers are flaunting nigh.

Oft, in the sunless April day,
  Thy early smile has stayed my walk;
But midst the gorgeous blooms of May,
  I passed thee on thy humble stalk.

So they, who climb to wealth, forget
  The friends in darker fortunes tried.
I copied them—but I regret
  That I should ape the ways of pride.

And when again the genial hour
  Awakes the painted tribes of light,
I'll not o'erlook the modest flower
  That made the woods of April bright.

<center>~~~~~******~~~~~</center>

INSCRIPTION FOR THE ENTRANCE TO A WOOD.

STRANGER, if thou hast learned a truth which needs
No school of long experience, that the world
Is full of guilt and misery, and hast seen
Enough of all its sorrows, crimes, and cares,
To tire thee of it, enter this wild wood
The calm shade
Shall bring a kindred calm, and the sweet breeze
That makes the green leaves dance, shall waft a balm
To thy sick heart. Thou wilt find nothing here
Of all that pained thee in the haunts of men,
And made thee loathe thy life. The primal curse
Fell, it is true, upon the unsinning earth,
But not in vengeance. God hath yoked to guilt
Her pale tormentor, misery. Hence, these shades
Are still the abodes of gladness; the thick roof
And view the haunts of Nature.
Of green and stirring branches is alive
And musical with birds, that sing and sport
In wantonness of spirit; while below
The squirrel, with raised paws and form erect,
Chirps merrily. Throngs of insects in the shade
Try their thin wings and dance in the warm beam
That waked them into life. Even the green trees
Partake the deep contentment; as they bend
To the soft winds, the sun from the blue sky
Looks in and sheds a blessing on the scene.
Scarce less the cleft-born wild-flower seems to enjoy
Existence, than the winged plunderer
That sucks its sweets. The mossy rocks themselves,
And the old and ponderous trunks of prostrate trees
That lead from knoll to knoll a causey rude
Or bridge the sunken brook, and their dark roots,
With all their earth upon them, twisting high,
Breathe fixed tranquillity. The rivulet
Sends forth glad sounds, and tripping o'er its bed
Of pebbly sands, or leaping down the rocks,
Seems, with continuous laughter, to rejoice
In its own being. Softly tread the marge,
Lest from her midway perch thou scare the wren
That dips her bill in water. The cool wind,
That stirs the stream in play, shall come to thee,
Like one that loves thee nor will let thee pass
Ungreeted, and shall give its light embrace.

<center>~~~~~******~~~~~</center>

29

SONG.

SOON as the glazed and gleaming snow
   Reflects the day-dawn cold and clear,
The hunter of the West must go
   In depth of wood to seek the deer.

His rifle on his shoulder placed,
   His stores of death arranged with skill,
His moccasins and snow-shoes laced—
   Why lingers he beside the hill?

Far, in the dim and doubtful light,
   Where woody slopes a valley leave,
He sees what none but lover might,
   The dwelling of his Genevieve.

And oft he turns his truant eye,
   And pauses oft, and lingers near;
But when he marks the reddening sky,
   He bounds away to hunt the deer.

~~~~~******~~~~~

TO A WATERFOWL.

WHITHER, midst falling dew,
While glow the heavens with the last steps of day,
Far, through their rosy depths, dost thou pursue
   Thy solitary way?

   Vainly the fowler's eye
Might mark thy distant flight to do thee wrong,
As, darkly seen against the crimson sky,
   Thy figure floats along.

   Seek'st thou the plashy brink
Of weedy lake, or marge of river wide,
Or where the rocking billows rise and sink
   On the chafed ocean-side?

   There is a Power whose care
Teaches thy way along that pathless coast—
The desert and illimitable air—
   Lone wandering, but not lost.

   All day thy wings have fanned,
At that far height, the cold, thin atmosphere,
Yet stoop not, weary, to the welcome land,
   Though the dark night is near.

   And soon that toil shall end;
Soon shalt thou find a summer home, and rest,
And scream among thy fellows; reeds shall bend,
   Soon, o'er thy sheltered nest.

Thou'rt gone, the abyss of heaven
Hath swallowed up thy form; yet, on my heart
Deeply hath sunk the lesson thou hast given,
    And shall not soon depart.

He who, from zone to zone,
Guides through the boundless sky thy certain flight,
In the long way that I must tread alone,
    Will lead my steps aright.

⁓⁓⁓******⁓⁓⁓

GREEN RIVER.

WHEN breezes are soft and skies are fair,
I steal an hour from study an(l care,
And hie me away to the woodland scene,
Where wanders the stream with waters of green,
As if the bright fringe of herbs on its brink
Had given their stain to the wave they drink;
And they, whose meadows it murmurs through,
Have named the stream from its own fair hue.

Yet pure its waters—its shallows are bright
With colored pebbles and sparkles of light,
And clear the depths where its eddies play,
And dimples deepen and whirl away,
And the plane-tree's speckled arms o'ershoot
The swifter current that mines its root,
Through whose shifting leaves, as you walk the hill,
The quivering glimmer of sun and rill
With a sudden flash on the eye is thrown,
Like the ray that streams from the diamond-stone.
Oh, loveliest there the spring days come,
With blossoms, and birds, and wild-bees' hum;
The flowers of summer are fairest there,
And freshest the breath of the summer air;
And sweetest the golden autumn day
In silence and sunshine glides away.

Yet fair as thou art, thou shunnest to glide,
Beautiful stream! by the village side;
But windest away from haunts of men,
To quiet valley and shaded glen;
And forest, and meadow, and slope of hill,
Around thee, are lonely, lovely, and still,
Lonely—save when, by thy rippling tides,
From thicket to thicket the angler glides;
Or the simpler comes, with basket and book
For herbs of power on thy banks to look;
Or haply, some idle dreamer, like me,
To wander, and muse, and gaze on thee,
Still—save the chirp of birds that feed
On the river cherry and seedy reed,
And thy own wild music gushing out
With mellow murmur of fairy shout,

31

From dawn to the blush of another day,
Like traveller singing along his way.

   That fairy music I never hear,
Nor gaze on those waters so green and clear,
And mark them winding away from sight,
Darkened with shade or flashing with light,
While o'er them the vine to its thicket clings,
And the zephyr stoops to freshen his wings,
But I wish that fate had left me free
To wander these quiet haunts with thee,
Till the eating cares of earth should depart,
And the peace of the scene pass into my heart;
And I envy thy stream, as it glides along
Through its beautiful banks in a trance of song.

   Though forced to drudge for the dregs of men,
And scrawl strange words with the barbarous pen,
And mingle among the jostling crowd,
Where the sons of strife are subtle and loud—
I often come to this quiet place,
To breathe the airs that ruffle thy face,
And gaze upon thee in silent dream,
For in thy lonely and lovely stream
An image of that calm life appears
That won my heart in my greener years.

——*****——

A WINTER PIECE.

   THE time has been that these wild solitudes,
Yet beautiful as wild, were trod by me
Oftener than now; and when the ills of life
Had chafed my spirit—when the unsteady pulse
Beat with strange flutterings—I would wander forth
And seek the woods. The sunshine on my path
Was to me as a friend. The swelling hills,
The quiet dells retiring far between,
With gentle invitation to explore
Their windings, were a calm society
That talked with me and soothed me. Then the chant
Of birds, and chime of brooks, and soft caress
Of the fresh sylvan air, made me forget
The thoughts that broke my peace, and I began
To gather simples by the fountain's brink,
And lose myself in day-dreams. While I stood
In Nature's loneliness, I was with one
With whom I early grew familiar, one
Who never had a frown for me, whose voice
Never rebuked me for the hours I stole
From cares I loved not, but of which the world
Deems highest, to converse with her. When shrieked
The bleak November winds, and smote the woods,
And the brown fields were herbless, and the shades,
That met above the merry rivulet,

Were spoiled, I sought, I loved them still; they seemed
Like old companions in adversity.
Still there was beauty in my walks; the brook,
Bordered with sparkling frost-work, was as gay
As with its fringe of summer flowers. Afar,
The village with its spires, the path of streams
And dim receding valleys, hid before
By interposing trees, lay visible
Through the bare grove, and my familiar haunts
Seemed new to me. Nor was I slow to come
Among them, when the clouds, from their still skirts,
Had shaken down on earth the feathery snow,
And all was white. The pure keen air abroad,
Albeit it breathed no scent of herb, nor heard
Love-call of bird nor merry hum of bee,
Was not the air of death. Bright mosses crept
Over the spotted trunks, and the close buds,
That lay along the boughs, instinct with life,
Patient, and waiting the soft breath of Spring,
Feared not the piercing spirit of the North.
The snow-bird twittered on the beechen bough,
And 'neath the hemlock, whose thick branches bent
Beneath its bright cold burden, and kept dry
A circle, on the earth, of withered leaves,
The partridge found a shelter. Through the snow
The rabbit sprang away. The lighter track
Of fox, and the raccoon's broad path, were there,
Crossing each other. From his hollow tree
The squirrel was abroad, gathering the nuts
Just fallen, that asked the winter cold and sway
Of winter blast, to shake them from their hold.

But Winter has yet brighter scenes—he boasts
Splendors beyond what gorgeous Summer knows;
Or Autumn with his many fruits, and woods
All flushed with many hues. Come when the rains
Have glazed the snow and clothed the trees with ice,
While the slant sun of February pours
Into the bowers a flood of light. Approach!
The incrusted surface shall upbear thy steps,
And the broad arching portals of the grove
Welcome thy entering. Look! the massy trunks
Are cased in the pure crystal; each light spray,
Nodding and tinkling in the breath of heaven,
Is studded with its trembling water-drops,
That glimmer with an amethystine light.
But round the parent-stem the long low boughs
Bend, in a glittering ring, and arbors hide
The glassy floor. Oh! you might deem the spot
The spacious cavern of some virgin mine,
Deep in the womb of earth—where the gems grow,
And diamonds put forth radiant rods and bud
With amethyst and topaz—and the place
Lit up, most royally, with the pure beam
That dwells in them. Or haply the vast hall
Of fairy palace, that outlasts the night,

And fades not in the glory of the sun;—
Where crystal columns send forth slender shafts
And crossing arches; and fantastic aisles
Wind from the sight in brightness, and are lost
Among the crowded pillars. Raise thine eye;
Thou seest no cavern roof, no palace vault;
There the blue sky and the white drifting cloud
Look in. Again the wildered fancy dreams
Of spouting fountains, frozen as they rose,
And fixed, with all their branching jets, in air,
And all their sluices sealed. All, all is light;
Light without shade. But all shall pass away
With the next sun. From numberless vast trunks
Loosened, the crashing ice shall make a sound
Like the far roar of rivers, and the eve
Shall close o'er the brown woods as it was wont.

　　And it is pleasant, when the noisy streams
Are just set free, and milder suns melt off
The plashy snow, save only the firm drift
In the deep glen or the close shade of pines—
'Tis pleasant to behold the wreaths of smoke
Roll up among the maples of the hill,
Where the shrill sound of youthful voices wakes
The shriller echo, as the clear pure lymph,
That from the wounded trees, in twinkling drops,
Falls, mid the golden brightness of the morn,
Is gathered in with brimming pails, and oft,
Wielded by sturdy hands, the stroke of axe
Makes the woods ring. Along the quiet air,
Come and float calmly off the soft light clouds,
Such as you see in summer, and the winds
Scarce stir the branches. Lodged in sunny cleft,
Where the cold breezes come not, blooms alone
The little wind-flower, whose just opened eye

Is blue as the spring heaven it gazes at—
Startling the loiterer in the naked groves
With unexpected beauty, for the time
Of blossoms and green leaves is yet afar.
And ere it comes, the encountering winds shall oft
Muster their wrath again, and rapid clouds
Shade heaven, and bounding on the frozen earth
Shall fall their volleyed stores, rounded like hail
And white like snow, and the loud North again
Shall buffet the vexed forest in his rage.

—⁓⁓⁓******⁓⁓⁓—

THE WEST WIND.

BENEATH the forest's skirt I rest,
　　Whose branching pines rise dark and high,
And hear the breezes of the West
　　Among the thread-like foliage sigh.

Sweet Zephyr! why that sound of woe?
  Is not thy home among the flowers?
Do not the bright June roses blow,
  To meet thy kiss at morning hours?

And lo! thy glorious realm outspread—
  Yon stretching valleys, green and gay,
And yon free hill-tops, o'er whose head
  The loose white clouds are borne away.

And there the full broad river runs,
  And many a fount wells fresh and sweet,
To cool thee when the mid-day suns
  Have made thee faint beneath their heat.

Thou wind of joy, and youth, and love;
  Spirit of the new-wakened year!
The sun in his blue realm above
  Smooths a bright path when thou art here.

In lawns the murmuring bee is heard,
  The wooing ring-dove in the shade;
On thy soft breath, the new-fledged bird
  Takes wing, half happy, half afraid.

Ah! thou art like our wayward race;—
  When not a shade of pain or ill
Dims the bright smile of Nature's face,
  Thou lov'st to sigh and murmur still.

<div align="center">~~~~******~~~~</div>

THE BURIAL-PLACE. [2]

A FRAGMENT.

  EREWHILE. on England's pleasant shores, our sires
Left not their churchyards unadorned with shades
Or blossoms, but indulgent to the strong
And natural dread of man's last home, the grave,
Its frost and silence—they disposed around,
To soothe the melancholy spirit that dwelt
Too sadly on life's close, the forms and hues
Of vegetable beauty. There the yew,
Green even amid the snows of winter, told
Of immortality, and gracefully
The willow, a perpetual mourner, drooped;
And there the gadding woodbine crept about,
And there the ancient ivy. From the spot
Where the sweet maiden, in her blossoming years

---

[2] The first half of this fragment may seem to the reader borrowed from the essay on Rural Funerals in the fourth number of "The Sketch-book." The lines were, however, written more than a year before that number appeared. The poem, unfinished as it is, would hardly have been admitted into this collection, had not the author been unwilling to lose what had the honor of resembling so beautiful a composition.

Cut off, was laid with streaming eyes, and hands
That trembled as they placed her there, the rose
Sprung modest, on bowed stalk, and better spoke
Her graces, than the proudest monument.
There children set about their playmate's grave
The pansy. On the infant's little bed,
Wet at its planting with maternal tears,
Emblem of early sweetness, early death,
Nestled the lowly primrose. Childless dames.
And maids that would not raise the reddened eye—
Orphans, from whose young lids the light of joy
Fled early—silent lovers, who had given
All that they lived for to the arms of earth,
Came often, o'er the recent graves to strew
Their offerings, rue, and rosemary, and flowers.

The pilgrim bands who passed the sea to keep
Their Sabbaths in the eye of God alone,
In his wide temple of the wilderness,
Brought not these simple customs of the heart
With them. It might be, while they laid their dead
By the vast solemn skirts of the old groves,
And the fresh virgin soil poured forth strange flowers
About their graves; and the familiar shades
Of their own native isle, and wonted blooms,
And herbs were wanting, which the pious hand
Might plant or scatter there, these gentle rites
Passed out of use. Now they are scarcely known,
And rarely in our borders may you meet
The tall larch, sighing in the burial—place,
Or willow, trailing low its boughs to hide
The gleaming marble. Naked rows of graves
And melancholy ranks of monuments
Are seen instead, where the coarse grass, between,
Shoots up its dull green spikes, and in the wind
Hisses, and the neglected bramble nigh,
Offers its berries to the school boy's hand,
In vain—they grow too near the dead. Yet here,
Nature, rebuking the neglect of man,
Plants often, by the ancient mossy stone,
The brier-rose, and upon the broken turf
That clothes the fresher grave, the strawberry plant
Sprinkles its swell with blossoms, and lays forth
Her ruddy, pouting fruit.

~~~~~******~~~~~

"BLESSED ARE THEY THAT MOURN."

OH, deem not they are blest alone
    Whose lives a peaceful tenor keep;
The Power who pities man, hath shown
    A blessing for the eyes that weep.

The light of smiles shall fill again
    The lids that overflow with tears;

And weary hours of woe and pain
  Are promises of happier years.

There is a day of sunny rest
  For every dark and troubled night:
And grief may hide an evening guest,
  But joy shall come with early light.

And thou, who, o'er thy friend's low bier,
  Dost shed the bitter drops like rain,
Hope that a brighter, happier sphere
  Will give him to thy arms again.

Nor let the good man's trust depart,
  Though life its common gifts deny,—
Though with a pierced and bleeding heart
  And spurned of men, he goes to die.

For God hath marked each sorrowing day
  And numbered every secret tear,
And heaven's long age of bliss shall pay
  For all his children suffer here.

<div align="center">~~~~~******~~~~~</div>

"NO MAN KNOWETH HIS SEPULCHRE."

WHEN he, who, from the scourge of wrong,
  Aroused the Hebrew tribes to fly,
Saw the fair region, promised long,
  And bowed him on the hills to die;

God made his grave, to men unknown,
  Where Moab's rocks a vale infold,
And laid the aged seer alone
  To slumber while the world grows old.

Thus still, whene'er the good and just
  Close the dim eye on life and pain,
Heaven watches o'er their sleeping dust
  Till the pure spirit comes again.

Though nameless, trampled, and forgot,
  His servant's humble ashes lie,
Yet God hath marked and sealed the spot,
  To call its inmate to the sky.

<div align="center">~~~~~******~~~~~</div>

A WALK AT SUNSET.

WHEN insect wings are glistening in the beam
  Of the low sun, and mountain-tops are bright,
Oh, let me, by the crystal valley-stream.
  Wander amid the mild and yellow light;
And while the wood-thrush pipes his evening lay,

Give me one lonely hour to hymn the setting day.

Oh, sun! that o'er the western mountains now
   Go'st down in glory! ever beautiful
And blessed is thy radiance, whether thou
   Colorest the eastern heaven and night-mist cool,
Till the bright day-star vanish, or on high
Climbest and streamest thy white splendors from mid-sky.

Yet, loveliest are thy setting smiles, and fair,
   Fairest of all that earth beholds, the hues
That live among the clouds, and flush the air,
   Lingering and deepening at the hour of dews.
Then softest gales are breathed, and softest heard
The plaining voice of streams, and pensive note of bird.

They who here roamed, of yore, the forest wide,
   Felt by such charm, their simple bosoms won;
They deemed their quivered warrior, when he died,
   Went to bright isles beneath the setting sun;
Where winds are aye at peace, and skies are fair,
And purple-skirted clouds curtain the crimson air.

So, with the glories of the dying day,
   Its thousand trembling lights and changing hues,
The memory of the brave who passed away
   Tenderly mingled;—fitting hour to muse
On such grave theme, and sweet the dream that shed
Brightness and beauty round the destiny of the dead.

For ages, on the silent forests here,
   Thy beams did fall before the red man came
To dwell beneath them; in the shade the deer
   Fed, and feared not the arrow's deadly aim.
Nor tree was felled, in all that world of woods,
Save by the beaver's tooth, or winds, or rush of floods.

Then came the hunter tribes, and thou didst look,
   For ages, on their deeds in the hard chase,
And well-fought wars; green sod and silver brook
   Took the first stain of blood; before thy face
The warrior generations came and passed,
And glory was laid up for many an age to last.

Now they are gone, gone as thy setting blaze
   Goes down the west, while night is pressing on,
And with them the old tale of better days,
   And trophies of remembered power, are gone.
You field that gives the harvest, where the plough
Strikes the white bone, is all that tells their story now.

I stand upon their ashes in thy beam,
   The offspring of another race, I stand,
Beside a stream they loved, this valley-stream;
   And where the night-fire of the quivered band
Showed the gray oak by fits, and war-song rung,

I teach the quiet shades the strains of this new tongue.

Farewell! but thou shalt come again—thy light
   Must shine on other changes, and behold
The place of the thronged city still as night—
   States fallen—new empires built upon the old—
But never shall thou see these realms again
Darkened by boundless groves, and roamed by savage men.

<div align="center">~~~~~******~~~~~</div>

HYMN TO DEATH.

   OH! could I hope the wise and pure in heart
Might hear my song without a frown, nor deem
My voice unworthy of the theme it tries,—
I would take up the hymn to Death, and say
To the grim power, The world hath slandered thee
And mocked thee. On thy dim and shadowy brow
They place an iron crown, and call thee king
Of terrors, and the spoiler of the world,
Deadly assassin, that strik'st down the fair,
The loved, the good—that breathest on the lights
Of virtue set along the vale of life,
And they go out in darkness. I am come,
Not with reproaches, not with cries and prayers,
Such as have stormed thy stern, insensible ear
From the beginning; I am come to speak
Thy praises. True it is, that I have wept
Thy conquests, and may weep them yet again,
And thou from some I love will take a life
Dear to me as my own. Yet while the spell
Is on my spirit, and I talk with thee
In sight of all thy trophies, face to face,
Meet is it that my voice should utter forth
Thy nobler triumphs; I will teach the world
To thank thee. Who are thine accusers?—Who?
The living!—they who never felt thy power,
And know thee not. The curses of the wretch
Whose crimes are ripe, his sufferings when thy hand
Is on him, and the hour he dreads is come,
Are writ among thy praises. But the good—
Does he whom thy kind hand dismissed to peace,
Upbraid the gentle violence that took off
His fetters, and unbarred his prison-cell?

   Raise then the hymn to Death. Deliverer!
God hath anointed thee to free the oppressed
And crush the oppressor. When the armed chief,
The conqueror of nations, walks the world,
And it is changed beneath his feet, and all
Its kingdoms melt into one mighty realm-
Thou, while his head is loftiest and his heart
Blasphemes, imagining his own right hand
Almighty, thou dost set thy sudden grasp
Upon him, and the links of that strong chain

39

Which bound mankind are crumbled; thou dost break
Sceptre and crown, and beat his throne to dust.
Then the earth shouts with gladness, and her tribes
Gather within their ancient bounds again.
Else had the mighty of the olden time,
Nimrod, Sesostris, or the youth who feigned
His birth from Libyan Ammon, smitten yet
The nations with a rod of iron, and driven
Their chariot o'er our necks. Thou dost avenge,
In thy good time, the wrongs of those who know
No other friend. Nor dost thou interpose
Only to lay the sufferer asleep,
Where he who made him wretched troubles not
His rest—thou dost strike down his tyrant too.
Oh, there is joy when hands that held the scourge
Drop lifeless, and the pitiless heart is cold.
Thou too dost purge from earth its horrible
And old idolatries;—from the proud fanes
Each to his grave their priests go out, till none
Is left to teach their worship; then the fires
Of sacrifice are chilled, and the green moss
O'er creeps their altars ; the fallen images
Cumber the weedy courts, and for loud hymns,
Chanted by kneeling multitudes, the wind
Shrieks in the solitary aisles. When he
Who gives his life to guilt, and laughs at all
The laws that God or man has made, and round
Hedges his seat with power, and shines in wealth,—
Lifts up his atheist front to scoff at Heaven,
And celebrates his shame in open day,
Thou, in the pride of all his crimes, cutt'st off
The horrible example. Touched by thine,
The extortioner's hard hand foregoes the gold
Wrung from the o'er-worn, poor. The perjurer,
Whose tongue was lithe, e'en now, and soluble
Against his neighbor's life, and he who laughed
And leaped for joy to see a spotless fame
Blasted before his own foul calumnies,
Are smit with deadly silence. He, who sold
His conscience to preserve a worthless life,
Even while he hugs himself on his escape,
Trembles, as, doubly terrible, at length,
Thy steps o'ertake him, and there is no time
For parley, nor will bribes unclench thy grasp.
Oft, too, dost thou reform thy victim, long
Ere his last hour. And when the reveller,
Mad in the chase of pleasure, stretches on,
And strains each nerve, and clears the path of life
Like wind, thou point'st him to the dreadful goal,
And shak'st thy hour-glass in his reeling eye.
And check'st him in mid course. Thy skeleton hand
Shows to the faint of spirit the right path,
And he is warned, and fears to step aside.
Thou sett'st between the ruffian and his crime
Thy ghastly countenance, and his slack hand
Drops the drawn knife. But, oh, most fearfully

Dost thou show forth Heaven's justice, when thy shafts
Drink up the ebbing spirit—then the hard
Of heart and violent of hand restores
The treasure to the friendless wretch he wronged.
Then from the writhing bosom thou dost pluck
The guilty secret; lips, for ages sealed,
Are faithless to their dreadful trust at length,
And give it up; the felon's latest breath
Absolves the innocent man who bears his crime;
The slanderer, horror-smitten, and in tears,
Recalls the deadly obloquy he forged
To work his brother's ruin. Thou dost make
Thy penitent victim utter to the air
The dark conspiracy that strikes at life,
And aims to whelm the laws; ere yet the hour
Is come, and the dread sign of murder given.

    Thus, from the first of time, hast thou been found
On virtue's side; the wicked, but for thee,
Had been too strong for the good; the great of earth
Had crushed the weak for ever. Schooled in guile
For ages, while each passing year had brought
Its baneful lesson, they had filled the world
With their abominations; while its tribes,
Trodden to earth, imbruted, and despoiled,
Had knelt to them in worship; sacrifice
Had smoked on many an altar, temple-roofs
Had echoed with the blasphemous prayer and hymn:
But thou, the great reformer of the world,
Tak'st off the sons of violence and fraud
In their green pupilage, their lore half learned—
Ere guilt had quite o'errun the simple heart
God gave them at their birth, and blotted out
His image. Thou dost mark them flushed with hope,
As on the threshold of their vast designs
Doubtful and loose they stand, and strik'st them down.

*   *   *   *   *   *   *   *   *   *   *   *   *   *

    Alas! I little thought that the stern power,
Whose fearful praise I sang, would try me thus
Before the strain was ended. It must cease—
For he is in his grave who taught my youth
The art of verse, and in the bud of life
Offered me to the Muses. Oh, cut off
Untimely! when thy reason in its strength,
Ripened by years of toil and studious search,
And watch of Nature's silent lessons, taught
Thy hand to practise best the lenient art
To which thou gayest thy laborious days,
And, last, thy life. And, therefore, when the earth
Received thee, tears were in unyielding eyes
And on hard cheeks, and they who deemed thy skill
Delayed their death-hour, shuddered and turned pale
When thou wert gone. This faltering verse, which thou
Shalt not, as wont, o'erlook, is all I have

To offer at thy grave—this—and the hope
To copy thy example, and to leave
A name of which the wretched shall not think
As of an enemy's, whom they forgive
As all forgive the dead. Rest, therefore, thou
Whose early guidance trained my infant steps—
Rest, in the bosom of God, till the brief sleep
Of death is over, and a happier life
Shall dawn to waken thine insensible dust.

   Now thou art not—and yet the men whose guilt
Has wearied Heaven for vengeance—he who bears
False witness—he who takes the orphan's bread,
And robs the widow—he who spreads abroad
Polluted hands in mockery of prayer,
Arc left to cumber earth. Shuddering I look
On what is written, yet I blot not out
The desultory numbers; let them stand,
The record of an idle revery.

<div align="center">~~~~~~******~~~~~~</div>

THE MASSACRE AT SCIO. [3]

WEEP not for Scio's children slain;
   Their blood, by Turkish falchions shed,
Sends not its cry to Heaven in vain
   For vengeance on the murderer's head.

Though high the warm red torrent ran
   Between the flames that lit the sky,
Yet, for each drop, an armed man
   Shall rise, to free the land, or die.

And for each corpse, that in the sea
   Was thrown, to feast the scaly herds,
A hundred of the foe shall be
   A banquet for the mountain-birds.

Stern rites and sad shall Greece ordain
   To keep that day along her shore,
Till the last link of slavery's chain
   Is shattered, to be worn no more.

<div align="center">~~~~~~******~~~~~~</div>

THE INDIAN GIRL'S LAMENT.

AN Indian girl was sitting where
   Her lover, slain in battle, slept;
Her maiden veil, her own black hair,[4]

---

[3] This poem, written about the time of the horrible butchery of the Sciotes by the Turks, in 1824, has been more fortunate than most poetical predictions. The independence of the Greek nation which it foretold, has come to pass, and the massacre, by inspiring deeper detestation of their oppressors, did much to promote that event.

[4] "The unmarried females have a modest falling down of the hair over the eyes." —ELIOT.

Came down o'er eyes that wept;
And wildly, in her woodland tongue,
This sad and simple lay she sung;

"I've pulled away the shrubs that grew
  Too close above thy sleeping head,
And broke the forest-boughs that threw
  Their shadows o'er thy bed,
That, shining from the sweet southwest,
The sunbeams might rejoice thy rest.

"It was a weary, weary road
  That led thee to the pleasant coast,
Where thou, in his serene abode,
  Hast met thy father's ghost;
Where everlasting autumn lies
On yellow woods and sunny skies.

"'Twas I the broidered mocsen made,
  That shod thee for that distant land
'Twas I thy bow and arrows laid
  Beside thy still cold hand;
Thy bow in many a battle bent,
Thy arrows never vainly sent.

"With wampum-belts I crossed thy breast.
  And wrapped thee in the bison's hide,
And laid the food that pleased the best,
  In plenty, by thy side,
And decked thee bravely, as became
A warrior of illustrious name.

"Thou 'rt happy now, for thou hast passed
  The long dark journey of the grave,
And in the land of light, at last,
  Hast joined the good and brave;
Amid the flushed and balmy air,
The bravest and the loveliest there.

"Yet, oft to thine own Indian maid
  Even there thy thoughts will earthward stray-
To her who sits where thou wert laid,
  And weeps the hours away,
Yet almost can her grief forget,
To think that thou dost love her yet.

"And thou, by one of those still lakes
  That in a shining cluster lie,
On which the south wind scarcely breaks
  The image of the sky,
A bower for thee and me hast made
Beneath the many-colored shade.

"And thou dost wait and watch to meet
   My spirit sent to join the blessed,
And, wondering what detains my feet
   From that bright land of rest,
Dost seem, in every sound, to hear
The rustling of my footsteps near."

            ******

ODE FOR AN AGRICULTURAL CELEBRATION.

FAR back in the ages,
   The plough with wreaths was crowned;
The hands of kings and sages
   Entwined the chaplet round;
Till men of spoil disdained the toil
   By which the world was nourished,
And dews of blood enriched the soil
   Where green their laurels flourished.
—Now the world her fault repairs—
   The guilt that stains her story;
And weeps her crimes amid the cares
   That formed her earliest glory.

The proud throne shall crumble,
   The diadem shall wane,
The tribes of earth shall humble
   The pride of those who reign;
And War shall lay his pomp away,—
   The fame that heroes cherish,
The glory earned in deadly fray
   Shall fade, decay, and perish.
Honor waits, o'er all the earth,
   Through endless generations,
The art that calls her harvests forth,
   And feeds th' expectant nations.

            ******

RIZPAH.

And he delivered them into the hands of the Gibeonites, and they hanged them in the hill before the Lord; and they fell all seven together, and were put to death in the days of the harvest, in the first days, in the beginning of barley-harvest.
And Rizpah, the daughter of Aiah, took sackcloth, and spread it for her upon the rock, from the beginning of harvest until the water dropped upon them out of heaven, and suffered neither the birds of the air to rest upon them by day, nor the beasts of the field by night. 2 SAMUEL, xxi. 10.

   Hear what the desolate Rizpah said,
As on Gibeah's rocks she watched the dead.
The sons of Michal before her lay,
And her own fair children, dearer than they:
By a death of shame they all had died,
And were stretched on the bare rock, side by side.
And Rizpah, once the loveliest of all
That bloomed and smiled in the court of Saul,
All wasted with watching and famine now,
And scorched by the sun her haggard brow,

44

Sat mournfully guarding their corpses there,
And murmured a strange and solemn air;
The low, heart-broken, and wailing strain
Of a mother that mourns her children slain:

"I have made the crags my home, and spread
On their desert backs my sackcloth bed;
I have eaten the bitter herb of the rocks,
And drunk the midnight dew in my locks;
I have wept till I could not weep, and the pain
Of my burning eyeballs went to my brain.
Seven blackened corpses before me lie,
In the blaze of the sun and the winds of the sky.
I have watched them through the burning day,
And driven the vulture and raven away;
And the cormorant wheeled in circles round,
Yet feared to alight on the guarded ground.
And when the shadows of twilight came,
I have seen the hyena's eyes of flame,
And heard at my side his stealthy tread,
But aye at my shout the savage fled:
And I threw the lighted brand to fright
The jackal and wolf that yelled in the night.

"Ye were foully murdered, my hapless sons,
By the hands of wicked and cruel ones;
Ye fell, in your fresh and blooming prime,
All innocent, for your father's crime.
He sinned—but he paid the price of his guilt
When his blood by a nameless hand was spilt;
When he strove with the heathen host in vain,
And fell with the flower of his people slain,
And the sceptre his children's hands should sway
From his injured lineage passed away.

"But I hoped that the cottage roof would be
A safe retreat for my sons and me;
And that while they ripened to manhood fast,
They should wean my thoughts from the woes of the past.
And my bosom swelled with a mother's pride,
As they stood in their beauty and strength by my side,
Tall like their sire, with the princely grace
Of his stately form, and the bloom of his face.

"Oh, what an hour for a mother's heart,
When the pitiless ruffians tore us apart!
When I clasped their knees and wept and prayed,
And struggled and shrieked to Heaven for aid,
And clung to my sons with desperate strength,
Till the murderers loosed my hold at length,
And bore me breathless and faint aside,
In their iron arms, while my children died.
They died—and the mother that gave them birth
Is forbid to cover their bones with earth.

"The barley-harvest was nodding white,

When my children died on the rocky height,
And the reapers were singing on hill and plain,
When I came to my task of sorrow and pain.
But now the season of rain is nigh,
The sun is dim in the thickening sky,
And the clouds in sullen darkness rest
Where he hides his light at the doors of the west.
I hear the howl of the wind that brings
The long drear storm on its heavy wings;
But the howling wind and the driving rain
Will beat on my houseless head in vain:
I shall stay, from my murdered sons to scare
The beasts of the desert, and fowls of air."

<center>~~~~~******~~~~~</center>

THE OLD MAN'S FUNERAL.

I SAW an aged man upon his bier,
  His hair was thin and white, and on his brow
A record of the cares of many a year;—
  Cares that were ended and forgotten now.
And there was sadness round, and faces bowed,
And woman's tears fell fast, and children wailed aloud.

Then rose another hoary man and said,
  In faltering accents, to that weeping train:
"Why mourn ye that our aged friend is dead?
  Ye are not sad to see the gathered grain,
Nor when their mellow fruit the orchards cast,
Nor when the yellow woods let fall the ripened mast.

"Ye sigh not when the sun, his course fulfilled,
  His glorious course, rejoicing earth and sky,
In the soft evening, when the winds are stilled,
  Sinks where his islands of refreshment lie,
And leaves the smile of his departure, spread
O'er the warm-colored heaven and ruddy mountain-head.

"Why weep ye then for him, who, having won
  The bound of man's appointed years, at last,
Life's blessings all enjoyed, life's labors done,
  Serenely to his final rest has passed;
While the soft memory of his virtues, yet,
Lingers like twilight hues, when the bright sun is set?

"His youth was innocent; his riper age
  Marked with some act of goodness every day;
And watched by eyes that loved him, calm and sage,
  Faded his late declining years away.
Meekly he gave his being up, and went
To share the holy rest that waits a life well spent.

"That life was happy; every day he gave
  Thanks for the fair existence that was his;
For a sick fancy made him not her slave,

To mock him with her phantom miseries.
No chronic tortures racked his aged limb,
For luxury and sloth had nourished none for him.

"And I am glad that he has lived thus long,
    And glad that he has gone to his reward;
Nor can I deem that Nature did him wrong,
    Softly to disengage the vital cord.
For when his hand grew palsied, and his eye
Dark with the mists of age, it was his time to die."

~~~~~******~~~~~

THE RIVULET.

THIS little rill, that from the springs
Of yonder grove its current brings,
Plays on the slope awhile, and then
Goes prattling into groves again,
Oft to its warbling waters drew
My little feet, when life was new.
When woods in early green were dressed,
And from the chambers of the west
The warmer breezes, travelling out,
Breathed the new scent of flowers about,
My truant steps from home would stray,
Upon its grassy side to play,
List the brown thrasher's vernal hymn,
And crop the violet on its brim,
With blooming cheek and open brow,
As young and gay, sweet rill, as thou.

And when the days of boyhood came,
And I had grown in love with fame,
Duly I sought thy banks, and tried
My first rude numbers by thy side.
Words cannot tell how bright and gay
The scenes of life before me lay.
Then glorious hopes, that now to speak
Would bring the blood into my cheek,
Passed o'er me; and I wrote, on high,
A name I deemed should never die.

Years change thee not. Upon yon hill
The tall old maples, verdant still,
Yet tell, in grandeur of decay,
How swift the years have passed away
Since first, a child, and half afraid,
I wandered in the forest shade.
Thou, ever-joyous rivulet,
Dost dimple, leap, and prattle yet;
And sporting with the sands that pave
The windings of thy silver wave,
And dancing to thy own wild chime,
Thou laughest at the lapse of time.
The same sweet sounds are in my ear

47

My early childhood loved to hear;
As pure thy limpid waters run;
As bright they sparkle to the sun;
As fresh and thick the bending ranks
Of herbs that line thy oozy banks;
The violet there, in soft May dew,
Comes up, as modest and as blue;
As green amid thy current's stress,
Floats the scarce-rooted watercress;
And the brown ground-bird, in thy glen,
Still chirps as merrily as then.

Thou changest not—but I am changed
Since first thy pleasant banks I ranged;
And the grave stranger, come to see
The play-place of his infancy,
Has scarce a single trace of him
Who sported once upon thy brim.
The visions of my youth are past—
Too bright, too beautiful to last.
I've tried the world—it wears no more
The coloring of romance it wore.
Yet well has Nature kept the truth
She promised in my earliest youth.
The radiant beauty shed abroad
On all the glorious works of God,
Shows freshly, to my sobered eye,
Each charm it wore in days gone by.

Yet a few years shall pass away,
And I, all trembling, weak, and gray,
Bowed to the earth, which waits to fold
My ashes in the embracing mould,
(If haply the dark will of Fate
Indulge my life so long a date),
May come for the last time to look
Upon my childhood's favorite brook.
Then dimly on my eye shall gleam
The sparkle of thy dancing stream;
And faintly on my ear shall fall
Thy prattling current's merry call;
Yet shalt thou flow as glad and bright
As when thou met'st my infant sight.

And I shall sleep—and on thy side,
As ages after ages glide,
Children their early sports shall try,
And pass to hoary age and die.
But thou unchanged from year to year,
Gayly shalt play and glitter here;
Amid young flowers and tender grass
Thy endless infancy shall pass;
And, singing down thy narrow glen,
Shalt mock the fading race of men.

~~~~~******~~~~~

MARCH.

THE stormy March is come at last,
   With wind, and cloud, and changing skies;
I hear the rushing of the blast,
   That through the snowy valley flies.

Ah, passing few are they who speak,
   Wild, stormy month! in praise of thee;
Yet, though thy winds are loud and bleak,
   Thou art a welcome month to me.

For thou, to northern lands, again
   The glad and glorious sun dost bring,
And thou hast joined the gentle train
   And wear'st the gentle name of Spring.

And, in thy reign of blast and storm,
   Smiles many a long, bright, sunny day,
When the changed winds are soft and warm,
   And heaven puts on the blue of May.

Then sing aloud the gushing rills
   In joy that they again are free,
And, brightly leaping down the hills,
   Renew their journey to the sea.

The year's departing beauty hides
   Of wintry storms the sullen threat;
But in thy sternest frown abides
   A look of kindly promise yet.

Thou bring'st the hope of those calm skies,
   And that soft time of sunny showers,
When the wide bloom, on earth that lies,
   Seems of a brighter world than ours.

<div align="center">~~~~******~~~~</div>

CONSUMPTION.

AY, thou art for the grave; thy glances shine
   Too brightly to shine long; another Spring
Shall deck her for men's eyes—but not for thine—
   Sealed in a sleep which knows no wakening.
The fields for thee have no medicinal leaf,
   And the vexed ore no mineral of power;
And they who love thee wait in anxious grief
   Till the slow plague shall bring the fatal hour.
Glide softly to thy rest, then; Death should come
   Gently, to one of gentle mould like thee,
As light winds wandering through groves of bloom
   Detach the delicate blossom from the tree.
Close thy sweet eyes, calmly, and without pain:
   And we will trust in God to see thee yet again.

AN INDIAN STORY.

"I KNOW where the timid fawn abides
  In the depths of the shaded dell,
Where the leaves are broad and the thicket hides,
With its many stems and its tangled sides,
  From the eye of the hunter well.

"I know where the young May violet grows,
  In its lone and lowly nook,
On the mossy bank, where the larch-tree throws
Its broad dark boughs, in solemn repose,
  Far over the silent brook.

"And that timid fawn starts not with fear
  When I steal to her secret bower;
And that young May violet to me is dear,
And I visit the silent streamlet near,
  To look on the lovely flower."

Thus Maquon sings as he lightly walks
  To the hunting-ground on the hills;
'Tis a song of his maid of the woods and rocks,
With her bright black eyes and long black locks,
  And voice like the music of rills.

He goes to the chase—but evil eyes
  Are at watch in the thicker shades;
For she was lovely that smiled on his sighs,
And he bore, from a hundred lovers, his prize,
  The flower of the forest maids.

The boughs in the morning wind are stirred,
  And the woods their song renew,
With the early carol of many a bird,
And the quickened tune of the streamlet heard
  Where the hazels trickle with dew.

And Maquon has promised his dark-haired maid,
  Ere eve shall redden the sky,
A good red deer from the forest shade,
That bounds with the herd through grove and glade,
  At her cabin-door shall lie.

The hollow woods, in the setting sun,
  Ring shrill with the fire-bird's lay;
And Maquon's sylvan labors are done,
And his shafts are spent, but the spoil they won
  He bears on his homeward way.

He stops near his bower—his eye perceives
  Strange traces along the ground—
At once to the earth his burden he heaves;

He breaks through the veil of boughs and leaves;
   And gains its door with a bound.

But the vines are torn on its walls that leant,
   And all from the young shrubs there
By struggling hands have the leaves been rent,
And there hangs on the sassafras, broken and bent,
   One tress of the well-known hair.

But where is she who, at this calm hour,
   Ever watched his coming to see?
She is not at the door, nor yet in the bower;
He calls—but he only hears on the flower
   The hum of the laden bee.

It is not a time for idle grief,
   Nor a time for tears to flow;
The horror that freezes his limbs is brief—
He grasps his war-axe and bow, and a sheaf
   Of darts made sharp for the foe.

And he looks for the print of the ruffian's feet
   Where he bore the maiden away;
And he darts on the fatal path more fleet
Than the blast hurries the vapor and sleet
   O'er the wild November day.

'Twas early summer when Maquon's bride
   Was stolen away from his door;
But at length the maples in crimson are dyed,
And the grape is black on the cabin-side—
   And she smiles at his hearth once more.

But far in the pine-grove, dark and cold,
   Where the yellow leaf falls not,
Nor the autumn shines in scarlet and gold,
   There lies a hillock of fresh dark mould,
In the deepest gloom of the spot.

And the Indian girls, that pass that way,
   Point out the ravisher's grave;
"And how soon to the bower she loved," they say,
   "Returned the maid that was borne away
From Maquon, the fond and the brave."

<center>~~~~~******~~~~~</center>

SUMMER WIND.

   IT is a sultry day; the sun has drunk
The dew that lay upon the morning grass;
There is no rustling in the lofty elm
That canopies my dwelling, and its shade
Scarce cools me. All is silent, save the faint
And interrupted murmur of the bee,
Settling on the sick flowers, and then again

Instantly on the wing. The plants around
Feel the two potent fervors: the tall maize
Rolls up its long green leaves; the clover droops
Its tender foliage, and declines its blooms.
But far in the fierce sunshine tower the hills,
With all their growth of woods, silent and stern,
As if the scorching heat and dazzling light
Were but an element they loved. Bright clouds,
Motionless pillars of the brazen heaven—
Their bases on the mountains—their white tops
Shining in the far ether—fire the air
With a reflected radiance, and make turn
The gazer's eye away. For me, I lie
Languidly in the shade, where the thick turf,
Yet virgin from the kisses of the sun,
Retains some freshness, and I woo the wind
That still delays his coming. Why so slow,
Gentle and voluble spirit of the air?
Oh, come and breathe upon the fainting earth
Coolness and life! Is it that in his caves
He hears me? See, on yonder woody ridge,
The pine is bending- his proud top, and now
Among the nearer groves, chestnut and oak
Are tossing their green boughs about. He comes;
Lo, where the grassy meadow runs in waves!
The deep distressful silence of the scene
Breaks up with mingling of unnumbered sounds
And universal motion. He is come,
Shaking a shower of blossoms from the shrubs,
And bearing on their fragrance; and he brings
Music of birds, and rustling of young boughs,
And sound of swaying branches, and the voice
Of distant waterfalls. All the green herbs
Are stirring in his breath; a thousand flowers,
By the road-side and the borders of the brook,
Nod gayly to each other; glossy leaves
Are twinkling in the sun, as if the dew
Were on them yet, and silver waters break
Into small waves and sparkle as he comes.

~~~~~******~~~~~

AN INDIAN AT THE BURIAL-PLACE OF HIS FATHERS.

It is the spot I came to seek,—
  My fathers' ancient burial-place
Ere from these vales, ashamed and weak,
  Withdrew our wasted race.
It is the spot—I know it well—
Of which our old traditions tell.

For here the upland bank sends out
  A ridge toward the river-side;
I know the shaggy hills about,
  The meadows smooth and wide,—
The plains, that, toward the southern sky,

Fenced east and west by mountains lie.

A white man, gazing on the scene,
  Would say a lovely spot was here,
And praise the lawns, so fresh and green,
  Between the hills so sheer.
I like it not—I would the plain
Lay in its tall old groves again.

The sheep are on the slopes around,
  The cattle in the meadows feed,
And labourers turn the crumbling ground,
  Or drop the yellow seed,
And prancing steeds, in trappings gay,
Whirl the bright chariot o'er the way.

Methinks it were a nobler sight
  To see these vales in woods arrayed,
Their summits in the golden light,
  Their trunks in grateful shade,
And herds of deer, that bounding go
O'er hills and prostrate trees below.

And then to mark the lord of all,
  The forest hero, trained to wars,
Quivered and plumed, and lithe and tall,
  And seamed with glorious scars,
Walk forth, amid his reign, to dare
The wolf, and grapple with the bear.

This bank, in which the dead were laid,
  Was sacred when its soil was ours;
Hither the artless Indian maid
  Brought wreaths of beads and flowers,
And the gray chief and gifted seer
Worshipped the god of thunders here.

But now the wheat is green and high
  On clods that hid the warrior's breast,
And scattered in the furrows lie
  The weapons of his rest;
And there, in the loose sand, is thrown
Of his large arm the mouldering bone.

Ah, little thought the strong and brave
  Who bore their lifeless chieftain forth—
Or the young wife, that weeping gave
  Her first-born to the earth,
That the pale race, who waste us now,
Among their bones should guide the plough.

They waste us—ay—like April snow
  In the warm noon, we shrink away;
And fast they follow, as we go
  Towards the setting day,—
Till they shall fill the land, and we

Are driven into the western sea.

But I behold a fearful sign,
  To which the white men's eyes are blind;
Their race may vanish hence, like mine,
  And leave no trace behind,
Save ruins o'er the region spread,
And the white stones above the dead.

Before these fields were shorn and tilled,
  Full to the brim our rivers flowed;
The melody of waters filled
  The fresh and boundless wood;
And torrents dashed and rivulets played,
And fountains spouted in the shade.

Those grateful sounds are heard no more,
  The springs are silent in the sun;
The rivers, by the blackened shore,
  With lessening current run;
The realm our tribes are crushed to get
May be a barren desert yet.

~~~~~******~~~~~

SONG.

DOST thou idly ask to hear
  At what gentle seasons
Nymphs relent, when lovers near
  Press the tenderest reasons?
Ah, they give their faith too oft
  To the careless wooer;
Maidens' hearts are always soft.
  Would that men's were truer!

Woo the fair one when around
  Early birds are singing;
When, o'er all the fragrant ground.
  Early herbs are springing:
When the brookside, bank, and grove,
  All with blossoms laden,
Shine with beauty, breathe of love,—
  Woo the timid maiden.

Woo her when, with rosy blush,
  Summer eve is sinking;
When, on rills that softly gush,
  Stars are softly winking;

When through boughs that knit the bower
  Moonlight gleams are stealing;
Woo her, till the gentle hour
  Wake a gentler feeling.

Woo her, when autumnal dyes

54

Tinge the woody mountain;
When the dropping foliage lies
 In the weedy fountain;
Let the scene, that tells how fast
 Youth is passing over,
Warn her, ere her bloom is past,
 To secure her lover.

Woo her when the north winds call
 At the lattice nightly;
When, within the cheerful hall,
 Blaze the fagots brightly;
While the wintry tempest round
 Sweeps the landscape hoary,
Sweeter in her ear shall sound
 Love's delightful story.

<center>~~~~~******~~~~~</center>

HYMN OF THE WALDENSES.

HEAR, Father, hear thy faint afflicted flock
Cry to thee, from the desert and the rock;
While those, who seek to slay thy children, hold
Blasphemous worship under roofs of gold;
And the broad goodly lands, with pleasant airs
That nurse the grape and wave the grain, are theirs.

Yet better were this mountain wilderness,
And this wild life of danger and distress—
Watchings by night and perilous flight by day,
And meetings in the depths of earth to pray—
Better, far better, than to kneel with them,
And pay the impious rite thy laws condemn.

Thou, Lord, dost hold the thunder; the firm land
Tosses in billows when it feels thy hand;
Thou dashest nation against nation, then
Stillest the angry world to peace again.
Oh, touch their stony hearts who hunt thy sons—
The murderers of our wives and little ones.

Yet, mighty God, yet shall thy frown look forth
Unveiled, and terribly shall shake the earth.
Then the foul power of priestly sin and all
Its long-upheld idolatries shall fall.
Thou shalt raise up the trampled and oppressed,
And thy delivered saints shall dwell in rest.

<center>~~~~~******~~~~~</center>

MONUMENT MOUNTAIN. [5]

THOU who wouldst see the lovely and the wild
Mingled in harmony on Nature's face,
Ascend our rocky mountains. Let thy foot
Fail not with weariness, for on their tops
The beauty and the majesty of earth,
Spread wide beneath, shall make thee to forget
The steep and toilsome way. There, as thou stand'st,
The haunts of men below thee, and around
The mountain-summits, thy expanding heart
Shall feel a kindred with that loftier world
To which thou art translated, and partake
The enlargement of thy vision. Thou shalt look
Upon the green and rolling forest-tops,
And down into the secrets of the glens,
And streams that with their bordering thickets strive
To hide their windings. Thou shalt gaze, at once,
Here on white villages, and tilth, and herds,
And swarming roads, and there on solitudes
That only hear the torrent, and the wind,
And eagle's shriek. There is a precipice
That seems a fragment of some mighty wall,
Built by the hand that fashioned the old world.
To separate its nations, and thrown down
When the flood drowned them. To the north, a path
Conducts you up the narrow battlement.
Steep is the western side, shaggy and wild
With mossy trees, and pinnacles of flint,
And many a hanging crag. But, to the east,
Sheer to the vale go down the bare old cliffs—
Huge pillars, that in middle heaven upbear
Their weather-beaten capitals, here dark
With moss, the growth of centuries, and there
Of chalky whiteness Where the thunderbolt
Has splintered them. It is a fearful thing
To stand upon the beetling verge, and see
Where storm and lightning, from that huge gray wall,
Have tumbled down vast blocks, and at the base
Dashed them in fragments, and to lay thine ear
Over the dizzy depth, and hear the sound
Of winds, that struggle with the woods below,
Come up like ocean-murmurs. But the scene
Is lovely round; a beautiful river there
Wanders amid the fresh and fertile meads,

---

[5] The mountain called by this name is a remarkable precipice in Great Barrington, overlooking the rich and picturesque valley of the Housatonic, in the western part of Massachusetts. At the southern extremity is, or was a few years since, a conical pile of small stones erected, according to the tradition of the surrounding country, by the Indians, in memory of a woman of the Stockbridge tribe who killed herself by leaping from the edge of the precipice. Until within a few years past, small parties of that tribe used to arrive from their settlement in the western part of the State of New York, on visits to Stockbridge, the place of their nativity and former residence. A young woman belonging to one of these parties related, to a friend of the author, the story on which the poem of Monument Mountain is founded. An Indian girl had formed an attachment for her cousin, which, according to the customs of the tribe, was unlawful. She was, in consequence, seized with a deep melancholy, and resolved to destroy herself. In company with a female friend she repaired to the mountain, decked out for the occasion in all her ornaments, and, after passing the day on the summit in singing with her companion the traditional songs of her nation, she threw herself headlong from the rock, and was killed.

The paradise he made unto himself,
Mining the soil for ages. On each side
The fields swell upward to the hills; beyond,
Above the hills, in the blue distance, rise
The mountain-columns with which earth props heaven.

There is a tale about these reverend rocks,
A sad tradition of unhappy love,
And sorrows borne and ended, long ago,
When over these fair vales the savage sought
His game in the thick woods. There was a maid
The fairest of the Indian maids, bright-eyed,
With wealth of raven tresses, a light form,
And a gay heart. About her cabin-door
The wide old woods resounded with her song
And fairy laughter all the summer day.
She loved her cousin; such a love was deemed,
By the morality of those stern tribes,
Incestuous, and she struggled hard and long
Against her love, and reasoned with her heart,
As simple Indian maiden might. In vain.
Then her eye lost its lustre, and her step
Its lightness, and the gray-haired men that passed
Her dwelling, wondered that they heard no more
The accustomed song and laugh of her, whose looks
Were like the cheerful smile of Spring, they said,
Upon the Winter of their age. She went
To weep where no eye saw, and was not found
When all the merry girls were met to dance.
And all the hunters of the tribe were out;
Nor when they gathered from the rustling husk
The shining ear; nor when, by the river's side,
They pulled the grape and startled the wild shades
With sounds of mirth. The keen—eyed Indian dames
Would whisper to each other, as they saw
Her wasting form, and say, *The girl will die.*

One day into the bosom of a friend,
A playmate of her young and innocent years,
She poured her griefs. "Thou know'st, and thou alone,
She said, "for I have told thee, all my love,
And guilt, and sorrow. I am sick of life.
All night I weep in darkness, and the morn
Glares on me. as upon a thing accursed,
That has no business on the earth. I hate
The pastimes and the pleasant toils that once
I loved; the cheerful voices of my friends
Sound in my ear like mockings, and, at night,
In dreams, my mother, from the land of souls,
Calls me and chides me. All that look on me
Do seem to know my shame; I cannot bear
Their eyes; I cannot from my heart root out
The love that wrings it so, and I must die."

It was a summer morning, and they went
To this old precipice. About the cliffs

Lay garlands, ears of maize, and shaggy skins
Of wolf and bear, the offerings of the tribe
Here made to the Great Spirit, for they deemed,
Like worshippers of the elder time, that God
Doth walk on the high places and affect
The earth-o'erlooking mountains. She had on
The ornaments with which her father loved
To deck the beauty of his bright-eyed girl,
And bade her wear when stranger warriors came
To be his guests. Here the friends sat them down,
And sang, all day, old songs of love and death,
And decked the poor wan victim's hair with flowers,
And prayed that safe and swift might be her way
To the calm world of sunshine, where no grief
Makes the heart heavy and the eyelids red.
Beautiful lay the region of her tribe
Below her—waters resting in the embrace
Of the wide forest, and maize-planted glades
Opening amid the leafy wilderness.
She gazed upon it long, and at the sight
Of her own village peeping through the trees,
And her own dwelling, and the cabin-roof
Of him she loved with an unlawful love,
And came to die for, a warm gush of tears
Ran from her eyes. But when the sun grew low
And the hill-shadows long, she threw herself
From the steep rock and perished. There was scooped,
Upon the mountain's southern slope, a grave;
And there they laid her, in the very garb
With which the maiden decked herself for death,
With the same withering wild-flowers in her hair.
And o'er the mould that covered her, the tribe
Built up a simple monument, a cone
Of small loose stones. Thenceforward all who passed,
Hunter, and dame, and virgin, laid a stone
In silence on the pile. It stands there yet.
And Indians from the distant West, who come
To visit where their fathers' bones are laid,
Yet tell the sorrowful tale, and to this day
The mountain where the hapless maiden died
Is called the Mountain of the Monument.

~~~~~~******~~~~~~

AFTER A TEMPEST.

THE day had been a day of wind and storm,
The wind was laid, the storm was overpast,
And stooping from the zenith, bright and warm,
Shone the great sun on the wide earth at last.
I stood upon the upland slope, and cast
Mine eye upon a broad and beauteous scene,
Where the vast plain lay girt by mountains vast,
And hills o'er hills lifted their heads of green,
With pleasant vales scooped out and villages between.

The rain-drops glistened on the trees around,
Whose shadows on the tall grass were not stirred,
Save when a shower of diamonds, to the ground,
Was shaken by the flight of startled bird;
For birds were warbling round, and bees were heard
About the flowers; the cheerful rivulet sung
And gossiped, as he hastened oceanward;
To the gray oak the squirrel, chiding, clung,
And chirping from the ground the grasshopper upsprung.

And from beneath the leaves that kept them dry
Flew many a glittering insect here and there,
And darted up and down the butterfly,
That seemed a living blossom of the air,
The flocks came scattering from the thicket, where
The violent rain had pent them; in the way
Strolled groups of damsels frolicsome and fair;
The farmer swung the scythe or turned the hay,
And 'twixt the heavy swaths his children were at play.

It was a scene of peace—and, like a spell,
Did that serene and golden sunlight fall
Upon the motionless wood that clothed the fell,
And precipice upspringing like a wall,
And glassy river and white waterfall,
And happy living things that trod the bright
And beauteous scene; while far beyond them all,
On many a lovely valley, out of sight,
Was poured from the blue heavens the same soft golden light.

I looked, and thought the quiet of the scene
An emblem of the peace that yet shall be,
When o'er earth's continents, and isles between,
The noise of war shall cease from sea to sea,
And married nations dwell in harmony;
When millions, crouching in the dust to one,
No more shall beg their lives on bended knee,
Nor the black stake be dressed, nor in the sun
The o'erlabored captive toil, and wish his life were done.

Too long, at clash of arms amid her bowers
And pools of blood, the earth has stood aghast,
The fair earth, that should only blush with flowers
And ruddy fruits; but not for aye can last
The storm, and sweet the sunshine when 'tis past.
Lo, the clouds roll away—they break—they fly,
And, like the glorious light of summer, cast
O'er the wide landscape from the embracing sky,
On all the peaceful world the smile of heaven shall he.

~~~~~******~~~~~

AUTUMN WOODS.

ERE, in the northern gale,
The summer tresses of the trees are gone,

The woods of Autumn, all around our vale,
    Have put their glory on.

The mountains that infold,
In their wide sweep, the colored landscape round,
Seem groups of giant kings, in purple and gold,
    That guard the enchanted ground.

I roam the woods that crown
The upland, where the mingled splendors glow,
Where the gay company of trees look down
    On the green fields below.

My steps are not alone
In these bright walks; the sweet southwest, at play
Flies, rustling, where the painted leaves are strown
    Along the winding way.

And far in heaven, the while,
The sun, that sends that gale to wander here,
Pours out on the fair earth his quiet smile—
    The sweetest of the year.

Where now the solemn shade,
Verdure and gloom where many branches meet;
So grateful, when the noon of summer made
    The valleys sick with heat?

Let in through all the trees
Come the strange rays; the forest depths are bright;
Their sunny colored foliage, in the breeze,
    Twinkles, like beams of light.

The rivulet, late unseen,
Where bickering through the shrubs its waters run,
Shines with the image of its golden screen,
    And glimmerings of the sun.

But 'neath yon crimson tree,
Lover to listening maid might breathe his flame,
Nor mark, within its roseate canopy,
    Her blush of maiden shame.

O Autumn! why so soon
Depart the hues that make thy forests glad,
Thy gentle wind and thy fair sunny noon,
    And leave thee wild and sad!

Ah! 'twere a lot too blest
Forever in thy colored shades to stray;
Amid the kisses of the soft southwest
    To rove and dream for aye;

And leave the vain low strife
That makes men mad—the tug for wealth and power,
The passions and the cares that wither life,

And waste its little hour.

~~~~~******~~~~~

MUTATION.

THEY talk of short-lived pleasure—be it so—
   Pain dies as quickly: stern, hard-featured Pain
Expires, and lets her weary prisoner go.
   The fiercest agonies have shortest reign;
   And after dreams of horror, comes again
The welcome morning with its rays of peace.
   Oblivion, softly wiping out the stain,
Makes the strong secret pangs of shame to cease:
Remorse is virtue's root; its fair increase
   Are fruits of innocence and blessedness:
Thus joy, o'erborne and bound, doth still release
   His young limbs from the chains that round him press.
Weep not that the world changes—did it keep
A stable, changeless state, 'twere cause indeed to weep.

~~~~~******~~~~~

NOVEMBER.

YET one smile more, departing, distant sun!
   One mellow smile through the soft vapory air,
Ere, o'er the frozen earth, the loud winds run,
   Or snows are sifted o'er the meadows bare.
One smile on the brown hills and naked trees,
   And the dark rocks whose summer wreaths are cast,
And the blue gentian—flower, that, in the breeze,
   Nods lonely, of her beauteous race the last.
Yet a few sunny days, in which the bee
   Shall murmur by the hedge that skirts the way,
The cricket chirp upon the russet lea,
   And man delight to linger in thy ray.
Yet one rich smile, and we will try to bear
The piercing winter frost, and winds, and darkened air.

~~~~~******~~~~~

SONG OF THE GREEK AMAZON.

I BUCKLE to my slender side
   The pistol and the scimitar,
And in my maiden flower and pride
   Am come to share the tasks of war.
And yonder stands my fiery steed,
   That paws the ground and neighs to go,
My charger of the Arab breed—
   I took him from the routed foe. I

My mirror is the mountain-spring,
   At which I dress my ruffled hair;
My dimmed and dusty arms I bring,

And wash away the blood-stain there.
Why should I guard from wind and sun
   This cheek, whose virgin rose is fled?
It was for one—oh, only one—
   I kept its bloom, and he is dead.

But they who slew him-unaware
   Of coward murderers lurking nigh—
And left him to the fowls of air,
   Are yet alive—and they must die!
They slew him—and my virgin years
   Are vowed to Greece and vengeance now,
And many an Othman dame, in tears,
   Shall rue the Grecian maiden's vow.

I touched the lute in better days,
   I led in dance the joyous band;
Ah! they may move to mirthful lays
   Whose hands can touch a lover's hand
The march of hosts that haste to meet
   Seems gayer than the dance to me;
The lute's sweet tones are not so sweet
   As the fierce shout of victory.

<div align="center">~~~~~******~~~~~</div>

TO A CLOUD.

BEAUTIFUL cloud! with folds so soft and fair,
   Swimming in the pure quiet air.
Thy fleeces bathed in sunlight, while below
   Thy shadow o'er the vale moves slow;
Where, midst their labor, pause the reaper train,
   As cool it comes along the grain.
Beautiful cloud! I would I were with thee
   In thy calm way o'er land and sea;
To rest on thy unrolling skirts, and look
   On Earth as on an open book;
On streams that tie her realms with silver bands,
   And the long ways that seam her lands;
And hear her humming cities, and the sound
   Of the great ocean breaking round.
Ay—I would sail, upon thy air-borne car,
   To blooming regions distant far,
To where the sun of Andalusia shines
   On his own olive-groves and vines,
Or the soft lights of Italy's clear sky
   In smiles upon her ruins lie.

But I would woo the winds to let us rest
   O'er Greece, long fettered and oppressed,
Whose sons at length have heard the call that comes
   From the old battle-fields and tombs,
And risen, and drawn the sword, and on the foe
   Have dealt the swift and desperate blow,
And the Othman power is cloven, and the stroke

Has touched its chains, and they are broke.
Ay, we would linger, till the sunset there
    Should come, to purple all the air,
And thou reflect upon the sacred ground
    The ruddy radiance streaming round.

Bright meteor! for the summer noontide made!
    Thy peerless beauty yet shall fade.

The sun, that fills with light each glistening fold,
    Shall set, and leave thee dark and cold:
The blast shall rend thy skirts, or thou mayst frown
    In the dark heaven when storms come down;
And weep in rain, till man's inquiring eye
    Miss thee, forever, from the sky.

<center>~~~~~******~~~~~</center>

THE MURDERED TRAVELLER. [6]

WHEN Spring, to woods and wastes around.
    Brought bloom and joy again,
The murdered traveller's bones were found,
    Far down a narrow glen.

The fragrant birch, above him, hung
    Her tassels in the sky:
And many a vernal blossom sprung,
    And nodded careless by.

The red-bird warbled, as he wrought
    His hanging nest o'erhead,
And fearless, near the fatal spot,
    Her young the partridge led.

But there was weeping far away,
    And gentle eyes, for him,
With watching many an anxious day,
    Were sorrowful and dim.

They little knew, who loved him so,
    The fearful death he met,
When shouting o'er the desert snow,
    Unarmed, and hard beset;—

---

[6] Some years since, in the month of May, the remains of a human body, partly devoured by wild animals, were found in a woody ravine, near a solitary road passing between the mountains west of the village of Stockbridge. It was supposed that the person came to his death by violence, but no traces could be discovered of his murderers. It was only recollected that one evening, in the course of the previous winter, a traveller had stopped at an inn in the village of West Stockbridge: that he had inquired the way to Stockbridge; and that, in paying the innkeeper for something he had ordered, it appeared that he had a considerable sum of money in his possession. Two ill-looking men were present, and went out about the same time that the traveller proceeded on his journey. During the winter, also, two men of shabby appearance, but plentifully supplied with money, had lingered for a while about the village of Stockbridge. Several years afterward, a criminal, about to be executed for a capital offence in Canada, confessed that he had been concerned in murdering a traveller in Stockbridge for the sake of his money. Nothing was ever discovered respecting the name or residence of the person murdered.

63

Nor how, when round the frosty pole
 The northern dawn was red,
The mountain wolf and wild-cat stole
 To banquet on the dead;—

Nor how, when strangers found his bones,
 They dressed the hasty bier,
And marked his grave with nameless stones,
 Unmoistened by a tear.

But long they looked, and feared, and wept,
 Within his distant home;
And dreamed, and started as they slept,
 For joy that he was come.

Long, long they looked—but never spied
 His welcome step again,

Nor knew the fearful death he died
 Far down that narrow glen.

<center>~~~~*****~~~~</center>

HYMN TO THE NORTH STAR.

THE sad and solemn night
Hath yet her multitude of cheerful fires;
 The glorious host of light
Walk the dark hemisphere till she retires;
All through her silent watches, gliding slow,
Her constellations come, and climb the heavens, and go.

 Day, too, hath many a star
To grace his gorgeous reign, as bright as they:
 Through the blue fields afar,
Unseen, they follow in his flaming way:
Many a bright lingerer, as the eve grows dim,
Tells what a radiant troop arose and set with him.

 And thou dost see them rise,
Star of the Pole! and thou dost see them set.
 Alone, in thy cold skies,
Thou keep'st thy old unmoving station yet,
Nor join'st the dances of that glittering train,
Nor dipp'st thy virgin orb in the blue western main.

 There, at morn's rosy birth,
Thou lookest meekly through the kindling air,
 And eve, that round the earth
Chases the day, beholds thee watching there;
There noontide finds thee, and the hour that calls
The shapes of polar flame to scale heaven's azure walls.

 Alike, beneath thine eye,
The deeds of darkness and of light are done;
 High toward the starlit sky

Towns blaze, the smoke of battle blots the sun,
The night-storm on a thousand hills is loud,
And the strong wind of day doth mingle sea and cloud.

On thy unaltering blaze
The half-wrecked mariner, his compass lost,
Fixes his steady gaze,
And steers, undoubting, to the friendly coast;
And they who stray in perilous wastes, by night,
Are glad when thou dost shine to guide their footsteps right.

And, therefore, bards of old,
Sages and hermits of the solemn wood,
Did in thy beams behold
A beauteous type of that unchanging good,
That bright eternal beacon, by whose ray
The voyager of time should shape his heedful way.

~~~~~******~~~~~

THE LAPSE OF TIME.

LAMENT who will, in fruitless tears,
    The speed with which our moments fly;
I sigh not over vanished years,
    But watch the years that hasten by.

Look, how they come—a mingled crowd
    Of bright and dark, but rapid clays;
Beneath them, like a summer cloud,
    The wide world changes as I gaze.

What! grieve that time has brought so soon
    The sober age of manhood on!
As idly might I weep, at noon,
    To see the blush of morning gone.

Could I give up the hopes that glow
    In prospect like Elysian isles;
And let the cheerful future go,
    With all her promises and smiles?

The future!—cruel were the power
    Whose doom would tear thee from my heart;
Thou sweetener of the present hour!
    We cannot—no—we will not part.

Oh, leave me, still, the rapid flight
    That makes the changing seasons gay,
The grateful speed that brings the night,
    The swift and glad return of day;

The months that touch, with added grace,
    This little prattler at my knee,
In whose arch eye and speaking face
    New meaning every hour I see;

The years, that o'er each sister land
   Shall lift the country of my birth,
And nurse her strength, till she shall stand
   The pride and pattern of the earth:

Till younger commonwealths, for aid,
   Shall cling about her ample robe,
And from her frown shall shrink afraid
   The crowned oppressors of the globe.

True—time will seam and blanch my brow—
   Well——I shall sit with aged men,
And my good glass will tell me how
   A grizzly beard becomes me then.

And then, should no dishonor lie
   Upon my head, when I am gray,
Love yet shall watch my fading eye,
   And smooth the path of my decay.

Then haste thee, Time—'tis kindness all
   That speeds thy winged feet so fast:
Thy pleasures stay not till they pall,
   And all thy pains are quickly past.

Thou fliest and bear'st away our woes,
   And as thy shadowy train depart,
The memory of sorrow grows
   A lighter burden on the heart.

～～～～＊＊＊＊＊＊～～～～

SONG OF THE STARS.

WHEN the radiant morn of creation broke,
And the world in the smile of God awoke,
And the empty realms of darkness and death
Were moved through their depths by his mighty breath,
And orbs of beauty and spheres of flame
From the void abyss by myriads came-
In the joy of youth as they darted away,
Through the widening wastes of space to play,
Their silver voices in chorus rang,
And this was the song the bright ones sang:

"Away, away, through the wide, wide sky,
The fair blue fields that before us lie—
Each sun with the worlds that round him roll,
Each planet, poised on her turning pole;
With her isles of green, and her clouds of white,
And her waters that lie like fluid light.

"For the source of glory uncovers his face,
And the brightness o'erflows unbounded space,
And we drink as we go the luminous tides

In our ruddy air and our blooming sides:
Lo, yonder the living splendors play;
Away, on our joyous path, away!

"Look, look, through our glittering ranks afar,
In the infinite azure, star after star,
How they brighten and bloom as they swiftly pass!
How the verdure runs o'er each rolling mass!
And the path of the gentle winds is seen,
Where the small waves dance, and the young woods lean.

"And see, where the brighter day-beams pour,
How the rainbows hang in the sunny shower;
And the morn and eve, with their pomp of hues,
Shift o'er the bright planets and shed their dews;
And 'twixt them both, o'er the teeming ground,
With her shadowy cone the night goes round!

"Away, away! in our blossoming bowers,
In the soft air wrapping these spheres of ours,
In the seas and fountains that shine with morn,
See, Love is brooding, and Life is born,
And breathing myriads are breaking from night,
To rejoice, like us, in motion and light.

"Glide on in your beauty, ye youthful spheres,
To weave the dance that measures the years;
Glide on, in the glory and gladness sent
To the farthest wall of the firmament—
The boundless visible smile of Him
To the veil of whose brow your lamps are dim."

—————******—————

A FOREST HYMN.

THE groves were God's first temples. Ere man learned
To hew the shaft, and lay the architrave,
And spread the roof above them—ere he framed
The lofty vault, to gather and roll back
The sound of anthems; in the darkling wood,
Amid the cool and silence, he knelt down,
And offered to the Mightiest solemn thanks
And supplication. For his simple heart
Might not resist the sacred influences
Which, from the stilly twilight of the place,
And from the gray old trunks that high in heaven
Mingled their mossy boughs, and from the sound
Of the invisible breath that swayed at once
All their green tops, stole over him, and bowed
His spirit with the thought of boundless power
And inaccessible majesty. Ah, why
Should we, in the world's riper years, neglect
God's ancient sanctuaries, and adore
Only among the crowd, and under roofs
That our frail hands have raised? Let me, at least,

Here, in the shadow of this aged wood,
Offer one hymn—thrice happy, if it find
Acceptance in His ear.

                      Father, thy hand
Hath reared these venerable columns, thou
Didst weave this verdant roof. Thou didst look down
Upon the naked earth, and, forthwith, rose
All these fair ranks of trees. They, in thy sun,
Budded, and shook their green leaves in thy breeze,
And shot toward heaven. The century—living crow
Whose birth was in their tops, grew old and died
Among their branches, till, at last, they stood,
As now they stand, massy, and tall, and dark,
Fit shrine for humble worshipper to hold
Communion with his Maker. These dim vaults,
These winding aisles, of human pomp or pride
Report not. No fantastic carvings show
The boast of our vain race to change the form
Of thy fair works. But thou art here—thou fill'st
The solitude. Thou art in the soft winds
That run along the summit of these trees
In music; thou art in the cooler breath
That from the inmost darkness of the place
Comes, scarcely felt; the barky trunks, the ground,
The fresh moist ground, are all instinct with thee.
Here is continual worship;—Nature, here,
In the tranquillity that thou dost love,
Enjoys thy presence. Noiselessly, around,
From perch to perch, the solitary bird
Passes; and yon clear spring, that, midst its herbs,
Wells softly forth and wandering steeps the roots
Of half the mighty forest, tells no tale
Of all the good it does. Thou hast not left
Thyself without a witness, in these shades,
Of thy perfections. Grandeur, strength, and grace,
Are here to speak of thee. This mighty oak—
By whose immovable stem I stand and seem
Almost annihilated—not a prince,
In all that proud old world beyond the deep,
E'er wore his crown as loftily as he
Wears the green coronal of leaves with which
Thy hand has graced him. Nestled at his root
Is beauty, such as blooms not in the glare
Of the broad sun. That delicate forest flower,
With scented breath and look so like a smile,
Seems, as it issues from the shapeless mould,
An emanation of the indwelling Life,
A visible token of the upholding Love,
That are the soul of this great universe.

    My heart is awed within me when I think
Of the great miracle that still goes on,
In silence, round me—the perpetual work
Of thy creation, finished, yet renewed
Forever. Written on thy works I read

The lesson of thy own eternity.
Lo! all grow old and die—but see again,
How on the faltering footsteps of decay
Youth presses—ever-gay and beautiful youth
In all its beautiful forms. These lofty trees
Wave not less proudly that their ancestors
Moulder beneath them. Oh, there is not lost
One of earth's charms: upon her bosom yet,
After the flight of untold centuries,
The freshness of her far beginning lies
And yet shall lie. Life mocks the idle hate
Of his arch-enemy Death—yea, seats himself
Upon the tyrant's throne—the sepulchre,
And of the triumphs of his ghastly foe
Makes his own nourishment. For he came forth
From thine own bosom, and shall have no end.

There have been holy men who hid themselves
Deep in the woody wilderness, and gave
Their lives to thought and prayer, till they outlived
The generation born with them, nor seemed
Less aged than the hoary trees and rocks
Around them;—and there have been holy men
Who deemed it were not well to pass life thus.
But let me often to these solitudes
Retire, and in thy presence reassure
My feeble virtue. Here its enemies,
The passions, at thy plainer footsteps shrink
And tremble and are still. O God! when thou
Dost scare the world with tempests, set on fire
The heavens with falling thunderbolts, or fill,
With all the waters of the firmament,
The swift dark whirlwind that uproots the woods
And drowns the villages; When, at thy call,
Uprises the great deep and throws himself
Upon the continent, and overwhelms
Its cities—who forgets not, at the sight
Of these tremendous tokens of thy power,
His pride, and lays his strifes and follies by?
Oh, from these sterner aspects of thy face
Spare me and mine, nor let us need the wrath
Of the mad, unchained elements to teach
Who rules them. Be it ours to meditate,
In these calm shades, thy milder majesty,
And to the beautiful order of thy works
Learn to conform the order of our lives.

~~~~~~~******~~~~~~~

"OH FAIREST OF THE RURAL MAIDS."

Oh fairest of the rural maids!
Thy birth was in the forest shades;
Green boughs, and glimpses of the sky,
Were all that met thine infant eye.

Thy sports, thy wanderings, when a child,
Were ever in the sylvan wild;
And all the beauty of the place
Is in thy heart and on thy face.

The twilight of the trees and rocks
Is in the light shade of thy locks;
Thy step is as the wind, that weaves
Its playful way among the leaves.

Thine eyes are springs, in whose serene
And silent waters heaven is seen;
Their lashes are the herbs that look
On their young figures in the brook.

The forest depths, by foot unpressed,
Are not more sinless than thy breast;
The holy peace, that fills the air
Of those calm solitudes, is there.

******

"I BROKE THE SPELL THAT HELD ME LONG."

I broke the spell that held me long,
The dear, dear witchery of song.
I said, the poet's idle lore
Shall waste my prime of years no more,
For Poetry, though heavenly born,
Consorts with poverty and scorn.

I broke the spell—nor deemed its power
Could fetter me another hour.
Ah, thoughtless! how could I forget
Its causes were around me yet?
For wheresoe'er I looked, the while,
Was Nature's everlasting smile.

Still came and lingered on my sight
Of flowers and streams the bloom and light,
And glory of the stars and sun; —
And these and poetry are one.
They, ere the world had held me long,
Recalled me to the love of song.

******

JUNE.

I gazed upon the glorious sky
    And the green mountains round,
And thought that when I came to lie
    At rest within the ground,
'Twere pleasant, that in flowery June,
When brooks send up a cheerful tune,
    And groves a joyous sound,

70

The sexton's hand, my grave to make,
The rich, green mountain-turf should break.

A cell within the frozen mould,
   A coffin borne through sleet,
And icy clods above it rolled,
   While fierce the tempests beat—
Away!—I will not think of these—
Blue be the sky and soft the breeze,
   Earth green beneath the feet,
And be the damp mould gently pressed
Into my narrow place of rest.

There through the long, long summer hours,
   The golden light should lie,
And thick young herbs and groups of flowers
   Stand in their beauty by.
The oriole should build and tell
His love-tale close beside my cell;
   The idle butterfly
Should rest him there, and there be heard
The housewife bee and humming-bird.

And what if cheerful shouts at noon
   Come, from the village sent,
Or songs of maids, beneath the moon
   With fairy laughter blent?
And what if, in the evening light,
Betrothed lovers walk in sight
   Of my low monument?
I would the lovely scene around
Might know no sadder sight nor sound.

I know that I no more should see
   The season's glorious show,
Nor would its brightness shine for me,
   Nor its wild music flow;
But if, around my place of sleep,
The friends I love should come to weep,
   They might not haste to go.
Soft airs, and song, and light, and bloom
Should keep them lingering by my tomb.

These to their softened hearts should bear
   The thought of what has been,
And speak of one who cannot share
   The gladness of the scene;
Whose part, in all the pomp that fills
The circuit of the summer hills,
   Is that his grave is green;
And deeply would their hearts rejoice
To hear again his living voice.

~~~~*****~~~~

71

A SONG OF PITCAIRN'S ISLAND.

Come, take our boy, and we will go
    Before our cabin-door;
The winds shall bring us, as they blow,
    The murmurs of the shore;
And we will kiss his young blue eyes,
And I will sing him, as he lies,
    Songs that were made of yore:
I'll sing, in his delighted ear,
The island lays thou lov'st to hear.

And thou, while stammering I repeat,
    Thy country's tongue shalt teach;
'Tis not so soft, but far more sweet
    Than my own native speech:
For thou no other tongue didst know,
When, scarcely twenty moons ago,
    Upon Tahete's beach,
Thou cam'st to woo me to be thine,
With many a speaking look and sign.

I knew thy meaning—thou didst praise
    My eyes, my locks of jet;
Ah! well for me they won thy gaze,
    But thine were fairer yet!
I'm glad to see my infant wear
Thy soft blue eyes and sunny hair,
    And when my sight is met
By his white brow and blooming cheek,
I feel a joy I cannot speak.

Come, talk of Europe's maids with me,
    Whose necks and cheeks, they tell,
Outshine the beauty of the sea,
    White foam and crimson shell.
I'll shape like theirs my simple dress,
And bind like them each jetty tress,
    A sight to please thee well;
And for my dusky brow will braid
A bonnet like an English maid.

Come, for the soft low sunlight calls,
    We lose the pleasant hours;
'Tis lovelier than these cottage walls,—
    That seat among the flowers.
And I will learn of thee a prayer,
To Him who gave a home so fair,
    A lot so blest as ours—
The God who made, for thee and me,
This sweet lone isle amid the sea.

*****

THE FIRMAMENT.

Ay! gloriously thou standest there,
  Beautiful, boundless firmament!
That, swelling wide o'er earth and air,
  And round the horizon bent,
With thy bright vault, and sapphire wall,
Dost overhang and circle all.

Far, far below thee, tall gray trees
  Arise, and piles built up of old,
And hills, whose ancient summits freeze
  In the fierce light and cold.
The eagle soars his utmost height,
Yet far thou stretchest o'er his flight.

Thou hast thy frowns—with thee on high
  The storm has made his airy seat,
Beyond that soft blue curtain lie
  His stores of hail and sleet.
Thence the consuming lightnings break,
There the strong hurricanes awake.

Yet art thou prodigal of smiles—
  Smiles, sweeter than thy frowns are stern.
Earth sends, from all her thousand isles,
  A shout at their return.
The glory that comes down from thee,
Bathes, in deep joy, the land and sea.

The sun, the gorgeous sun is thine,
  The pomp that brings and shuts the day,
The clouds that round him change and shine,
  The airs that fan his way.
Thence look the thoughtful stars, and there
The meek moon walks the silent air.

The sunny Italy may boast
  The beauteous tints that flush her skies,
And lovely, round the Grecian coast,
  May thy blue pillars rise.
I only know how fair they stand
Around my own beloved land.

And they are fair—a charm is theirs,
  That earth, the proud green earth, has not,
With all the forms, and hues, and airs,
  That haunt her sweetest spot.
We gaze upon thy calm pure sphere,
And read of Heaven's eternal year.

Oh, when, amid the throng of men,
  The heart grows sick of hollow mirth,
How willingly we turn us then

Away from this cold earth,
And look into thy azure breast,
For seats of innocence and rest!

~~~~~~******~~~~~~

"I CANNOT FORGET WITH WHAT FERVID DEVOTION."

I cannot forget with what fervid devotion
  I worshipped the visions of verse and of fame;
Each gaze at the glories of earth, sky, and ocean,
  To my kindled emotions, was wind over flame.

And deep were my musings in life's early blossom,
  Mid the twilight of mountain-groves wandering long;
How thrilled my young veins, and how throbbed my full bosom,
  When o'er me descended the spirit of song!

'Mong the deep-cloven fells that for ages had listened
  To the rush of the pebble-paved river between,
Where the kingfisher screamed and gray precipice glistened,
  All breathless with awe have I gazed on the scene;

Till I felt the dark power o'er my reveries stealing,
  From the gloom of the thicket that over me hung,
And the thoughts that awoke, in that rapture of feeling,
  Were formed into verse as they rose to my tongue.

Bright visions! I mixed with the world, and ye faded,
  No longer your pure rural worshipper now;
In the haunts your continual presence pervaded,
  Ye shrink from the signet of care on my brow.

In the old mossy groves on the breast of the mountains,
  In deep lonely glens where the waters complain,
By the shade of the rock, by the gush of the fountain,
  I seek your loved footsteps, but seek them in vain.

Oh, leave not forlorn and forever forsaken,
  Your pupil and victim to life and its tears!
But sometimes return, and in mercy awaken
  The glories ye showed to his earlier years.

~~~~~~******~~~~~~

TO A MOSQUITO.

Fair insect! that, with threadlike legs spread out,
  And blood-extracting bill and filmy wing,
Dost murmur, as thou slowly sail'st about,
  In pitiless ears full many a plaintive thing,
And tell how little our large veins would bleed,
Would we but yield them to thy bitter need.

Unwillingly, I own, and, what is worse,
  Full angrily men hearken to thy plaint;

Thou gettest many a brush, and many a curse,
  For saying thou art gaunt, and starved, and faint;
Even the old beggar, while he asks for food,
Would kill thee, hapless stranger, if he could.

I call thee stranger, for the town, I ween,
  Has not the honor of so proud a birth,—
Thou com'st from Jersey meadows, fresh and green,
  The offspring of the gods, though born on earth;
For Titan was thy sire, and fair was she,
The ocean-nymph that nursed thy infancy.

Beneath the rushes was thy cradle swung,
  And when at length thy gauzy wings grew strong,
Abroad to gentle airs their folds were flung,
  Rose in the sky and bore thee soft along;
The south wind breathed to waft thee on the way,
And danced and shone beneath the billowy bay.

Calm rose afar the city spires, and thence
  Came the deep murmur of its throng of men,
And as its grateful odors met thy sense,
  They seemed the perfumes of thy native fen.
Fair lay its crowded streets, and at the sight
Thy tiny song grew shriller with delight.

At length thy pinions fluttered in Broadway—
  Ah, there were fairy steps, and white necks kissed
By wanton airs, and eyes whose killing ray
  Shone through the snowy veils like stars through mist;
And fresh as morn, on many a cheek and chin,
Bloomed the bright blood through the transparent skin.

Sure these were sights to touch an anchorite!
  What! do I hear thy slender voice complain?
Thou wailest when I talk of beauty's light,
  As if it brought the memory of pain:
Thou art a wayward being—well—come near,
And pour thy tale of sorrow in my ear.

What sayest thou—slanderer!—rouge makes thee sick?
  And China bloom at best is sorry food?
And Rowland's Kalydor, if laid on thick,
  Poisons the thirsty wretch that bores for blood?
Go! 'twas a just reward that met thy crime—
But shun the sacrilege another time.

That bloom was made to look at, not to touch;
  To worship, not approach, that radiant white;
And well might sudden vengeance light on such
  As dared, like thee, most impiously to bite.
Thou shouldst have gazed at distance and admired,
Murmured thy adoration, and retired.

Thou'rt welcome to the town; but why come here
  To bleed a brother poet, gaunt like thee?

Alas! the little blood I have is dear,
  And thin will be the banquet drawn from me.
Look round—the pale-eyed sisters in my cell,
Thy old acquaintance, Song and Famine, dwell.

Try some plump alderman, and suck the blood
  Enriched by generous wine and costly meat;
On well-filled skins, sleek as thy native mud,
  Fix thy light pump and press thy freckled feet.
Go to the men for whom, in ocean's halls,
The oyster breeds, and the green turtle sprawls.

There corks are drawn, and the red vintage flows
  To fill the swelling veins for thee, and now
The ruddy cheek and now the ruddier nose
  Shall tempt thee, as thou flittest round the brow;
And when the hour of sleep its quiet brings,
No angry hands shall rise to brush thy wings.

~~~~~~******~~~~~~

LINES ON REVISITING THE COUNTRY.

I stand upon my native hills again,
  Broad, round, and green, that in the summer sky
With garniture of waving grass and grain,
  Orchards, and beechen forests, basking lie,
While deep the sunless glens are scooped between,
Where brawl o'er shallow beds the streams unseen.

A lisping voice and glancing eyes are near,
  And ever-restless feet of one, who, now,
Gathers the blossoms of her fourth bright year;
  There plays a gladness o'er her fair young brow
As breaks the varied scene upon her sight,
Upheaved and spread in verdure and in light.

For I have taught her, with delighted eye,
  To gaze upon the mountains,—to behold,
With deep affection, the pure ample sky
  And clouds along its blue abysses rolled,
To love the song of waters, and to hear
The melody of winds with charmed ear.

Here, have I 'scaped the city's stifling heat,
  Its horrid sounds, and its polluted air,
And, where the season's milder fervors beat,
  And gales, that sweep the forest borders, bear
The song of bird and sound of running stream,
Am come awhile to wander and to dream.

Ay, flame thy fiercest, sun! thou canst not wake,
  In this pure air, the plague that walks unseen.
The maize-leaf and the maple-bough but take,
  From thy strong heats, a deeper, glossier green.
The mountain wind, that faints not in thy ray,

Sweeps the blue steams of pestilence away.

The mountain wind! most spiritual thing of all
  The wide earth knows; when, in the sultry tune,
He stoops him from his vast cerulean hall,
  He seems the breath of a celestial clime!
As if from heaven's wide-open gates did flow
Health and refreshment on the world below.

<center>~~~~~******~~~~~</center>

THE DEATH OF THE FLOWERS.

The melancholy days are come, the saddest of the year,
Of wailing winds, and naked woods, and meadows brown and sere.
Heaped in the hollows of the grove, the autumn leaves lie dead;
They rustle to the eddying gust, and to the rabbit's tread;
The robin and the wren are flown, and from the shrubs the jay,
And from the wood-top calls the crow through all the gloomy day.

Where are the flowers, the fair young flowers, that lately sprang and stood
In brighter light and softer airs, a beauteous sisterhood?
Alas! they all are in their graves, the gentle race of flowers
Are lying in their lowly beds, with the fair and good of ours.
The rain is falling where they lie, but the cold November rain
Calls not from out the gloomy earth the lovely ones again.

The wind-flower and the violet, they perished long ago,
And the brier-rose and the orchis died amid the summer glow;
But on the hills the golden-rod, and the aster in the wood,
And the yellow sun-flower by the brook in autumn beauty stood,
Till fell the frost from the clear cold heaven, as falls the plague on men,
And the brightness of their smile was gone, from upland, glade, and glen.

And now, when comes the calm mild day, as still such days will come,
To call the squirrel and the bee from out their winter home;
When the sound of dropping nuts is heard, though all the trees' added are still,
And twinkle in the smoky light the waters of the rill,
The south wind searches for the flowers whose fragrance late he bore,
And sighs to find them in the wood and by the stream no more.

And then I think of one who in her youthful beauty died,
The fair meek blossom that grew up and faded by my side.
In the cold moist earth we laid her, when the forests cast the leaf,
And we wept that one so lovely should have a life so brief:
Yet not unmeet it was that one, like that young friend of ours,
So gentle and so beautiful, should perish with the flowers.

<center>~~~~~******~~~~~</center>

ROMERO.

When freedom, from the land of Spain,
  By Spain's degenerate sons was driven,
Who gave their willing limbs again
  To wear the chain so lately riven;

Romero broke the sword he wore—
  "Go, faithful brand," the warrior said,
"Go, undishonored, never more
  The blood of man shall make thee red.
  I grieve for that already shed;
And I am sick at heart to know,
That faithful friend and noble foe
Have only bled to make more strong
The yoke that Spain has worn so long.
Wear it who will, in abject fear—
  I wear it not who have been free;
The perjured Ferdinand shall hear
  No oath of loyalty from me."
Then, hunted by the hounds of power,
  Romero chose a safe retreat,
Where bleak Nevada's summits tower
  Above the beauty at their feet.
There once, when on his cabin lay
The crimson light of setting day,
When, even on the mountain's breast,
The chainless winds were all at rest,
And he could hear the river's flow
From the calm paradise below;
Warmed with his former fires again
He framed this rude but solemn strain:

I.

  "Here will I make my home—for here at least I see,
Upon this wild Sierra's side, the steps of Liberty;
Where the locust chirps unscared beneath the unpruned lime,
And the merry bee doth hide from man the spoil of the mountain-thyme;
Where the pure winds come and go, and the wild-vine strays at will,
An outcast from the haunts of men, she dwells with Nature still.

II.

  "I see the valleys, Spain! where thy mighty rivers run,
And the hills that lift thy harvests and vineyards to the sun,
And the flocks that drink thy brooks and sprinkle all the green,
Where lie thy plains, with sheep-walks seamed, and olive-shades between:
I see thy fig-trees bask, with the fair pomegranate near,
And the fragrance of thy lemon-groves can almost reach me here.

III.

  "Fair—fair—but fallen Spain! 'tis with a swelling heart,
That I think on all thou mightst have been, and look at what thou art;
But the strife is over now, and all the good and brave,
That would have raised thee up, are gone, to exile or the grave.
Thy fleeces are for monks, thy grapes for the convent feast,
And the wealth of all thy harvest-fields for the pampered lord and priest.

IV.

  "But I shall see the day—it will come before I die—

I shall see it in my silver hairs, and with an age-dimmed eye;
When the spirit of the land to liberty shall bound,
As yonder fountain leaps away from the darkness of the ground:
And to my mountain-cell, the voices of the free
Shall rise as from the beaten shore the thunders of the sea."

~~~~~******~~~~~

A MEDITATION ON RHODE ISLAND COAL.

"Decolor, obscurus, vilis, non ille repexam
Cesariem regum, non candida virginis ornat
Colla, nec insigni splendet per cingula morsu
Sed nova si nigri videas miracula saxi,
Tune superat pulchroa cultus et quicquid Eois
Indus litoribus rubra scrutatur in alga."
                                        CLAUDIAN.

I sat beside the glowing grate, fresh heaped
    With Newport coal, and as the flame grew bright
—The many-colored flame—and played and leaped,
    I thought of rainbows, and the northern light,
Moore's Lalla Rookh, the Treasury Report,
And other brilliant matters of the sort.

And last I thought of that fair isle which sent
    The mineral fuel; on a summer day
I saw it once, with heat and travel spent,
    And scratched by dwarf-oaks in the hollow way.
Now dragged through sand, now jolted over stone—
A rugged road through rugged Tiverton.

And hotter grew the air, and hollower grew
    The deep-worn path, and horror-struck, I thought,
Where will this dreary passage lead me to?
    This long dull road, so narrow, deep, and hot?
I looked to see it dive in earth outright;
I looked—but saw a far more welcome sight.

Like a soft mist upon the evening shore,
    At once a lovely isle before me lay,
Smooth, and with tender verdure covered o'er,
    As if just risen from its calm inland bay;
Sloped each way gently to the grassy edge,
And the small waves that dallied with the sedge.

The barley was just reaped; the heavy sheaves
    Lay on the stubble-field; the tall maize stood
Dark in its summer growth, and shook its leaves,
    And bright the sunlight played on the young wood—
For fifty years ago, the old men say,
The Briton hewed their ancient groves away.

I saw where fountains freshened the green land,
    And where the pleasant road, from door to door,
With rows of cherry-trees on either hand,
    Went wandering all that fertile region o'er—

79

Rogue's Island once—but when the rogues were dead,
Rhode Island was the name it took instead.

Beautiful island! then it only seemed
  A lovely stranger; it has grown a friend.
I gazed on its smooth slopes, but never dreamed
  How soon that green and quiet isle would send
The treasures of its womb across the sea,
To warm a poet's room and boil his tea.

Dark anthracite! that reddenest on my hearth,
  Thou in those island mines didst slumber long;
But now thou art come forth to move the earth,
  And put to shame the men that mean thee wrong:
Thou shalt be coals of fire to those that hate thee,
And warm the shins of all that underrate thee.

Yea, they did wrong thee foully—they who mocked
  Thy honest face, and said thou wouldst not burn;
Of hewing thee to chimney-pieces talked,
  And grew profane, and swore, in bitter scorn,
That men might to thy inner caves retire,
And there, unsinged, abide the day of fire.

Yet is thy greatness nigh. I pause to state,
  That I too have seen greatness—even I—
Shook hands with Adams, stared at La Fayette,
  When, barehead, in the hot noon of July,
He would not let the umbrella be held o'er him,
For which three cheers burst from the mob before him.

And I have seen—not many months ago—
  An eastern Governor in chapeau bras
And military coat, a glorious show!
  Ride forth to visit the reviews, and ah!
How oft he smiled and bowed to Jonathan!
How many hands were shook and votes were won!

'Twas a great Governor; thou too shalt be
  Great in thy turn, and wide shall spread thy fame
And swiftly; furthest Maine shall hear of thee,
  And cold New Brunswick gladden at thy name;
And, faintly through its sleets, the weeping isle
That sends the Boston folks their cod shall smile.

For thou shalt forge vast railways, and shalt heat
  The hissing rivers into steam, and drive
Huge masses from thy mines, on iron feet,
  Walking their steady way, as if alive,
Northward, till everlasting ice besets thee,
And South as far as the grim Spaniard lets thee.

Thou shalt make mighty engines swim the sea,
  Like its own monsters—boats that for a guinea
Will take a man to Havre—and shalt be
  The moving soul of many a spinning-jenny,

And ply thy shuttles, till a bard can wear
As good a suit of broadcloth as the mayor.

Then we will laugh at winter when we hear
  The grim old churl about our dwellings rave:
Thou, from that "ruler of the inverted year,"
  Shalt pluck the knotty sceptre Cowper gave,
And pull him from his sledge, and drag him in,
And melt the icicles from off his chin.

<div align="center">~~~~*******~~~~</div>

THE NEW MOON.

When, as the garish day is done,
Heaven burns with the descended sun,
    'Tis passing sweet to mark,
Amid that flush of crimson light,
The new moon's modest bow grow bright,
    As earth and sky grow dark.

Few are the hearts too cold to feel
A thrill of gladness o'er them steal,
    When first the wandering eye
Sees faintly, in the evening blaze,
That glimmering curve of tender rays
    Just planted in the sky.

The sight of that young crescent brings
Thoughts of all fair and youthful things—
    The hopes of early years;
And childhood's purity and grace,
And joys that like a rainbow chase
    The passing shower of tears.

The captive yields him to the dream
Of freedom, when that virgin beam
    Comes out upon the air;
And painfully the sick man tries
To fix his dim and burning eyes
    On the sweet promise there.

Most welcome to the lover's sight
Glitters that pure, emerging light;
    For prattling poets say,
That sweetest is the lovers' walk,
And tenderest is their murmured talk,
    Beneath its gentle ray.

And there do graver men behold
A type of errors, loved of old,
    Forsaken and forgiven;
And thoughts and wishes not of earth
Just opening in their early birth,
    Like that new light in heaven.

OCTOBER.

Ay, thou art welcome, heaven's delicious breath!
  When woods begin to wear the crimson leaf,
  And suns grow meek, and the meek suns grow brief,
And the year smiles as it draws near its death.
Wind of the sunny south! oh, still delay
  In the gay woods and in the golden air,
  Like to a good old age released from care,
Journeying, in long serenity, away.
In such a bright, late quiet, would that I
  Might wear out life like thee, mid bowers and brooks,
  And, dearer yet, the sunshine of kind looks,
And music of kind voices ever nigh;
And when my last sand twinkled in the glass,
Pass silently from men, as thou dost pass.

THE DAMSEL OF PERU.

Where olive-leaves were twinkling in every wind that blew,
There sat beneath the pleasant shade a damsel of Peru.
Betwixt the slender boughs, as they opened to the air,
Came glimpses of her ivory neck and of her glossy hair;
And sweetly rang her silver voice, within that shady nook,
As from the shrubby glen is heard the sound of hidden brook.

'Tis a song of love and valor, in the noble Spanish tongue,
That once upon the sunny plains of old Castile was sung;
When, from their mountain-holds, on the Moorish rout below,
Had rushed the Christians like a flood, and swept away the foe.
Awhile that melody is still, and then breaks forth anew
A wilder rhyme, a livelier note, of freedom and Peru.

For she has bound the sword to a youthful lover's side,
And sent him to the war the day she should have been his bride,
And bade him bear a faithful heart to battle for the right,
And held the fountains of her eyes till he was out of sight.
Since the parting kiss was given, six weary months are fled,
And yet the foe is in the land, and blood must yet be shed.

A white hand parts the branches, a lovely face looks forth,
And bright dark eyes gaze steadfastly and sadly toward the north.
Thou look'st in vain, sweet maiden, the sharpest sight would fail
To spy a sign of human life abroad in all the vale;
For the noon is coming on, and the sunbeams fiercely beat,
And the silent hills and forest-tops seem reeling in the heat.

That white hand is withdrawn, that fair sad face is gone,
But the music of that silver voice is flowing sweetly on,
Not as of late, in cheerful tones, but mournfully and low,—
A ballad of a tender maid heart-broken long ago,
Of him who died in battle, the youthful and the brave,

82

And her who died of sorrow, upon his early grave.

And see, along that mountain-slope, a fiery horseman ride;
Mark his torn plume, his tarnished belt, the sabre at his side.
His spurs are buried rowel-deep, he rides with loosened rain,
There's blood upon his charger's flank and foam upon the mane.
He speeds him toward the olive-grove, along that shaded hill!
God shield the helpless maiden there, if he should mean her ill!

And suddenly that song has ceased, and suddenly I hear
A shriek sent up amid the shade, a shriek—but not of fear.
For tender accents follow, and tender pauses speak
The overflow of gladness, when words are all too weak;
"I lay my good sword at thy feet, for now Peru is free,
And I am come to dwell beside the olive-grove with thee."

******

THE AFRICAN CHIEF.

Chained in the market-place he stood,[7]
  A man of giant frame,
Amid the gathering multitude
  That shrunk to hear his name—
All stern of look and strong of limb,
  His dark eye on the ground:—
And silently they gazed on him,
  As on a lion bound.

Vainly, but well, that chief had fought,
  He was a captive now,
Yet pride, that fortune humbles not,
  Was written on his brow.
The scars his dark broad bosom wore,
  Showed warrior true and brave;
A prince among his tribe before,
  He could not be a slave.

Then to his conqueror he spake—
  "My brother is a king;
Undo this necklace from my neck,
  And take this bracelet ring,
And send me where my brother reigns,
  And I will fill thy hands
With store of ivory from the plains,
  And gold-dust from the sands."

"Not for thy ivory nor thy gold
  Will I unbind thy chain;

---

[7] The story of the African chief, related in this ballad, may be found in the *African Repository* for April, 1825. The subject of it was a warrior of majestic stature, the brother of Yarradee, king of the Solima nation. He had been taken in battle, and was brought in chains for sale to the Rio Pongas, where he was exhibited in the market-place, his ankles still adorned with massy rings of gold which he wore when captured. The refusal of his captors to listen to his offers of ransom drove him mad, and he died a maniac.

83

That bloody hand shall never hold
  The battle-spear again.
A price thy nation never gave
  Shall yet be paid for thee;
For thou shalt be the Christian's slave,
  In lands beyond the sea."

Then wept the warrior chief, and bade
  To shred his locks away;
And one by one, each heavy braid
  Before the victor lay.
Thick were the platted locks, and long,
  And closely hidden there
Shone many a wedge of gold among
  The dark and crisped hair.

"Look, feast thy greedy eye with gold
  Long kept for sorest need:
Take it—thou askest sums untold,
  And say that I am freed.
Take it—my wife, the long, long day,
  Weeps by the cocoa-tree,
And my young children leave their play,
  And ask in vain for me."

"I take thy gold—but I have made
  Thy fetters fast and strong,
And ween that by the cocoa shade
  Thy wife will wait thee long."
Strong was the agony that shook
  The captive's frame to hear,
And the proud meaning of his look
  Was changed to mortal fear.

His heart was broken—crazed his brain:
  At once his eye grew wild;
He struggled fiercely with his chain,
  Whispered, and wept, and smiled;
Yet wore not long those fatal bands,
  And once, at shut of day,
They drew him forth upon the sands,
  The foul hyena's prey.

—————******—————

SPRING IN TOWN.

The country ever has a lagging Spring,
  Waiting for May to call its violets forth,
And June its roses; showers and sunshine bring,
  Slowly, the deepening verdure o'er the earth;
To put their foliage out, the woods are slack,
And one by one the singing-birds come back.

Within the city's bounds the time of flowers
  Comes earlier. Let a mild and sunny day,

Such as full often, for a few bright hours,
  Breathes through the sky of March the airs of May,
Shine on our roofs and chase the wintry gloom—
And lo! our borders glow with sudden bloom.

For the wide sidewalks of Broadway are then
  Gorgeous as are a rivulet's banks in June,
That overhung with blossoms, through its glen,
  Slides soft away beneath the sunny noon,
And they who search the untrodden wood for flowers
Meet in its depths no lovelier ones than ours.

For here are eyes that shame the violet,
  Or the dark drop that on the pansy lies,
And foreheads, white, as when in clusters set,
  The anemones by forest-mountains rise;
And the spring-beauty boasts no tenderer streak
Than the soft red on many a youthful cheek.

And thick about those lovely temples lie
  Locks that the lucky Vignardonne has curled,
Thrice happy man! whose trade it is to buy,
  And bake, and braid those love-knots of the world;
Who curls of every glossy color keepest,
And sellest, it is said, the blackest cheapest.

And well thou mayst—for Italy's brown maids
  Send the dark locks with which their brows are dressed,
And Gascon lasses, from their jetty braids,
  Crop half, to buy a ribbon for the rest;
But the fresh Norman girls their tresses spare,
And the Dutch damsel keeps her flaxen hair.

Then, henceforth, let no maid nor matron grieve,
  To see her locks of an unlovely hue,
Frouzy or thin, for liberal art shall give
  Such piles of curls as Nature never knew.
Eve, with her veil of tresses, at the sight
Had blushed, outdone, and owned herself a fright.

Soft voices and light laughter wake the street,
  Like notes of woodbirds, and where'er the eye
Threads the long way, plumes wave, and twinkling feet
  Fall light, as hastes that crowd of beauty by.
The ostrich, hurrying o'er the desert space,
Scarce bore those tossing plumes with fleeter pace.

No swimming Juno gait, of languor born,
  Is theirs, but a light step of freest grace,—
Light as Camilla's o'er the unbent corn, —
  A step that speaks the spirit of the place,
Since Quiet, meek old dame, was driven away
To Sing Sing and the shores of Tappan Bay.

Ye that dash by in chariots! who will care
  For steeds or footmen now? ye cannot show

Fair face, and dazzling dress, and graceful air,
  And last edition of the shape! Ah, no,
These sights are for the earth and open sky,
And your loud wheels unheeded rattle by.

~~~~~******~~~~~

THE GLADNESS OF NATURE.

Is this a time to be cloudy and sad,
  When our mother Nature laughs around;
When even the deep blue heavens look glad,
  And gladness breathes from the blossoming ground?

There are notes of joy from the hang-bird and wren,
  And the gossip of swallows through all the sky;
The ground-squirrel gayly chirps by his den,
  And the wilding bee hums merrily by.

The clouds are at play in the azure space
  And their shadows at play on the bright-green vale,
And here they stretch to the frolic chase,
  And there they roll on the easy gale.

There's a dance of leaves in that aspen bower,
  There's a titter of winds in that beechen tree,
There's a smile on the fruit, and a smile on the flower,
  And a laugh from the brook that runs to the sea.

And look at the broad-faced sun, how he smiles
  On the dewy earth that smiles in his ray,
On the leaping waters and gay young isles;
  Ay, look, and he'll smile thy gloom away.

~~~~~******~~~~~

THE DISINTERRED WARRIOR.

Gather him to his grave again,
  And solemnly and softly lay,
Beneath the verdure of the plain,
  The warrior's scattered bones away.
Pay the deep reverence, taught of old,
  The homage of man's heart to death;
Nor dare to trifle with the mould
  Once hallowed by the Almighty's breath.

The soul hath quickened every part—
  That remnant of a martial brow,
Those ribs that held the mighty heart,
  That strong arm—strong no longer now.
Spare them, each mouldering relic spare,
  Of God's own image; let them rest,
Till not a trace shall speak of where
  The awful likeness was impressed.

For he was fresher from the hand
  That formed of earth the human face,
And to the elements did stand
  In nearer kindred than our race.
In many a flood to madness tossed,
  In many a storm has been his path;
He hid him not from heat or frost,
  But met them, and defied their wrath.

Then they were kind—the forests here,
  Rivers, and stiller waters, paid
A tribute to the net and spear
  Of the red ruler of the shade.
Fruits on the woodland branches lay,
  Roots in the shaded soil below;
The stars looked forth to teach his way;
  The still earth warned him of the foe.

A noble race! but they are gone,
  With their old forests wide and deep,
And we have built our homes upon
  Fields where their generations sleep.
Their fountains slake our thirst at noon,
  Upon their fields our harvest waves,
Our lovers woo beneath their moon—
  Then let us spare, at least, their graves.

~~~~~******~~~~~

MIDSUMMER.

A power is on the earth and in the air
  From which the vital spirit shrinks afraid,
  And shelters him, in nooks of deepest shade,
From the hot steam and from the fiery glare.
Look forth upon the earth—her thousand plants
  Are smitten; even the dark sun-loving maize
  Faints in the field beneath the torrid blaze;
The herd beside the shaded fountain pants;
For life is driven from all the landscape brown;
  The bird has sought his tree, the snake his den,
  The trout floats dead in the hot stream, and men
Drop by the sun-stroke in the populous town;
  As if the Day of Fire had dawned, and sent
  Its deadly breath into the firmament.

~~~~~******~~~~~

THE GREEK PARTISAN.

Our free flag is dancing
  In the free mountain air,
And burnished arms are glancing,
  And warriors gathering there;
And fearless is the little train
  Whose gallant bosoms shield it;

The blood that warms their hearts shall stain
 That banner, ere they yield it.
—Each dark eye is fixed on earth,
 And brief each solemn greeting;
There is no look nor sound of mirth,
 Where those stern men are meeting.

They go to the slaughter
 To strike the sudden blow,
And pour on earth, like water,
 The best blood of the foe;
To rush on them from rock and height,
 And clear the narrow valley,
Or fire their camp at dead of night,
 And fly before they rally.
—Chains are round our country pressed,
 And cowards have betrayed her,
And we must make her bleeding breast
 The grave of the invader.

Not till from her fetters
 We raise up Greece again,
And write, in bloody letters,
 That tyranny is slain,—
Oh, not till then the smile shall steal
 Across those darkened faces,
Nor one of all those warriors feel
 His children's dear embraces.
—Reap we not the ripened wheat,
 Till yonder hosts are flying,
And all their bravest, at our feet,
 Like autumn sheaves are lying.

******

THE TWO GRAVES.

 'Tis a bleak wild hill, but green and bright
In the summer warmth and the mid-day light;
There's the hum of the bee and the chirp of the wren
And the dash of the brook from the alder-glen.
There's the sound of a bell from the scattered flock,
And the shade of the beech lies cool on the rock,
And fresh from the west is the free wind's breath;—
There is nothing here that speaks of death.

 Far yonder, where orchards and gardens lie,
And dwellings cluster, 'tis there men die,
They are born, they die, and are buried near,
Where the populous graveyard lightens the bier.
For strict and close are the ties that bind
In death the children of human-kind;
Yea, stricter and closer than those of life,—
'Tis a neighborhood that knows no strife.
They are noiselessly gathered—friend and foe—
To the still and dark assemblies below.

Without a frown or a smile they meet,
Each pale and calm in his winding-sheet;
In that sullen home of peace and gloom,
Crowded, like guests in a banquet-room.

  Yet there are graves in this lonely spot,
Two humble graves, —but I meet them not.
I have seen them,—eighteen years are past
Since I found their place in the brambles last,—
The place where, fifty winters ago
An aged man in his locks of snow,
And an aged matron, withered with years,
Were solemnly laid!—but not with tears.
For none, who sat by the light of their hearth,
Beheld their coffins covered with earth;
Their kindred were far, and their children dead,
When the funeral-prayer was coldly said.

  Two low green hillocks, two small gray stones,
Rose over the place that held their bones;
But the grassy hillocks are levelled again,
And the keenest eye might search in vain,
'Mong briers, and ferns, and paths of sheep,
For the spot where the aged couple sleep.

  Yet well might they lay, beneath the soil
Of this lonely spot, that man of toil,
And trench the strong hard mould with the spade,
Where never before a grave was made;
For he hewed the dark old woods away,
And gave the virgin fields to the day;
And the gourd and the bean, beside his door,
Bloomed where their flowers ne'er opened before;
And the maize stood up, and the bearded rye
Bent low in the breath of an unknown sky.

  'Tis said that when life is ended here,
The spirit is borne to a distant sphere;
That it visits its earthly home no more,
Nor looks on the haunts it loved before.
But why should the bodiless soul be sent
Far off, to a long, long banishment?
Talk not of the light and the living green!
It will pine for the dear familiar scene;
It will yearn, in that strange bright world, to behold
The rock and the stream it knew of old.

  'Tis a cruel creed, believe it not!
Death to the good is a milder lot.
They are here,—they are here,—that harmless pair,
In the yellow sunshine and flowing air,
In the light cloud-shadows that slowly pass,
In the sounds that rise from the murmuring grass.
They sit where their humble cottage stood,
They walk by the waving edge of the wood,
And list to the long-accustomed flow

Of the brook that wets the rocks below,
Patient, and peaceful, and passionless,
As seasons on seasons swiftly press,
They watch, and wait, and linger around,
Till the day when their bodies shall leave the ground.

~~~~~~******~~~~~~

THE CONJUNCTION OF JUPITER AND VENUS. [8]

I would not always reason. The straight path
Wearies us with the never-varying lines,
And we grow melancholy. I would make
Reason my guide, but she should sometimes sit
Patiently by the way-side, while I traced
The mazes of the pleasant wilderness
Around me. She should be my counsellor,
But not my tyrant. For the spirit needs
Impulses from a deeper source than hers,
And there are motions, in the mind of man,
That she must look upon with awe. I bow
Reverently to her dictates, but not less
Hold to the fair illusions of old time—
Illusions that shed brightness over life,
And glory over Nature. Look, even now,
Where two bright planets in the twilight meet,
Upon the saffron heaven,—the imperial star
Of Jove, and she that from her radiant urn
Pours forth the light of love. Let me believe,
Awhile, that they are met for ends of good,
Amid the evening glory, to confer
Of men and their affairs, and to shed down
Kind influence. Lo! they brighten as we gaze,
And shake out softer fires! The great earth feels
The gladness and the quiet of the time.
Meekly the mighty river, that infolds
This mighty city, smooths his front, and far
Glitters and burns even the rocky base
Of the dark heights that bound him to the west;
And a deep murmur, from the many streets,
Rises like a thanksgiving. Put we hence
Dark and sad thoughts awhile—there's time for them
Hereafter—on the morrow we will meet,
With melancholy looks, to tell our griefs,
And make each other wretched; this calm hour,
This balmy, blessed evening, we will give
To cheerful hopes and dreams of happy days,
Born of the meeting of those glorious stars.

Enough of drought has parched the year, and scared
The land with dread of famine. Autumn, yet,

---

[8] This conjunction was said in the common calendars to have taken place on the 2d of August, 1826. This, I believe, was an error, but
the apparent approach of the planets was sufficiently near for poetical purposes.

90

Shall make men glad with unexpected fruits.
The dog-star shall shine harmless: genial days
Shall softly glide away into the keen
And wholesome cold of winter; he that fears
The pestilence, shall gaze on those pure beams,
And breathe, with confidence, the quiet air.

 Emblems of power and beauty! well may they
Shine brightest on our borders, and withdraw
Toward the great Pacific, marking out
The path of empire. Thus in our own land,
Ere long, the better Genius of our race,
Having encompassed earth, and tamed its tribes,
Shall sit him down beneath the farthest west,
By the shore of that calm ocean, and look back
On realms made happy.

        Light the nuptial torch,
And say the glad, yet solemn rite, that knits
The youth and maiden. Happy days to them
That wed this evening!—a long life of love,
And blooming sons and daughters! Happy they
Born at this hour, for they shall see an age
Whiter and holier than the past, and go
Late to their graves. Men shall wear softer hearts,
And shudder at the butcheries of war,
As now at other murders.

        Hapless Greece!
Enough of blood has wet thy rocks, and stained
Thy rivers; deep enough thy chains have worn
Their links into thy flesh; the sacrifice
Of thy pure maidens, and thy innocent babes,
And reverend priests, has expiated all
Thy crimes of old. In yonder mingling lights
There is an omen of good days for thee.
Thou shalt arise from midst the dust and sit
Again among the nations. Thine own arm
Shall yet redeem thee. Not in wars like thine
The world takes part. Be it a strife of kings,—
Despot with despot battling for a throne,—
And Europe shall be stirred throughout her realms,
Nations shall put on harness, and shall fall
Upon each other, and in all their bounds
The wailing of the childless shall not cease.
Thine is a war for liberty, and thou
Must fight it single-handed. The old world
Looks coldly on the murderers of thy race,
And leaves thee to the struggle; and the new,—
I fear me thou couldst tell a shameful tale
Of fraud and lust of gain;—thy treasury drained,
And Missolonghi fallen. Yet thy wrongs
Shall put new strength into thy heart and hand,
And God and thy good sword shall yet work out,
For thee, a terrible deliverance.

A SUMMER RAMBLE.

The quiet August noon has come;
  A slumberous silence fills the sky,
The fields are still, the woods are dumb,
  In glassy sleep the waters lie.

And mark yon soft white clouds that rest
  Above our vale, a moveless throng;
The cattle on the mountain's breast
  Enjoy the grateful shadow long.

Oh, how unlike those merry hours,
  In early June, when Earth laughs out,
When the fresh winds make love to flowers,
  And woodlands sing and waters shout.

When in the grass sweet voices talk,
  And strains of tiny music swell
From every moss-cup of the rock,
  From every nameless blossom's bell.

But now a joy too deep for sound,
  A peace no other season knows,
Hushes the heavens and wraps the ground,
  The blessing of supreme repose.

Away! I will not be, to-day,
  The only slave of toil and care,
Away from desk and dust! away!
  I'll be as idle as the air.

Beneath the open sky abroad,
  Among the plants and breathing things,
The sinless, peaceful works of God,
  I'll share the calm the season brings.

Come, thou, in whose soft eyes I see
  The gentle meanings of thy heart,
One day amid the woods with me,
  From men and all their cares apart.

And where, upon the meadow's breast,
  The shadow of the thicket lies,
The blue wild-flowers thou gatherest
  Shall glow yet deeper near thine eyes.

Come, and when mid the calm profound,
  I turn, those gentle eyes to seek,
They, like the lovely landscape round,
  Of innocence and peace shall speak.

Rest here, beneath the unmoving shade,
  And on the silent valleys gaze,

Winding and widening, till they fade
  In yon soft ring of summer haze.

The village trees their summits rear
  Still as its spire, and yonder flock
At rest in those calm fields appear
  As chiselled from the lifeless rock.

One tranquil mount the scene o'erlooks—
  There the hushed winds their sabbath keep,
While a near hum from bees and brooks
  Comes faintly like the breath of sleep.

Well may the gazer deem that when,
  Worn with the struggle and the strife,
And heart-sick at the wrongs of men,
  The good forsakes the scene of life;

Like this deep quiet that, awhile,
  Lingers the lovely landscape o'er,
Shall be the peace whose holy smile
  Welcomes him to a happier shore.

<center>~~~~~******~~~~~</center>

A SCENE ON THE BANKS OF THE HUDSON.

Cool shades and dews are round my way,
And silence of the early day;
Mid the dark rocks that watch his bed,
Glitters the mighty Hudson spread,
Unrippled, save by drops that fall
From shrubs that fringe his mountain wall;
And o'er the clear still water swells
The music of the Sabbath bells.

All, save this little nook of land,
Circled with trees, on which I stand;
All, save that line of hills which lie
Suspended in the mimic sky—
Seems a blue void, above, below,
Through which the white clouds come and go;
And from the green world's farthest steep
I gaze into the airy deep.

Loveliest of lovely things are they,
On earth, that soonest pass away.
The rose that lives its little hour
Is prized beyond the sculptured flower.
Even love, long tried and cherished long,
Becomes more tender and more strong
At thought of that insatiate grave
From which its yearnings cannot save.

River! in this still hour thou hast
Too much of heaven on earth to last;

Nor long may thy still waters lie,
An image of the glorious sky.
Thy fate and mine are not repose,
And ere another evening close,
Thou to thy tides shalt turn again,
And I to seek the crowd of men.

~~~~~******~~~~~

THE HURRICANE. [9]

Lord of the winds! I feel thee nigh,
I know thy breath in the burning sky!
And I wait, with a thrill in every vein,
For the coming of the hurricane!

And lo! on the wing of the heavy gales,
Through the boundless arch of heaven he sails;
Silent and slow, and terribly strong,
The mighty shadow is borne along,
Like the dark eternity to come;
While the world below, dismayed and dumb,
Through the calm of the thick hot atmosphere,
Looks up at its gloomy folds with fear.

They darken fast; and the golden blaze
Of the sun is quenched in the lurid haze,
And he sends through the shade a funeral ray—
A glare that is neither night nor day,
A beam that touches, with hues of death,
The clouds above and the earth beneath.
To its covert glides the silent bird,
While the hurricane's distant voice is heard
Uplifted among the mountains round,
And the forests hear and answer the sound.

He is come! he is come! do ye not behold
His ample robes on the wind unrolled?
Giant of air! we bid thee hail!—
How his gray skirts tops in the whirling gale;
How his huge and writhing arms are bent
To clasp the zone of the firmament,
And fold at length, in their dark embrace,
From mountain to mountain the visible space.

Darker—still darker! the whirlwinds bear
The dust of the plains to the middle air:
And hark to the crashing, long and loud,
Of the chariot of God in the thunder-cloud!
You may trace its path by the flashes that start
From the rapid wheels where'er they dart,

---

[9] This poem is nearly a translation from one by Jose Maria de Heredia, a native of the island of Cuba, who published at New York about the year 1825, a volume of poems in the Spanish language.

94

As the fire-bolts leap to the world below,
And flood the skies with a lurid glow.

What roar is that?—'tis the rain that breaks
In torrents away from the airy lakes,
Heavily poured on the shuddering ground,
And shedding a nameless horror round.
Ah! well-known woods, and mountains, and skies,
With the very clouds!—ye are lost to my eyes.

I seek ye vainly, and see in your place
The shadowy tempest that sweeps through space,
A whirling ocean that fills the wall
Of the crystal heaven, and buries all
And I, cut off from the world, remain
Alone with the terrible hurricane.

~~~******~~~

WILLIAM TELL. [10]

Chains may subdue the feeble spirit, but thee,
  TELL, of the iron heart! they could not tame!
  For thou wert of the mountains; they proclaim
The everlasting creed of liberty.
That creed is written on the untrampled snow,
  Thundered by torrents which no power can hold,
  Save that of God, when He sends forth His cold,
And breathed by winds that through the free heaven blow.
Thou, while thy prison-walls were dark around,
  Didst meditate the lesson Nature taught,
  And to thy brief captivity was brought
A vision of thy Switzerland unbound.
  The bitter cup they mingled, strengthened thee
  For the great work to set thy country free.

~~~******~~~

THE HUNTER'S SERENADE.

Thy bower is finished, fairest!
  Fit bower for hunter's bride,
Where old woods overshadow
  The green savanna's side.
I've wandered long, and wandered far,
  And never have I met,
In all this lovely Western land,
  A spot so lovely yet.
But I shall think it fairer
  When thou art come to bless,
With thy sweet smile and silver voice,

---

[10] Neither this, nor any of the other sonnets in the collection, with the exception of the one from the Portuguese, is framed according to the legitimate Italian model, which, in the author's opinion, possesses no peculiar beauty for an ear accustomed only to the metrical forms of our own language. The sonnets in this collection are rather poems in fourteen lines than sonnets.

Its silent loveliness.

For thee the wild-grape glistens
  On sunny knoll and tree,
The slim papaya ripens[11]
  Its yellow fruit for thee.
For thee the duck, on glassy stream,
  The prairie-fowl shall die;
My rifle for thy feast shall bring
  The wild-swan from the sky.
The forest's leaping panther,
  Fierce, beautiful, and fleet,
Shall yield his spotted hide to be
  A carpet for thy feet.

I know, for thou hast told me,
  Thy maiden love of flowers;
Ah, those that deck thy gardens
  Are pale compared with ours.
When our wide woods and mighty lawns
  Bloom to the April skies,
The earth has no more gorgeous sight
  To show to human eyes.
In meadows red with blossoms,
  All summer long, the bee
Murmurs, and loads his yellow thighs,
  For thee, my love, and me.

Or wouldst thou gaze at tokens
  Of ages long ago—
Our old oaks stream with mosses,
  And sprout with mistletoe;
And mighty vines, like serpents, climb
  The giant sycamore;
And trunks, o'erthrown for centuries,
  Cumber the forest floor;
And in the great savanna,
  The solitary mound,
Built by the elder world, o'erlooks
  The loneliness around.

Come, thou hast not forgotten
  Thy pledge and promise quite,
With many blushes murmured,
  Beneath the evening light.
Come, the young violets crowd my door,

---

[11] Papaya—papaw, custard-apple. Flint, in his excellent work on the *Geography and History of the Western States*, thus describes the tree and its fruit:

"A papaw-shrub hanging full of fruits, of a size and weight sod is proportioned to the stem, and from under long and rich-looking leaves, of the same yellow with the ripened fruit, and of an African luxuriance of growth, is to us one of the richest spectacles that we have ever contemplated in the array of the woods. The fruit contains from two to six seeds like those of the tamarind, except that they are double the size. The pulp of the fruit resembles egg-custard inconsistence and appearance. It has the same creamy feeling in the mouth, and unites the taste of eggs, cream, sugar, and spice. It is a natural custard, too luscious for the relish of most people."

Chateaubriand, in his Travels, speaks disparagingly of the fruit of the papaw; but on the authority of Mr. Flint, who must know more of the matter, I have ventured to make my Western lover enumerate it among the delicacies of the wilderness.

Thy earliest look to win,
And at my silent window-sill
  The jessamine peeps in.
All day the red-bird warbles
  Upon the mulberry near,
And the night-sparrow trills her song
  All night, with none to hear.

~~~~******~~~~

THE GREEK BOY.

Gone are the glorious Greeks of old,
    Glorious in mien and mind;
Their bones are mingled with the mould,
    Their dust is on the wind;
The forms they hewed from living stone
Survive the waste of years, alone,
And, scattered with their ashes, show
What greatness perished long ago.

Yet fresh the myrtles there; the springs
    Gush brightly as of yore;
Flowers blossom from the dust of kings,
    As many an age before.
There Nature moulds as nobly now,
As e'er of old, the human brow;
And copies still the martial form
That braved Plataea's battle-storm.

Boy! thy first looks were taught to seek
    Their heaven in Hellas' skies;
Her airs have tinged thy dusky cheek,
    Her sunshine lit thine eyes;
Thine ears have drunk the woodland strains
Heard by old poets, and thy veins
Swell with the blood of demigods,
That slumber in thy country's sods.

Now is thy nation free, though late;
    Thy elder brethren broke—
Broke, ere thy spirit felt its weight—
    The intolerable yoke.
And Greece, decayed, dethroned, doth see
Her youth renewed in such as thee:
A shoot of that old vine that made
The nations silent in its shade.

~~~~******~~~~

THE PAST.

    Thou unrelenting Past!
Strong are the barriers round thy dark domain,
    And fetters, sure and fast,
Hold all that enter thy unbreathing reign.

97

Far in thy realm withdrawn,
Old empires sit in sullenness and gloom,
  And glorious ages gone
Lie deep within the shadow of thy womb.

  Childhood, with all its mirth,
Youth, Manhood, Age that draws us to the ground,
  And last, Man's Life on earth,
Glide to thy dim dominions, and are bound.

  Thou hast my better years;
Thou hast my earlier friends, the good, the kind,
  Yielded to thee with tears—
The venerable form, the exalted mind.

  My spirit yearns to bring
The lost ones back—yearns with desire intense,
  And struggles hard to wring
Thy bolts apart, and pluck thy captives thence.

  In vain; thy gates deny
All passage save to those who hence depart;
  Nor to the streaming eye
Thou giv'st them back—nor to the broken heart.

  In thy abysses hide
Beauty and excellence unknown; to thee
  Earth's wonder and her pride
Are gathered, as the waters to the sea;

  Labors of good to man,
Unpublished charity, unbroken faith,
  Love, that midst grief began,
And grew with years, and faltered not in death.

  Full many a mighty name
Lurks in thy depths, unuttered, unrevered;
  With thee are silent fame,
Forgotten arts, and wisdom disappeared.

  Thine for a space are they—
Yet shalt thou yield thy treasures up at last:
  Thy gates shall yet give way,
Thy bolts shall fall, inexorable Past!

  All that of good and fair
Has gone into thy womb from earliest time,
  Shall then come forth to wear
The glory and the beauty of its prime.

  They have not perished—no!
Kind words, remembered voices once so sweet,
  Smiles, radiant long ago,
And features, the great soul's apparent seat.

All shall come back; each tie
Of pure affection shall be knit again;
   Alone shall Evil die,
And Sorrow dwell a prisoner in thy reign.

   And then shall I behold
Him, by whose kind paternal side I sprung,
   And her, who, still and cold,
Fills the next grave—the beautiful and young.

<div align="center">~~~~******~~~~</div>

"UPON THE MOUNTAIN'S DISTANT HEAD."

Upon the mountain's distant head,
  With trackless snows forever white,
Where all is still, and cold, and dead,
  Late shines the day's departing light.

But far below those icy rocks,
  The vales, in summer bloom arrayed,
Woods full of birds, and fields of flocks,
  Are dim with mist and dark with shade.

'Tis thus, from warm and kindly hearts,
  And eyes where generous meanings burn,
Earliest the light of life departs,
  But lingers with the cold and stern.

<div align="center">~~~~******~~~~</div>

THE EVENING WIND.

Spirit that breathest through my lattice, thou
  That cool'st the twilight of the sultry day,
Gratefully flows thy freshness round my brow;
  Thou hast been out upon the deep at play,
Riding all day the wild blue waves till now,
  Roughening their crests, and scattering high their spray,
And swelling the white sail. I welcome thee
To the scorched land, thou wanderer of the sea!

Nor I alone; a thousand bosoms round
  Inhale thee in the fulness of delight;
And languid forms rise up, and pulses bound
  Livelier, at coming of the wind of night;
And, languishing to hear thy grateful sound,
  Lies the vast inland stretched beyond the sight.
Go forth into the gathering shade; go forth,
God's blessing breathed upon the fainting earth!

Go, rock the little wood-bird in his nest,
  Curl the still waters, bright with stars, and rouse
The wide old wood from his majestic rest,
  Summoning from the innumerable boughs
The strange, deep harmonies that haunt his breast:

99

Pleasant shall be thy way where meekly bows
The shutting flower, and darkling waters pass,
And where the o'ershadowing branches sweep the grass.

The faint old man shall lean his silver head
  To feel thee; thou shalt kiss the child asleep,
And dry the moistened curls that overspread
  His temples, while his breathing grows more deep;
And they who stand about the sick man's bed,
  Shall joy to listen to thy distant sweep,
And softly part his curtains to allow
Thy visit, grateful to his burning brow.

Go—but the circle of eternal change,
  Which is the life of Nature, shall restore,
With sounds and scents from all thy mighty range,
  Thee to thy birthplace of the deep once more;
Sweet odors in the sea-air, sweet and strange,
  Shall tell the home-sick mariner of the shore;
And, listening to thy murmur, he shall deem
He hears the rustling leaf and running stream.

******

"WHEN THE FIRMAMENT QUIVERS WITH DAYLIGHT'S YOUNG BEAM."

When the firmament quivers with daylight's young beam,
  And the woodlands awaking burst into a hymn,
And the glow of the sky blazes back from the stream,
  How the bright ones of heaven in the brightness grow dim!

Oh! 'tis sad, in that moment of glory and song,
  To see, while the hill-tops are waiting the sun,
The glittering band that kept watch all night long
  O'er Love and o'er Slumber, go out one by one:

Till the circle of ether, deep, ruddy, and vast,
  Scarce glimmers with one of the train that were there;
And their leader, the day-star, the brightest and last,
  Twinkles faintly and fades in that desert of air.

Thus, Oblivion, from midst of whose shadow we came,
  Steals o'er us again when life's twilight is gone;
And the crowd of bright names, in the heaven of fame,
  Grow pale and are quenched as the years hasten on.

Let them fade—but we'll pray that the age, in whose flight,
  Of ourselves and our friends the remembrance shall die,
May rise o'er the world, with the gladness and light
  Of the morning that withers the stars from the sky.

******

"INNOCENT CHILD AND SNOW-WHITE FLOWER."

Innocent child and snow-white flower!

100

Well are ye paired in your opening hour.
Thus should the pure and the lovely meet,
Stainless with stainless, and sweet with sweet.

White as those leaves, just blown apart;
Are the folds of thy own young heart;
Guilty passion and cankering care
Never have left their traces there.

Artless one! though thou gazest now
O'er the white blossom with earnest brow,
Soon will it tire thy childish eye;
Fair as it is, thou wilt throw it by.

Throw it aside in thy weary hour,
Throw to the ground the fair white flower;
Yet, as thy tender years depart,
Keep that white and innocent heart.

~~~~~~******~~~~~~

TO THE RIVER ARVE.

SUPPOSED TO BE WRITTEN AT A HAMLET NEAR THE FOOT OF MONT BLANC.

Not from the sands or cloven rocks,
  Thou rapid Arve! thy waters flow;
Nor earth, within her bosom, locks
  Thy dark unfathomed wells below.
Thy springs are in the cloud, thy stream
  Begins to move and murmur first
Where ice-peaks feel the noonday beam,
  Or rain-storms on the glacier burst.

Born where the thunder and the blast
  And morning's earliest light are born,
Thou rushest swoln, and loud, and fast,
  By these low homes, as if in scorn:
Yet humbler springs yield purer waves;
  And brighter, glassier streams than thine,
Sent up from earth's unlighted caves,
  With heaven's own beam and image shine.

Yet stay; for here are flowers and trees;
  Warm rays on cottage-roofs are here;
And laugh of girls, and hum of bees,
  Here linger till thy waves are clear.
Thou heedest not—thou hastest on;
  From steep to steep thy torrent falls;
Till, mingling with the mighty Rhone,
  It rests beneath Geneva's walls.

Rush on—but were there one with me
  That loved me, I would light my hearth
Here, where with God's own majesty
  Are touched the features of the earth.

101

By these old peaks, white, high, and vast,
  Still rising as the tempests beat,
Here would I dwell, and sleep, at last,
  Among the blossoms at their feet.

******

TO COLE, THE PAINTER, DEPARTING FOR EUROPE.

Thine eyes shall see the light of distant skies;
    Yet, COLE! thy heart shall bear to Europe's strand
    A living image of our own bright land,
Such as upon thy glorious canvas lies;
Lone lakes—savannas where the bison roves—
    Rocks rich with summer garlands—solemn streams—
    Skies, where the desert eagle wheels and screams—

Spring bloom and autumn blaze of boundless groves.
Fair scenes shall greet thee where thou goest—fair,
    But different—everywhere the trace of men,
    Paths, homes, graves, ruins, from the lowest glen
To where life shrinks from the fierce Alpine air.
    Gaze on them, till the tears shall dim thy sight,
    But keep that earlier, wilder image bright.

******

TO THE FRINGED GENTIAN.

Thou blossom bright with autumn dew,
And colored with the heaven's own blue,
That openest when the quiet light
Succeeds the keen and frosty night.

Thou comest not when violets lean
O'er wandering brooks and springs unseen,
Or columbines, in purple dressed,
Nod o'er the ground-bird's hidden nest.

Thou waitest late and com'st alone,
When woods are bare and birds are flown,
And frosts and shortening days portend
The aged year is near his end.

Then doth thy sweet and quiet eye
Look through its fringes to the sky,
Blue—blue—as if that sky let fall
A flower from its cerulean wall.

I would that thus, when I shall see
The hour of death draw near to me,
Hope, blossoming within my heart,
May look to heaven as I depart.

******

THE TWENTY-SECOND OF DECEMBER.

Wild was the day; the wintry sea
  Moaned sadly on New-England's strand,
When first the thoughtful and the free,
  Our fathers, trod the desert land.

They little thought how pure a light,
  With years, should gather round that day;
How love should keep their memories bright,
  How wide a realm their sons should sway.

Green are their bays; but greener still
  Shall round their spreading fame be wreathed,
And regions, now untrod, shall thrill
  With reverence when their names are breathed.

Till where the sun, with softer fires,
  Looks on the vast Pacific's sleep,
The children of the pilgrim sires
  This hallowed day like us shall keep.

****

HYMN OF THE CITY.

Not in the solitude
Alone may man commune with Heaven, or see,
  Only in savage wood
And sunny vale, the present Deity;
  Or only hear his voice
Where the winds whisper and the waves rejoice.

  Even here do I behold
Thy steps, Almighty!—here, amidst the crowd
  Through the great city rolled,
With everlasting murmur deep and loud—
  Choking the ways that wind
'Mongst the proud piles, the work of human kind.

  Thy golden sunshine comes
From the round heaven, and on their dwellings lies
  And lights their inner homes;
For them thou fill'st with air the unbounded skies,
  And givest them the stores
Of ocean, and the harvests of its shores.

  Thy Spirit is around,
Quickening the restless mass that sweeps along;
  And this eternal sound—
Voices and footfalls of the numberless throng—
  Like the resounding sea,
Or like the rainy tempest, speaks of Thee.

  And when the hour of rest
Comes, like a calm upon the mid-sea brine,

Hushing its billowy breast—
The quiet of that moment too is thine;
It breathes of Him who keeps
The vast and helpless city while it sleeps.

~~~~~******~~~~~

THE PRAIRIES.

These are the gardens of the Desert, these
The unshorn fields, boundless and beautiful,
For which the speech of England has no name—
The Prairies. I behold them for the first,
And my heart swells, while the dilated sight
Takes in the encircling vastness. Lo! they stretch,
In airy undulations, far away,
As if the ocean, in his gentlest swell,
Stood still, with all his rounded billows fixed,
And motionless forever.—Motionless?—
No—they are all unchained again. The clouds
Sweep over with their shadows, and, beneath,
The surface rolls and fluctuates to the eye;[12]
Dark hollows seem to glide along and chase
The sunny ridges. Breezes of the South!
Who toss the golden and the flame-like flowers,
And pass the prairie-hawk that, poised on high,
Flaps his broad wings, yet moves not[13]—ye have played
Among the palms of Mexico and vines
Of Texas, and have crisped the limpid brooks
That from the fountains of Sonora glide
Into the calm Pacific—have ye fanned
A nobler or a lovelier scene than this?
Man hath no power in all this glorious work:
The hand that built the firmament hath heaved
And smoothed these verdant swells, and sown their slopes
With herbage, planted them with island groves,
And hedged them round with forests. Fitting floor
For this magnificent temple of the sky—
With flowers whose glory and whose multitude
Rival the constellations! The great heavens
Seem to stoop down upon the scene in love,—
A nearer vault, and of a tenderer blue,
Than that which bends above our eastern hills.

As o'er the verdant waste I guide my steed,
Among the high rank grass that sweeps his sides
The hollow beating of his footstep seems
A sacrilegious sound. I think of those
Upon whose rest he tramples. Are they here—
The dead of other days?—and did the dust

---

[12] The prairies of the West, with an undulating surface, *rolling prairies*, as they are called, present to the unaccustomed eye a singula[r]
spectacle when the shadows of the clouds are passing rapidly over them. The face of the ground seems to fluctuate and toss lik[e]
billows of the sea.

[13] I have seen the prairie-hawk balancing himself in the air for hours together, apparently over the same spot; probably watching hi[s]
prey.

Of these fair solitudes once stir with life
And burn with passion? Let the mighty mounds
That overlook the rivers, or that rise
In the dim forest crowded with old oaks,
Answer. A race, that long has passed away,
Built them; —a disciplined and populous race
Heaped, with long toil, the earth, while yet the Greek
Was hewing the Pentelicus to forms
Of symmetry, and rearing on its rock
The glittering Parthenon. These ample fields
Nourished their harvests,[14] here their herds were fed,
When haply by their stalls the bison lowed,
And bowed his maned shoulder to the yoke.
All day this desert murmured with their toils,
Till twilight blushed, and lovers walked, and wooed
In a forgotten language, and old tunes,
From instruments of unremembered form,
Gave the soft winds a voice. The red man came—
The roaming hunter tribes, warlike and fierce,
And the mound-builders vanished from the earth.
The solitude of centuries untold
Has settled where they dwelt. The prairie-wolf
Hunts in their meadows, and his fresh-dug den
Yawns by my path. The gopher mines the ground
Where stood their swarming cities. All is gone;
All—save the piles of earth that hold their bones,
The platforms where they worshipped unknown gods,
The barriers which they builded from the soil
To keep the foe at bay—till o'er the walls
The wild beleaguerers broke, and, one by one,
The strongholds of the plain were forced, and heaped
With corpses. The brown vultures of the wood
Flocked to those vast uncovered sepulchres,
And sat unscared and silent at their feast.
Haply some solitary fugitive,
Lurking in marsh and forest, till the sense
Of desolation and of fear became
Bitterer than death, yielded himself to die.
Man's better nature triumphed then. Kind words
Welcomed and soothed him; the rude conquerors
Seated the captive with their chiefs;[15] he chose
A bride among their maidens, and at length
Seemed to forget—yet ne'er forgot—the wife
Of his first love, and her sweet little ones,
Butchered, amid their shrieks, with all his race.

   Thus change the forms of being. Thus arise
Races of living things, glorious in strength,
And perish, as the quickening breath of God

---

[14] The size and extent of the mounds in the valley of the Mississippi indicate the existence, at a remote period, of a nation at once populous and laborious, and therefore probably subsisting by agriculture.

[15] Instances ace not wanting of generosity like this among the North American Indians toward a captive or survivor of a hostile tribe on which the greatest cruelties had been exercised.

Fills them, or is withdrawn. The red man, too,
Has left the blooming wilds he ranged so long,
And nearer to the Rocky Mountains, sought
A wilder hunting-ground. The beaver builds
No longer by these streams, but far away,
On waters whose blue surface ne'er gave back
The white man's face—among Missouri's springs,
And pools whose issues swell the Oregon—
He rears his little Venice. In these plains
The bison feeds no more. Twice twenty leagues
Beyond remotest smoke of hunter's camp,
Roams the majestic brute, in herds that shake
The earth with thundering steps—yet here I meet
His ancient footprints stamped beside the pool.

   Still this great solitude is quick with life.
Myriads of insects, gaudy as the flowers
They flutter over, gentle quadrupeds,
And birds, that scarce have learned the fear of man,
Are here, and sliding reptiles of the ground,
Startlingly beautiful. The graceful deer
Bounds to the wood at my approach. The bee,
A more adventurous colonist than man,
With whom he came across the eastern deep,
Fills the savannas with his murmurings,
And hides his sweets, as in the golden age,
Within the hollow oak. I listen long
To his domestic hum, and think I hear
The sound of that advancing multitude
Which soon shall fill these deserts. From the ground
Comes up the laugh of children, the soft voice
Of maidens, and the sweet and solemn hymn
Of Sabbath worshippers. The low of herds
Blends with the rustling of the heavy grain
Over the dark brown furrows. All at once
A fresher wind sweeps by, and breaks my dream,
And I am in the wilderness alone.

<div align="center">~~~~******~~~~</div>

SONG OF MARION'S MEN. [16]

Our band is few but true and tried,
  Our leader frank and bold;
The British soldier trembles
  When Marion's name is told.
Our fortress is the good greenwood,
  Our tent the cypress-tree;
We know the forest round us,
  As seamen know the sea.

---

[16] The exploits of General Francis Marion, the famous partisan warrior of South Carolina, form an interesting chapter in the annals of the American Revolution. The British troops were so harassed by the irregular and successful warfare which he kept up at the head of a few daring followers, that they sent an officer to remonstrate with him for not coming into the open field and fighting "like gentleman and a Christian."

We know its walls of thorny vines,
  Its glades of reedy grass,
Its safe and silent islands
  Within the dark morass.

Woe to the English soldiery
  That little dread us near!
On them shall light at midnight
  A strange and sudden fear:
When, waking to their tents on fire,
  They grasp their arms in vain,
And they who stand to face us
  Are beat to earth again;
And they who fly in terror deem
  A mighty host behind,
And hear the tramp of thousands
  Upon the hollow wind.

Then sweet the hour that brings release
  From danger and from toil:
We talk the battle over,
  And share the battle's spoil.
The woodland rings with laugh and shout,
  As if a hunt were up,
And woodland flowers are gathered
  To crown the soldier's cup.
With merry songs we mock the wind
  That in the pine-top grieves,
And slumber long and sweetly
  On beds of oaken leaves.

Well knows the fair and friendly moon
  The band that Marion leads—
The glitter of their rifles,
  The scampering of their steeds.
'Tis life to guide the fiery barb
  Across the moonlight plain;
'Tis life to feel the night-wind
  That lifts the tossing mane.
A moment in the British camp—
  A moment—and away
Back to the pathless forest,
  Before the peep of day.

Grave men there are by broad Santee,
  Grave men with hoary hairs;
Their hearts are all with Marion,
  For Marion are their prayers.
And lovely ladies greet our band
  With kindliest welcoming,
With smiles like those of summer,
  And tears like those of spring.
For them we wear these trusty arms,
  And lay them down no more
Till we have driven the Briton,
  Forever, from our shore.

THE ARCTIC LOVER.

Gone is the long, long winter night;
  Look, my beloved one!
How glorious, through his depths of light,
  Rolls the majestic sun!
The willows, waked from winter's death,
Give out a fragrance like thy breath—
  The summer is begun!

Ay, 'tis the long bright summer day:
  Hark to that mighty crash!
The loosened ice-ridge breaks away—
  The smitten waters flash;
Seaward the glittering mountain rides,
While, down its green translucent sides,
  The foamy torrents dash.

See, love, my boat is moored for thee
  By ocean's weedy floor—
The petrel does not skim the sea
  More swiftly than my oar.
We'll go where, on the rocky isles,
Her eggs the screaming sea-fowl piles
  Beside the pebbly shore.

Or, bide thou where the poppy blows,
  With wind-flowers frail and fair,
While I, upon his isle of snow,
  Seek and defy the bear.
Fierce though he be, and huge of frame,
This arm his savage strength shall tame,
  And drag him from his lair.

When crimson sky and flamy cloud
  Bespeak the summer o'er,
And the dead valleys wear a shroud
  Of snows that melt no more,
I'll build of ice thy winter home,
With glistening walls and glassy dome,
  And spread with skins the floor.

The white fox by thy couch shall play;
  And, from the frozen skies,
The meteors of a mimic day
  Shall flash upon thine eyes.
And I—for such thy vow—meanwhile
Shall hear thy voice and see thy smile.
  Till that long midnight flies.

THE JOURNEY OF LIFE.

Beneath the waning moon I walk at night,
  And muse on human life—for all around
Are dim uncertain shapes that cheat the sight,
  And pitfalls lurk in shade along the ground,
And broken gleams of brightness, here and there,
Glance through, and leave unwarmed the death-like air.

The trampled earth returns a sound of fear—
  A hollow sound, as if I walked on tombs;
And lights, that tell of cheerful homes, appear
  Far off, and die like hope amid the glooms.
A mournful wind across the landscape flies,
And the wide atmosphere is full of sighs.

And I, with faltering footsteps, journey on,
  Watching the stars that roll the hours away,
Till the faint light that guides me now is gone,
  And, like another life, the glorious day
Shall open o'er me from the empyreal height,
With warmth, and certainty, and boundless light.

****

TRANSLATIONS.

**

VERSION OF A FRAGMENT OF SIMONIDES.

The night winds howled, the billows dashed
  Against the tossing chest,
As Danae to her broken heart
  Her slumbering infant pressed.

"My little child" —in tears she said—
  "To wake and weep is mine,
But thou canst sleep—thou dost not know
  Thy mother's lot, and thine.

"The moon is up, the moonbeams smile—
  They tremble on the main;
But dark, within my floating cell,
  To me they smile in vain.

"Thy folded mantle wraps thee warm,
  Thy clustering locks are dry;
Thou dost not hear the shrieking gust,
  Nor breakers booming high.

"As o'er thy sweet unconscious face
  A mournful watch I keep,
I think, didst thou but know thy fate,
  How thou wouldst also weep.

"Yet, dear one, sleep, and sleep, ye winds,
    That vex the restless brine—
When shall these eyes, my babe, be sealed
    As peacefully as thine!"

~~~~~******~~~~~

FROM THE SPANISH OF VILLEGAS.

'Tis sweet, in the green Spring,
To gaze upon the wakening fields around;
    Birds in the thicket sing,
Winds whisper, waters prattle from the ground.
    A thousand odors rise,
Breathed up from blossoms of a thousand dyes.

    Shadowy, and close, and cool,
The pine and poplar keep their quiet nook;
    Forever fresh and full,
Shines, at their feet, the thirst-inviting brook;
    And the soft herbage seems
Spread for a place of banquets and of dreams.

    Thou, who alone art fair,
And whom alone I love, art far away.
    Unless thy smile be there,
It makes me sad to see the earth so gay;
    I care not if the train
Of leaves, and flowers, and zephyrs go again.

~~~~~******~~~~~

MARY MAGDALEN. [17]

FROM THE SPANISH OF BARTOLOME LEONARDO DE ARGENSOLA.

Blessed, yet sinful one, and broken-hearted!
    The crowd are pointing at the thing forlorn,
        In wonder and in scorn!
Thou weepest days of innocence departed;
    Thou weepest, and thy tears have power to move
        The Lord to pity and love.

The greatest of thy follies is forgiven,
    Even for the least of all the tears that shine
        On that pale cheek of thine.
Thou didst kneel down, to Him who came from heaven,
    Evil and ignorant, and thou shalt rise

---

[17] Several learned divines, with much appearance of reason, in particular Dr. Lardner, have maintained that the common notion respecting the dissolute life of Mary Magdalen is erroneous, and that she was always a person of excellent character. Charles Taylor the editor of *Calmet'sDictionary of the Bible* takes the same view of the subject. The verses of the Spanish poet here translated refer to the "woman who had been a sinner," mentioned in the seventh chapter of St. Luke's Gospel, and who is commonly confounded with Mary Magdalen.

Holy, and pure, and wise.

It is not much that to the fragrant blossom
  The ragged brier should change, the bitter fir
    Distil Arabian myrrh;
Nor that, upon the wintry desert's bosom,
  The harvest should rise plenteous, and the swain
    Bear home the abundant grain.

But come and see the bleak and barren mountains
  Thick to their tops with roses; come and see
    Leaves on the dry dead tree.
The perished plant, set out by lining fountains,
  Grows fruitful, and its beauteous branches rise,
    Forever, toward the skies.

******

THE LIFE OF THE BLESSED.

FROM THE SPANISH OF LUIS PONCE DE LEON.

    Region of life and light!
Land of the good whose earthly toils are o'er!
    Nor frost nor heat may blight
    Thy vernal beauty, fertile shore,
Yielding thy blessed fruits for evermore.

    There, without crook or sling,
Walks the good shepherd; blossoms white and red
    Round his meek temples cling;
    And to sweet pastures led,
The flock he loves beneath his eye is fed.

    He guides, and near him they
Follow delighted, for he makes them go
    Where dwells eternal May,
    And heavenly roses blow,
Deathless, and gathered but again to grow.

    He leads them to the height
Named of the infinite and long-sought Good,
    And fountains of delight;
    And where his feet have stood
Springs up, along the way, their tender food.

    And when, in the mid skies,
The climbing sun has reached his highest bound,
    Reposing as he lies,
    With all his flock around,
He witches the still air with numerous sound.

    From his sweet lute flow forth
Immortal harmonies, of power to still
    All passions born of earth,
    And draw the ardent will

Its destiny of goodness to fulfil.

Might but a little part,
A wandering breath of that high melody,
Descend into my heart,
And change it till it be
Transformed and swallowed up, oh love, in thee!

Ah! then my soul should know,
Beloved! where thou liest at noon of day,
And from this place of woe
Released, should take its way
To mingle with thy flock and never stray.

~~~~~******~~~~~

FATIMA AND RADUAN. [18]

FROM THE SPANISH.

Diamante falso y fingido,
Engastado en pedernal, etc.

"False diamond set in flint! hard heart in haughty breast!
By a softer, warmer bosom the tiger's couch is prest.
Thou art fickle as the sea, thou art wandering as the wind,
And the restless ever-mounting flame is not more hard to bind.
If the tears I shed were tongues, yet all too few would be
To tell of all the treachery that thou hast shown to me.
Oh! I could chide thee sharply—but every maiden knows
That she who chides her lover, forgives him ere he goes.

"Thou hast called me oft the flower of all Granada's maids,
Thou hast said that by the side of me the first and fairest fades;
And they thought thy heart was mine, and it seemed to every one
That what thou didst to win my love, for love of me was done.
Alas! if they but knew thee, as mine it is to know,
They well might see another mark to which thine arrows go;
But thou giv'st me little heed—for I speak to one who knows
That she who chides her lover, forgives him ere he goes.

"It wearies me, mine enemy, that I must weep and bear
What fills thy heart with triumph, and fills my own with care.
Thou art leagued with those that hate me, and ah! thou know'st I feel
That cruel words as surely kill as sharpest blades of steel.
'Twas the doubt that thou wert false that wrung my heart with pain;
But, now I know thy perfidy, I shall be well again.
I would proclaim thee as thou art—but every maiden knows
That she who chides her lover, forgives him ere he goes."

Thus Fatima complained to the valiant Raduan,

---

[18] This and the following poems belong to that class of ancient Spanish ballads, by unknown authors, called *Romances Moriscos-* Moriscan Romances or ballads. They were composed in the fourteenth century, some of them, probably, by the Moors, who then live intermingled with the Christians; and they relate the loves and achievements of the knights of Granada.

Where underneath the myrtles Alhambra's fountains ran.
The Moor was inly moved, and blameless as he was,
He took her white hand in his own, and pleaded thus his cause:
"Oh lady, dry those star-like eyes—their dimness does me wrong;
If my heart be made of flint, at least 'twill keep thy image long.
Thou hast uttered cruel words—but I grieve the less for those,
Since she who chides her lover, forgives him ere he goes."

~~~~******~~~~

LOVE AND FOLLY. [19]

FROM LA FONTAINE.

Love's worshippers alone can know
  The thousand mysteries that are his;
His blazing torch, his twanging bow,
  His blooming age are mysteries.
A charming science—but the day
  Were all too short to con it o'er;
So take of me this little lay,
  A sample of its boundless lore.

As once, beneath the fragrant shade
  Of myrtles fresh in heaven's pure air,
The children, Love and Folly, played,
  A quarrel rose betwixt the pair.
Love said the gods should do him right—
  But Folly vowed to do it then,
And struck him, o'er the orbs of sight,
  So hard he never saw again.

His lovely mother's grief was deep,
  She called for vengeance on the deed;
A beauty does not vainly weep,
  Nor coldly does a mother plead.
A shade came o'er the eternal bliss
  That fills the dwellers of the skies;
Even stony-hearted Nemesis,
  And Rhadamanthus, wiped their eyes.

"Behold," she said, "this lovely boy,"
  While streamed afresh her graceful tears—
"Immortal, yet shut out from joy
  And sunshine, all his future years.
The child can never take, you see,
  A single step without a staff—
The hardest punishment would be
  Too lenient for the crime by half."

All said that Love had suffered wrong,
  And well that wrong should be repaid;
Then weighed the public interest long,
  And long the party's interest weighed.

---

[19] This is rather an imitation than a translation of the poem of the graceful French fabulist.

And thus decreed the court above:
  "Since Love is blind from Folly's blow,
Let Folly be the guide of Love,
  Where'er the boy may choose to go."

~~~~~******~~~~~

THE SIESTA.

FROM THE SPANISH.

Vientecico murmurador,
Que lo gozas y andas todo, etc.

Airs, that wander and murmur round,
  Bearing delight where'er ye blow!
Make in the elms a lulling sound,
  While my lady sleeps in the shade below.

Lighten and lengthen her noonday rest,
  Till the heat of the noonday sun is o'er.
Sweet be her slumbers! though in my breast
  The pain she has waked may slumber no more.

Breathing soft from the blue profound,
  Bearing delight where'er ye blow,
Make in the elms a lulling sound,
  While my lady sleeps in the shade below.

Airs! that over the bending boughs,
  And under the shade of pendent leaves,
Murmur soft, like my timid vows
  Or the secret sighs my bosom heaves—

Gently sweeping the grassy ground,
  Bearing delight where'er ye blow,
Make in the elms a lulling sound,
  While my lady sleeps in the shade below.

~~~~~******~~~~~

THE ALCAYDE OF MOLINA.

FROM THE SPANISH.

To the town of Atienza, Molina's brave Alcayde,
The courteous and the valorous, led forth his bold brigade.
The Moor came back in triumph, he came without a wound,
With many a Christian standard, and Christian captive bound.
He passed the city portals, with swelling heart and vain,
And toward his lady's dwelling he rode with slackened rein;
Two circuits on his charger he took, and at the third,
From the door of her balcony Zelinda's voice was heard.
"Now if thou wert not shameless," said the lady to the Moor,
"Thou wouldst neither pass my dwelling, nor stop before my door.
Alas for poor Zelinda, and for her wayward mood,

That one in love with peace should have loved a man of blood!
Since not that thou wert noble I chose thee for my knight,
But that thy sword was dreaded in tournay and in fight.
Ah, thoughtless and unhappy! that I should fail to see
How ill the stubborn flint and the yielding wax agree.
Boast not thy love for me, while the shrieking of the fife
Can change thy mood of mildness to fury and to strife.
Say not my voice is magic—thy pleasure is to hear
The bursting of the carbine, and shivering of the spear.
Well, follow thou thy choice—to the battle-field away,
To thy triumphs and thy trophies, since I am less than they.
Thrust thy arm into thy buckler, gird on thy crooked brand,
And call upon thy trusty squire to bring thy spears in hand.
Lead forth thy band to skirmish, by mountain and by mead,
On thy dappled Moorish barb, or thy fleeter border steed.
Go, waste the Christian hamlets, and sweep away their flocks,
From Almazan's broad meadows to Siguenza's rocks.
Leave Zelinda altogether, whom thou leavest oft and long,
And in the life thou lovest, forget whom thou dost wrong.
These eyes shall not recall thee, though they meet no more thine own,[20]
Though they weep that thou art absent, and that I am all alone."
She ceased, and turning from him her flushed and angry cheek,
Shut the door of her balcony before the Moor could speak.

~~~~~~******~~~~~~

THE DEATH OF ALIATAR.

FROM THE SPANISH.

'Tis not with gilded sabres
  That gleam in baldricks blue,
Nor nodding plumes in caps of Fez,
  Of gay and gaudy hue—
But, habited in mourning weeds,
  Come marching from afar,
By four and four, the valiant men
  Who fought with Aliatar.
All mournfully and slowly
  The afflicted warriors come,
To the deep wail of the trumpet,
  And beat of muffled drum.

The banner of the Phoenix,
  The flag that loved the sky,
That scarce the wind dared wanton with,

---

[20] This is the very expression of the original—*No te llamaran mis ojos*,etc. The Spanish poets early adopted the practice of calling a lady by the name of the most expressive feature of her countenance, her eyes. The lover styled his mistress "ojos bellos," beautiful eyes; "ojos serenos," serene eyes. Green eyes seem to have been anciently thought a great beauty in Spain, and there is a very pretty ballad by an absent lover, in which he addressed his lady by the title of "green eyes;" supplicating that he may remain in her remembrance:

  "Ay ojuelos verdes!
  Ay los mis ojuelos!
  Ay, hagan los cielos
  Que de mi te acuerdes!"

It flew so proud and high—
Now leaves its place in battle-field,
　And sweeps the ground in grief,
The bearer drags its glorious folds
　Behind the fallen chief,
As mournfully and slowly
　The afflicted warriors come,
To the deep wail of the trumpet,
　And beat of muffled drum.

Brave Aliatar led forward
　A hundred Moors to go
To where his brother held Motril
　Against the leaguering foe.
On horseback went the gallant Moor,
　That gallant band to lead;
And now his bier is at the gate,
　From which he pricked his steed.
While mournfully and slowly
　The afflicted warriors come,
To the deep wail of the trumpet,
　And beat of muffled drum.

The knights of the Grand Master
　In crowded ambush lay;
They rushed upon him where the reeds
　Were thick beside the way;
They smote the valiant Aliatar,
　They smote the warrior dead,
And broken, but not beaten, were
　The gallant ranks he led.
Now mournfully and slowly
　The afflicted warriors come,
To the deep wail of the trumpet,
　And beat of muffled drum.

Oh! what was Zayda's sorrow,
　How passionate her cries!
Her lover's wounds streamed not more free
　Than that poor maiden's eyes.
Say, Love—for didst thou see her tears—[21]
　Oh, no! he drew more tight
The blinding fillet o'er his lids
　To spare his eyes the sight.
While mournfully and slowly
　The afflicted warriors come,
To the deep wail of the trumpet,
　And beat of muffled drum.

---

[21] The stanza beginning with this line stands thus in the original:
"Dilo tu, amor, si lo viste;
　¡Mas ay! que de lastimado
Diste otro nudo a la venda,
　Para no ver lo que la pasado."
I am sorry to find so poor a conceit deforming so spirited a composition as this old ballad, but I have preserved it in the version. It one of those extravagances which afterward became so common in Spanish poetry, when Gongora introduced the *estilo culto*, as was called.

Nor Zayda weeps him only,
  But all that dwell between
The great Alhambra's palace walls
  And springs of Albaicin.
The ladies weep the flower of knights,
  The brave the bravest here;
The people weep a champion,
  The Alcaydes a noble peer.
While mournfully and slowly
  The afflicted warriors come,
To the deep wail of the trumpet,
  And beat of muffled drum.

~~~~~******~~~~~

LOVE IN THE AGE OF CHIVALRY. [22]

FROM PEYRE VIDAL, THE TROUBADOUR.

The earth was sown with early flowers,
  The heavens were blue and bright—
I met a youthful cavalier
  As lovely as the light.
I knew him not—but in my heart
  His graceful image lies,
And well I marked his open brow,
  His sweet and tender eyes,
His ruddy lips that ever smiled,
  His glittering teeth betwixt,
And flowing robe embroidered o'er,
  With leaves and blossoms mixed.
He wore a chaplet of the rose;
  His palfrey, white and sleek,
Was marked with many an ebon spot,
  And many a purple streak;
Of jasper was his saddle-bow,
  His housings sapphire stone,
And brightly in his stirrup glanced
  The purple calcedon.
Fast rode the gallant cavalier,
  As youthful horsemen ride;
"Peyre Vidal! know that I am Love,"
  The blooming stranger cried;
"And this is Mercy by my side,
  A dame of high degree;
This maid is Chastity," he said,
  "This squire is Loyalty."

~~~~~******~~~~~

---

[22] This personification of the passion of Love, by Peyre Vidal, has been referred to as a proof of how little the Provencal poets were indebted to the authors of Greece and Rome for the imagery of their poems.

117

THE LOVE OF GOD. [23]

FROM THE PROVENCAL OF BERNARD RASCAS.

All things that are on earth shall wholly pass away,
Except the love of God, which shall live and last for aye.
The forms of men shall be as they had never been;
The blasted groves shall lose their fresh and tender green;
The birds of the thicket shall end their pleasant song,
And the nightingale shall cease to chant the evening long;
The kine of the pasture shall feel the dart that kills,
And all the fair white flocks shall perish from the hills.
The goat and antlered stag, the wolf and the fox,
The wild-boar of the wood, and the chamois of the rocks,
And the strong and fearless bear, in the trodden dust shall lie;
And the dolphin of the sea, and the mighty whale, shall die.
And realms shall be dissolved, and empires be no more,
And they shall bow to death, who ruled from shore to shore;
And the great globe itself, so the holy writings tell,
With the rolling firmament, where the starry armies dwell,
Shall melt with fervent heat—they shall all pass away,
Except the love of God, which shall live and last for aye.

~~~~~******~~~~~

FROM THE SPANISH OF PEDRO DE CASTRO Y ANAYA. [24]

Stay rivulet, nor haste to leave
  The lovely vale that lies around thee.
Why wouldst thou be a sea at eve,
  When but a fount the morning found thee?

Born when the skies began to glow,
  Humblest of all the rock's cold daughters,

---

[23] The original of these lines is thus given by John of Nostradamus, in his Lives of the Troubadours, in a barbarous Frenchified orthography:

"Touta kausa mortala una fes perira,
Fors que l'amour de Dieu, que touiours durara.
Tous nostres cors vendran essuchs, come fa l'eska,
Lous Aubres leyssaran lour verdour tendra e fresca,
Lous Ausselets del bosc perdran lour kant subtyeu,
E non s'auzira plus lou Rossignol gentyeu.
Lous Buols al Pastourgage, e las blankas fedettas
Sent'ran lous agulhons de las mortals Sagettas,
Lous crestas d'Aries fiers, Renards, e Loups espars
Kabrols, Cervys, Chamous, Senglars de toutes pars,
Lous Ours hardys e forts, seran poudra, e Arena.
Lou Daulphin en la Mar, lou Ton, e la Balena,
Monstres impetuous, Ryaumes, e Comtas,
Lous Princes, e lous Reys, seran per mort domtas.
E nota ben eysso kascun: la Terra granda,
(Ou l'Escritura ment) lou fermament que branda,
Prendra autra figura. Enfin tout perira,
Fors que l'Amour de Dieu, que touiours durara."

[24] *Las Auroras de Diana*, in which the original of these lines is contained, is, notwithstanding it was praised by Lope de Vega, one of the worst of the old Spanish Romances, being a tissue of riddles and affectations, with now and then a little poem of considerable beauty.

No blossom bowed its stalk to show
  Where stole thy still and scanty waters.

Now on the stream the noonbeams look,
  Usurping, as thou downward driftest,
Its crystal from the clearest brook,
  Its rushing current from the swiftest.

Ah! what wild haste! —and all to be
  A river and expire in ocean.
Each fountain's tribute hurries thee
  To that vast grave with quicker motion.

Far better 'twere to linger still
  In this green vale, these flowers to cherish,
And die in peace, an aged rill,
  Than thus, a youthful Danube, perish.

~~~~~******~~~~~

SONNET.

FROM THE PORTUGUESE OF SEMEDO.

It is a fearful night; a feeble glare
  Streams from the sick moon in the o'erclouded sky;
  The ridgy billows, with a mighty cry,
Rush on the foamy beaches wild and bare;
No bark the madness of the waves will dare;
  The sailors sleep; the winds are loud and high.
  Ah, peerless Laura! for whose love I die,
Who gazes on thy smiles while I despair?
  As thus, in bitterness of heart, I cried,
I turned, and saw my Laura, kind and bright,
  A messenger of gladness, at my side;
To my poor bark she sprang with footstep light,
  And as we furrowed Tago's heaving tide,
I never saw so beautiful a night.

~~~~~******~~~~~

SONG.

FROM THE SPANISH OF IGLESIAS.

Alexis calls me cruel:
  The rifted crags that hold
The gathered ice of winter,
  He says, are not more cold.

When even the very blossoms
  Around the fountain's brim,
And forest-walks, can witness
  The love I bear to him.

I would that I could utter

119

My feelings without shame,
And tell him how I love him,
  Nor wrong my virgin fame.

Alas! to seize the moment
  When heart inclines to heart,
And press a suit with passion,
  Is not a woman's part.

If man come not to gather
  The roses where they stand,
They fade among their foliage;
  They cannot seek his hand.

~~~~~~******~~~~~~

THE COUNT OF GREIERS.

FROM THE GERMAN OF UHLAND.

At morn the Count of Greiers before his castle stands;
He sees afar the glory that lights the mountain-lands;
The horned crags are shining, and in the shade between
A pleasant Alpine valley lies beautifully green.

"Oh, greenest of the valleys, how shall I come to thee!
Thy herdsmen and thy maidens, how happy must they be!
I have gazed upon thee coldly, all lovely as thou art,
But the wish to walk thy pastures now stirs my inmost heart."

He hears a sound of timbrels, and suddenly appear
A troop of ruddy damsels and herdsmen drawing near:
They reach the castle greensward, and gayly dance across;
The white sleeves flit and glimmer, the wreaths and ribbons toss.

The youngest of the maidens, slim as a spray of spring,
She takes the young count's fingers, and draws him to the ring;
They fling upon his forehead a crown of mountain flowers,
"And ho, young Count of Greiers! this morning thou art ours!"

Then hand in hand departing, with dance and roundelay,
Through hamlet after hamlet, they lead the Count away.
They dance through wood and meadow, they dance across the linn,
Till the mighty Alpine summits have shut the music in.

The second morn is risen, and now the third is come;
Where stays the Count of Greiers? has he forgot his home?
Again the evening closes, in thick and sultry air;
There's thunder on the mountains, the storm is gathering there.

The cloud has shed its waters, the brook comes swollen down;
You see it by the lightning—a river wide and brown.
Around a struggling swimmer the eddies dash and roar,
Till, seizing on a willow, he leaps upon the shore.

"Here am I cast by tempests far from your mountain-dell.

Amid our evening dances the bursting deluge fell.
Ye all, in cots and caverns, have 'scaped the water-spout,
While me alone the tempest overwhelmed and hurried out.

"Farewell, with thy glad dwellers, green vale among the rocks!
Farewell the swift sweet moments, in which I watched thy flocks!
Why rocked they not my cradle in that delicious spot,
That garden of the happy, where Heaven endures me not?

"Rose of the Alpine valley! I feel, in every vein,
Thy soft touch on my fingers; oh, press them not again!
Bewitch me not, ye garlands, to tread that upward track,
And thou, my cheerless mansion, receive thy master back."

~~~~~~******~~~~~~

THE SERENADE.

FROM THE SPANISH.

If slumber, sweet Lisena!
  Have stolen o'er thine eyes,
As night steals o'er the glory
  Of spring's transparent skies;

Wake, in thy scorn and beauty,
  And listen to the strain
That murmurs my devotion,
  That mourns for thy disdain.

Here, by thy door at midnight,
  I pass the dreary hour,
With plaintive sounds profaning
  The silence of thy bower;

A tale of sorrow cherished
  Too fondly to depart,
Of wrong from love the flatterer
  And my own wayward heart.

Twice, o'er this vale, the seasons
  Have brought and borne away
The January tempest,
  The genial wind of May;

Yet still my plaint is uttered,
  My tears and sighs are given
To earth's unconscious waters,
  And wandering winds of heaven.

I saw, from this fair region,
  The smile of summer pass,
And myriad frost-stars glitter
  Among the russet grass.

While winter seized the streamlets

That fled along the ground,
  And fast in chains of crystal
  The truant murmurers bound.

I saw that to the forest
  The nightingales had flown,
And every sweet-voiced fountain
  Had hushed its silver tone.

The maniac winds, divorcing
  The turtle from his mate,
Raved through the leafy beeches,
  And left them desolate.

Now May, with life and music,
  The blooming valley fills,
And rears her flowery arches
  For all the little rills.

The minstrel bird of evening
  Comes back on joyous wings,
And, like the harp's soft murmur,
  Is heard the gush of springs.

And deep within the forest
  Are wedded turtles seen,
Their nuptial chambers seeking,
  Their chambers close and green.

The rugged trees are mingling
  Their flowery sprays in love;
The ivy climbs the laurel,
  To clasp the boughs above.

They change—but thou, Lisena,
  Art cold while I complain:
Why to thy lover only
  Should spring return in vain?

~~~~~******~~~~~

A NORTHERN LEGEND.

FROM THE GERMAN OF UHLAND.

There sits a lovely maiden,
  The ocean murmuring nigh;
She throws the hook, and watches;
  The fishes pass it by.

A ring, with a red jewel,
  Is sparkling on her hand;
Upon the hook she binds it,
  And flings it from the land.

Uprises from the water

A hand like ivory fair.
What gleams upon its finger?
  The golden ring is there.

Uprises from the bottom
  A young and handsome knight;
In golden scales he rises,
  That glitter in the light.

The maid is pale with terror—
  "Nay, Knight of Ocean, nay,
It was not thou I wanted;
  Let go the ring, I pray."

"Ah, maiden, not to fishes
  The bait of gold is thrown;
Thy ring shall never leave me,
  And thou must be my own."

<div align="center">~~~~~~******~~~~~</div>

THE PARADISE OF TEARS.

FROM THE GERMAN OF N. MUELLER.

Beside the River of Tears, with branches low,
And bitter leaves, the weeping-willows grow;
The branches stream like the dishevelled hair
Of women in the sadness of despair.

On rolls the stream with a perpetual sigh;
The rocks moan wildly as it passes by;
Hyssop and wormwood border all the strand,
And not a flower adorns the dreary land.

Then comes a child, whose face is like the sun,
And dips the gloomy waters as they run,
And waters all the region, and behold
The ground is bright with blossoms manifold.

Where fall the tears of love the rose appears,
And where the ground is bright with friendship's tears,
Forget-me-not, and violets, heavenly blue,
Spring, glittering with the cheerful drops like dew.

The souls of mourners, all whose tears are dried,
Like swans, come gently floating down the tide,
Walk up the golden sands by which it flows,
And in that Paradise of Tears repose.

There every heart rejoins its kindred heart;
There in a long embrace that none may part,
Fulfilment meets desire, and that fair shore
Beholds its dwellers happy evermore.

<div align="center">~~~~~~******~~~~~</div>

THE LADY OF CASTLE WINDECK.

FROM THE GERMAN OF CHAMISSO.

Rein in thy snorting charger!
  That stag but cheats thy sight;
He is luring thee on to Windeck,
  With his seeming fear and flight.

Now, where the mouldering turrets
  Of the outer gate arise,
The knight gazed over the ruins
  Where the stag was lost to his eyes.

The sun shone hot above him;
  The castle was still as death;
He wiped the sweat from his forehead,
  With a deep and weary breath.

"Who now will bring me a beaker
  Of the rich old wine that here,
In the choked-up vaults of Windeck,
  Has lain for many a year?"

The careless words had scarcely
  Time from his lips to fall,
When the lady of Castle Windeck,
  Came round the ivy-wall.

He saw the glorious maiden
  In her snow-white drapery stand,
The bunch of keys at her girdle,
  The beaker high in her hand.

He quaffed that rich old vintage;
  With an eager lip he quaffed;
But he took into his bosom
  A fire with the grateful draught.

Her eyes' unfathomed brightness!
  The flowing gold of her hair!
He folded his hands in homage,
  And murmured a lover's prayer.

She gave him a look of pity,
  A gentle look of pain;
And, quickly as he had seen her,
  She passed from his sight again.

And ever, from that moment,
  He haunted the ruins there,
A sleepless, restless wanderer,
  A watcher with despair.

Ghost-like and pale he wandered,

With a dreamy, haggard eye;
He seemed not one of the living,
    And yet he could not die.

'Tis said that the lady met him,
    When many years had past,
And kissing his lips, released him
    From the burden of life at last.

~~~~~~********~~~~~~

LATER POEMS.

~~**~~

TO THE APENNINES.

Your peaks are beautiful, ye Apennines!
    In the soft light of these serenest skies;
From the broad highland region, black with pines,
    Fair as the hills of Paradise they rise,
Bathed in the tint Peruvian slaves behold
In rosy flushes on the virgin gold.

There, rooted to the aerial shelves that wear
    The glory of a brighter world, might spring
Sweet flowers of heaven to scent the unbreathed air,
    And heaven's fleet messengers might rest the wing
To view the fair earth in its summer sleep,
Silent, and cradled by the glimmering deep.

Below you lie men's sepulchres, the old
    Etrurian tombs, the graves of yesterday;
The herd's white bones lie mixed with human mould,
    Yet up the radiant steeps that I survey
Death never climbed, nor life's soft breath, with pain,
Was yielded to the elements again.

Ages of war have filled these plains with fear;
    How oft the hind has started at the clash
Of spears, and yell of meeting armies here,
    Or seen the lightning of the battle flash
From clouds, that rising with the thunder's sound,
Hung like an earth-born tempest o'er the ground!

Ah me! what armed nations—Asian horde,
    And Libyan host, the Scythian and the Gaul
Have swept your base and through your passes poured,
    Like ocean-tides uprising at the call
Of tyrant winds—against your rocky side
The bloody billows dashed, and howled, and died!

How crashed the towers before beleaguering foes,
    Sacked cities smoked and realms were rent in twain;
And commonwealths against their rivals rose,

Trode out their lives and earned the curse of Cain!
While, in the noiseless air and light that flowed
Round your fair brows, eternal Peace abode.

Here pealed the impious hymn, and altar-flames
  Rose to false gods, a dream-begotten throng,
Jove, Bacchus, Pan, and earlier, fouler names;
  While, as the unheeding ages passed along,
Ye, from your station in the middle skies,
Proclaimed the essential Goodness, strong and wise.

In you the heart that sighs for freedom seeks
  Her image; there the winds no barrier know,
Clouds come and rest and leave your fairy peaks;
  While even the immaterial Mind, below,
And Thought, her winged offspring, chained by power,
Pine silently for the redeeming hour.

<p style="text-align:center">~~~~~~******~~~~~~</p>

EARTH. [25]

A midnight black with clouds is in the sky;
I seem to feel, upon my limbs, the weight
Of its vast brooding shadow. All in vain
Turns the tired eye in search of form; no star
Pierces the pitchy veil; no ruddy blaze,
From dwellings lighted by the cheerful hearth,
Tinges the flowering summits of the grass.
No sound of life is heard, no village hum,
Nor measured tramp of footstep in the path,
Nor rush of wind, while, on the breast of Earth,
I lie and listen to her mighty voice:
A voice of many tones—sent up from streams

---

[25] The author began this poem in rhyme. The following is the first draught of it as far as he proceeded, in a stanza which he found it convenient to abandon:

A midnight black with clouds is on the sky;
  A shadow like the first original night
Folds in, and seems to press me as I lie;
  No image meets the vainly wandering sight,
And shot through rolling mists no starlight gleam
Glances on glassy pool or rippling stream.

No ruddy blaze, from dwellings bright within,
  Tinges the flowering summits of the grass;
No sound of life is heard, no village din,
  Wings rustling overhead or steps that pass,
While, on the breast of Earth at random thrown,
I listen to her mighty voice alone.

A voice of many tones: deep murmurs sent
  From waters that in darkness glide away,
From woods unseen by sweeping breezes bent,
  From rocky chasms where darkness dwells all day,
And hollows of the invisible hills around,
Blent in one ceaseless, melancholy sound.

O Earth! dost thou, too, sorrow for the past?
  Mourn'st thou thy childhood's unreturning hours,
Thy springs, that briefly bloomed and faded fast,
  The gentle generations of thy flowers,
Thy forests of the elder time, decayed
And gone with all the tribes that loved their shade?

Mourn'st thou that first fair time so early lost,
  The golden age that lives in poets' strains,
Ere hail or lightning, whirlwind, flood, or frost
  Scathed thy green breast, or earthquakes whelmed thy plains,
Ere blood upon the shuddering ground was spilt,
Or night was haunted by disease and guilt?

Or haply dost thou grieve for those who die?
  For living things that trod a while thy face,
The love of thee and heaven, and now they lie
  Mixed with the shapeless dust the wild winds chase?
I, too, must grieve, for never on thy sphere
Shall those bright forms and faces reappear.

Ha! with a deeper and more thrilling tone,
  Rises that voice around me: 'tis the cry
Of Earth for guilt and wrong, the eternal moan
  Sent to the listening and long-suffering sky,
I hear and tremble, and my heart grows faint,
As midst the night goes up that great complaint.

That wander through the gloom, from woods unseen
Swayed by the sweeping of the tides of air,
From rocky chasms where darkness dwells all day,
And hollows of the great invisible hills,
And sands that edge the ocean, stretching far
Into the night—a melancholy sound!

  O Earth! dost thou too sorrow for the past
Like man thy offspring? Do I hear thee mourn
Thy childhood's unreturning hours, thy springs
Gone with their genial airs and melodies,
The gentle generations of thy flowers,
And thy majestic groves of olden time,
Perished with all their dwellers? Dost thou wail
For that fair age of which the poets tell,
Ere yet the winds grew keen with frost, or fire
Fell with the rains or spouted from the hills,
To blast thy greenness, while the virgin night
Was guiltless and salubrious as the day?
Or haply dost thou grieve for those that die—
For living things that trod thy paths awhile,
The love of thee and heaven—and now they sleep
Mixed with the shapeless dust on which thy herds
Trample and graze? I too must grieve with thee,
O'er loved ones lost. Their graves are far away
Upon thy mountains; yet, while I recline
Alone, in darkness, on thy naked soil,
The mighty nourisher and burial-place
Of man, I feel that I embrace their dust.

  Ha! how the murmur deepens! I perceive
And tremble at its dreadful import. Earth
Uplifts a general cry for guilt and wrong,
And heaven is listening. The forgotten graves
Of the heart-broken utter forth their plaint.
The dust of her who loved and was betrayed,
And him who died neglected in his age;
The sepulchres of those who for mankind
Labored, and earned the recompense of scorn;
Ashes of martyrs for the truth, and bones
Of those who, in the strife for liberty,
Were beaten down, their corses given to dogs,
Their names to infamy, all find a voice.
The nook in which the captive, overtoiled,
Lay down to rest at last, and that which holds
Childhood's sweet blossoms, crushed by cruel hands,
Send up a plaintive sound. From battle-fields,
Where heroes madly drave and dashed their hosts
Against each other, rises up a noise,
As if the armed multitudes of dead
Stirred in their heavy slumber. Mournful tones
Come from the green abysses of the sea—
A story of the crimes the guilty sought
To hide beneath its waves. The glens, the groves,
Paths in the thicket, pools of running brook,
And banks and depths of lake, and streets and lanes

128

Of cities, now that living sounds are hushed,
Murmur of guilty force and treachery.

Here, where I rest, the vales of Italy
Are round me, populous from early time,
And field of the tremendous warfare waged
'Twixt good and evil. Who, alas! shall dare
Interpret to man's ear the mingled voice
That comes from her old dungeons yawning now
To the black air, her amphitheatres,
Where the dew gathers on the mouldering stones,
And fanes of banished gods, and open tombs,
And roofless palaces, and streets and hearths
Of cities dug from their volcanic graves?
I hear a sound of many languages,
The utterance of nations now no more,
Driven out by mightier, as the days of heaven
Chase one another from the sky. The blood
Of freemen shed by freemen, till strange lords
Came in their hour of weakness, and made fast
The yoke that yet is worn, cries out to heaven.

What then shall cleanse thy bosom, gentle Earth,
From all its painful memories of guilt?
The whelming flood, or the renewing fire,
Or the slow change of time? —that so, at last,
The horrid tale of perjury and strife,
Murder and spoil, which men call history,
May seem a fable, like the inventions told
By poets of the gods of Greece. O thou,
Who sittest far beyond the Atlantic deep,
Among the sources of thy glorious streams,
My native Land of Groves! a newer page
In the great record of the world is thine;
Shall it be fairer? Fear, and friendly Hope,
And Envy, watch the issue, while the lines,
By which thou shalt be judged, are written down.

~~~~~~******~~~~~~

THE KNIGHT'S EPITAPH.

This is the church which Pisa, great and free,
Reared to St. Catharine. How the time-stained walls,
That earthquakes shook not from their poise, appear
To shiver in the deep and voluble tones
Rolled from the organ! Underneath my feet
There lies the lid of a sepulchral vault.
The image of an armed knight is graven
Upon it, clad in perfect panoply—
Cuishes, and greaves, and cuirass, with barred helm,
Gauntleted hand, and sword, and blazoned shield.
Around, in Gothic characters, worn dim
By feet of worshippers, are traced his name,
And birth, and death, and words of eulogy.
Why should I pore upon them? This old tomb,

This effigy, the strange disused form
Of this inscription, eloquently show
His history. Let me clothe in fitting words
The thoughts they breathe, and frame his epitaph:

"He whose forgotten dust for centuries
Has lain beneath this stone, was one in whom
Adventure, and endurance, and emprise,
Exalted the mind's faculties and strung
The body's sinews. Brave he was in fight,
Courteous in banquet, scornful of repose,
And bountiful, and cruel, and devout,
And quick to draw the sword in private feud,
He pushed his quarrels to the death, yet prayed
The saints as fervently on bended knees
As ever shaven cenobite. He loved
As fiercely as he fought. He would have borne
The maid that pleased him from her bower by night
To his hill castle, as the eagle bears
His victim from the fold, and rolled the rocks
On his pursuers. He aspired to see
His native Pisa queen and arbitress
Of cities; earnestly for her he raised
His voice in council, and affronted death
In battle-field, and climbed the galley's deck,
And brought the captured flag of Genoa back,
Or piled upon the Arno's crowded quay
The glittering spoils of the tamed Saracen.
He was not born to brook the stranger's yoke,
But would have joined the exiles that withdrew
Forever, when the Florentine broke in
The gates of Pisa, and bore off the bolts
For trophies—but he died before that day.

"He lived, the impersonation of an age
That never shall return. His soul of fire
Was kindled by the breath of the rude time
He lived in. Now a gentler race succeeds,
Shuddering at blood; the effeminate cavalier,
Turning his eyes from the reproachful past,
And from the hopeless future, gives to ease,
And love, and music, his inglorious life."

******

THE HUNTER OF THE PRAIRIES.

Ay, this is freedom! —these pure skies
   Were never stained with village smoke:
The fragrant wind, that through them flies,
   Is breathed from wastes by plough unbroke.
Here, with my rifle and my steed,
   And her who left the world for me,
I plant me, where the red deer feed
   In the green desert—and am free.

For here the fair savannas know
  No barriers in the bloomy grass;
Wherever breeze of heaven may blow,
  Or beam of heaven may glance, I pass.
In pastures, measureless as air,
  The bison is my noble game;
The bounding elk, whose antlers tear
  The branches, falls before my aim.

Mine are the river-fowl that scream
  From the long stripe of waving sedge;
The bear that marks my weapon's gleam,
  Hides vainly in the forest's edge;
In vain the she-wolf stands at bay;
  The brinded catamount, that lies
High in the boughs to watch his prey,
  Even in the act of springing, dies.

With what free growth the elm and plane
  Fling their huge arms across my way,
Gray, old, and cumbered with a train
  Of vines, as huge, and old, and gray!
Free stray the lucid streams, and find
  No taint in these fresh lawns and shades;
Free spring the flowers that scent the wind
  Where never scythe has swept the glades.

Alone the Fire, when frost-winds sere
  The heavy herbage of the ground,
Gathers his annual harvest here,
  With roaring like the battle's sound,
And hurrying flames that sweep the plain,
  And smoke-streams gushing up the sky:
I meet the flames with flames again,
  And at my door they cower and die.

Here, from dim woods, the aged past
  Speaks solemnly; and I behold
The boundless future in the vast
  And lonely river, seaward rolled.
Who feeds its founts with rain and dew?
  Who moves, I ask, its gliding mass,
And trains the bordering vines, whose blue
  Bright clusters tempt me as I pass?

Broad are these streams—my steed obeys,
  Plunges, and bears me through the tide.
Wide are these woods—I thread the maze
  Of giant stems, nor ask a guide.
I hunt till day's last glimmer dies
  O'er woody vale and grassy height;
And kind the voice and glad the eyes
  That welcome my return at night.

~~~~~******~~~~~

SEVENTY-SIX.

What heroes from the woodland sprung,
  When, through the fresh awakened land,
The thrilling cry of freedom rung,
And to the work of warfare strung
  The yeoman's iron hand!

Hills flung the cry to hills around,
  And ocean-mart replied to mart,
And streams whose springs were yet unfound,
Pealed far away the startling sound
  Into the forest's heart.

Then marched the brave from rocky steep,
  From mountain river swift and cold;
The borders of the stormy deep,
The vales where gathered waters sleep,
Sent up the strong and bold,—

As if the very earth again
  Grew quick with God's creating breath,
And, from the sods of grove and glen,
Rose ranks of lion-hearted men
  To battle to the death.

The wife, whose babe first smiled that day,
  The fair fond bride of yestereve,
And aged sire and matron gray,
Saw the loved warriors haste away,
  And deemed it sin to grieve.

Already had the strife begun;
  Already blood on Concord's plain
Along the springing grass had run,
And blood had flowed at Lexington,
  Like brooks of April rain.

That death-stain on the vernal sward
  Hallowed to freedom all the shore;
In fragments fell the yoke abhorred—
The footstep of a foreign lord
  Profaned the soil no more.

~~~~~******~~~~~

THE LIVING LOST.

Matron! the children of whose love,
  Each to his grave, in youth have passed;
And now the mould is heaped above
  The dearest and the last!
Bride! who dost wear the widow's veil
Before the wedding flowers are pale!
Ye deem the human heart endures
No deeper, bitterer grief than yours.

132

Yet there are pangs of keener woe,
  Of which the sufferers never speak,
Nor to the world's cold pity show
  The tears that scald the cheek,
Wrung from their eyelids by the shame
And guilt of those they shrink to name,
Whom once they loved with cheerful will,
And love, though fallen and branded, still.

Weep, ye who sorrow for the dead,
  Thus breaking hearts their pain relieve,
And reverenced are the tears they shed,
  And honored ye who grieve.
The praise of those who sleep in earth,
The pleasant memory of their worth,
The hope to meet when life is past,
Shall heal the tortured mind at last.

But ye, who for the living lost
  That agony in secret bear,
Who shall with soothing words accost
  The strength of your despair?
Grief for your sake is scorn for them
Whom ye lament and all condemn;
And o'er the world of spirits lies
A gloom from which ye turn your eyes.

<center>~~~~~******~~~~~</center>

CATTERSKILL FALLS.

Midst greens and shades the Catterskill leaps,
  From cliffs where the wood-flower clings;
All summer he moistens his verdant steeps,
  With the sweet light spray of the mountain-springs,
And he shakes the woods on the mountain-side,
When they drip with the rains of autumn-tide.

But when, in the forest bare and old,
  The blast of December calls,
He builds, in the starlight clear and cold,
  A palace of ice where his torrent falls,
With turret, and arch, and fretwork fair,
And pillars blue as the summer air.

For whom are those glorious chambers wrought,
  In the cold and cloudless night?
Is there neither spirit nor motion of thought
  In forms so lovely, and hues so bright?
Hear what the gray-haired woodmen tell
Of this wild stream and its rocky dell.

'Twas hither a youth of dreamy mood,
  A hundred winters ago,
Had wandered over the mighty wood,

133

When the panther's track was fresh on the snow,
And keen were the winds that came to stir
The long dark boughs of the hemlock-fir.

Too gentle of mien he seemed and fair,
  For a child of those rugged steeps;
His home lay low in the valley where
  The kingly Hudson rolls to the deeps;
But he wore the hunter's frock that day,
And a slender gun on his shoulder lay.

And here he paused, and against the trunk
  Of a tall gray linden leant,
When the broad clear orb of the sun had sunk,
  From his path in the frosty firmament,
And over the round dark edge of the hill
A cold green light was quivering still.

And the crescent moon, high over the green,
  From a sky of crimson shone,
On that icy palace, whose towers were seen
  To sparkle as if with stars of their own,
While the water fell with a hollow sound,
'Twixt the glistening pillars ranged around.

Is that a being of life, that moves
  Where the crystal battlements rise?
A maiden watching the moon she loves,
  At the twilight hour, with pensive eyes?
Was that a garment which seemed to gleam
Betwixt the eye and the falling stream?

'Tis only the torrent tumbling o'er,
  In the midst of those glassy walls,
Gushing, and plunging, and beating the floor
  Of the rocky basin in which it falls.
'Tis only the torrent—but why that start?
Why gazes the youth with a throbbing heart?

He thinks no more of his home afar,
  Where his sire and sister wait.
He heeds no longer how star after star
  Looks forth on the night as the hour grows late.
He heeds not the snow-wreaths, lifted and cast
From a thousand boughs, by the rising blast.

His thoughts are alone of those who dwell
  In the halls of frost and snow,
Who pass where the crystal domes upswell
  From the alabaster floors below,
Where the frost-trees shoot with leaf and spray,
And frost-gems scatter a silvery day.

"And oh that those glorious haunts were mine!"
  He speaks, and throughout the glen
Thin shadows swim in the faint moonshine,

And take a ghastly likeness of men,
As if the slain by the wintry storms
Came forth to the air in their earthly forms.

There pass the chasers of seal and whale,
  With their weapons quaint and grim,
And hands of warriors in glittering mail,
  And herdsmen and hunters huge of limb;
There are naked arms, with bow and spear,
And furry gauntlets the carbine rear.

There are mothers—and oh how sadly their eyes
  On their children's white brows rest!
There are youthful lovers—the maiden lies,
  In a seeming sleep, on the chosen breast;
There are fair wan women with moonstruck air,
The snow-stars necking their long loose hair.

They eye him not as they pass along,
  But his hair stands up with dread,
When he feels that he moves with that phantom throng,
  Till those icy turrets are over his head,
And the torrent's roar as they enter seems
Like a drowsy murmur heard in dreams.

The glittering threshold is scarcely passed,
  When there gathers and wraps him round
A thick white twilight, sullen and vast,
  In which there is neither form nor sound;
The phantoms, the glory, vanish all,
With the dying voice of the waterfall.

Slow passes the darkness of that trance,
  And the youth now faintly sees
Huge shadows and gushes of light that dance
  On a rugged ceiling of unhewn trees,
And walls where the skins of beasts are hung,
And rifles glitter on antlers strung.

On a couch of shaggy skins he lies;
  As he strives to raise his head,
Hard-featured woodmen, with kindly eyes,
  Come round him and smooth his furry bed,
And bid him rest, for the evening star
Is scarcely set and the day is far.

They had found at eve the dreaming one
  By the base of that icy steep,
When over his stiffening limbs begun
  The deadly slumber of frost to creep,
And they cherished the pale and breathless form,
Till the stagnant blood ran free and warm.

~~~~~~******~~~~~~

THE STRANGE LADY.

The summer morn is bright and fresh, the birds are darting by,
As if they loved to breast the breeze that sweeps the cool clear sky;
Young Albert, in the forest's edge, has heard a rustling sound,
An arrow slightly strikes his hand and falls upon the ground.

A dark-haired woman from the wood comes suddenly in sight;
Her merry eye is full and black, her cheek is brown and bright;
Her gown is of the mid-sea blue, her belt with beads is strung,
And yet she speaks in gentle tones, and in the English tongue.

"It was an idle bolt I sent, against the villain crow;
Fair sir, I fear it harmed thy hand; beshrew my erring bow!"
"Ah! would that bolt had not been spent! then, lady, might I wear
A lasting token on my hand of one so passing fair!"

"Thou art a flatterer like the rest, but wouldst thou take with me
A day of hunting in the wild beneath the greenwood tree,
I know where most the pheasants feed, and where the red-deer herd,
And thou shouldst chase the nobler game, and I bring down the bird."

Now Albert in her quiver lays the arrow in its place,
And wonders as he gazes on the beauty of her face:
"Those hunting-grounds are far away, and, lady, 'twere not meet
That night, amid the wilderness, should overtake thy feet."

"Heed not the night; a summer lodge amid the wild is mine—
'Tis shadowed by the tulip-tree, 'tis mantled by the vine;
The wild-plum sheds its yellow fruit from fragrant thickets nigh,
And flowery prairies from the door stretch till they meet the sky.

"There in the boughs that hide the roof the mock-bird sits and sings,
And there the hang-bird's brood within its little hammock swings;
A pebbly brook, where rustling winds among the hopples sweep,
Shall lull thee till the morning sun looks in upon thy sleep."

Away, into the forest depths by pleasant paths they go,
He with his rifle on his arm, the lady with her bow,
Where cornels arch their cool dark boughs o'er beds of winter-green,
And never at his father's door again was Albert seen.

That night upon the woods came down a furious hurricane,
With howl of winds and roar of streams, and beating of the rain;
The mighty thunder broke and drowned the noises in its crash;
The old trees seemed to fight like fiends beneath the lightning flash.

Next day, within a mossy glen, 'mid mouldering trunks were found
The fragments of a human form upon the bloody ground;
White bones from which the flesh was torn, and locks of glossy hair;
They laid them in the place of graves, yet wist not whose they were.

And whether famished evening wolves had mangled Albert so,
Or that strange dame so gay and fair were some mysterious foe,
Or whether to that forest-lodge, beyond the mountains blue,
He went to dwell with her, the friends who mourned him never knew.

~~~~~******~~~~~

LIFE.

Oh Life! I breathe thee in the breeze,
  I feel thee bounding in my veins,
I see thee in these stretching trees,
  These flowers, this still rock's mossy stains.

This stream of odors flowing by
  From clover-field and clumps of pine,
This music, thrilling all the sky,
  From all the morning birds, are thine.

Thou fill'st with joy this little one,
  That leaps and shouts beside me here,
Where Isar's clay-white rivulets run[26]
  Through the dark woods like frighted deer.

Ah! must thy mighty breath, that wakes
  Insect and bird, and flower and tree,
From the low-trodden dust, and makes
  Their daily gladness, pass from me—

Pass, pulse by pulse, till o'er the ground
  These limbs, now strong, shall creep with pain,
And this fair world of sight and sound
  Seem fading into night again?

The things, oh LIFE! thou quickenest, all
  Strive upward toward the broad bright sky,
Upward and outward, and they fall
  Back to earth's bosom when they die.

All that have borne the touch of death,
  All that shall live, lie mingled there,
Beneath that veil of bloom and breath,
  That living zone 'twixt earth and air.

There lies my chamber dark and still,
  The atoms trampled by my feet
There wait, to take the place I fill
  In the sweet air and sunshine sweet.

Well, I have had my turn, have been
  Raised from the darkness of the clod,
And for a glorious moment seen
  The brightness of the skirts of God;

---

[26] Close to the city of Munich, in Bavaria, lies the spacious and beautiful pleasure-ground, called the English Garden, in which these lines were written, originally projected and laid out by our countryman, Count Rumford, under the auspices of one of the sovereigns of the country. Winding walks, of great extent, pass through close thickets and groves interspersed with lawns; and streams, diverted from the river Isar, traverse the grounds swiftly in various directions, the water of which, stained with the clay of the soil it has corroded in its descent from the upper country, is frequently of a turbid-white color.

And knew the light within my breast,
  Though wavering oftentimes and dim,
The power, the will, that never rest,
  And cannot die, were all from him.

Dear child! I know that thou wilt grieve
  To see me taken from thy love,
Wilt seek my grave at Sabbath eve
  And weep, and scatter flowers above.

Thy little heart will soon be healed,
  And being shall be bliss, till thou
To younger forms of life must yield
  The place thou fill'st with beauty now.

When we descend to dust again,
  Where will the final dwelling be
Of thought and all its memories then,
  My love for thee, and thine for me?

～～～～＊＊＊＊＊＊～～～～

"EARTH'S CHILDREN CLEAVE TO EARTH."

Earth's children cleave to Earth—her frail
  Decaying children dread decay.
Yon wreath of mist that leaves the vale
  And lessens in the morning ray—
Look, how, by mountain rivulet,
  It lingers as it upward creeps,
And clings to fern and copsewood set
  Along the green and dewy steeps:
Clings to the flowery kalmia, clings
  To precipices fringed with grass,
Dark maples where the wood-thrush sings,
  And bowers of fragrant sassafras.
Yet all in vain—it passes still
  From hold to hold, it cannot stay,
And in the very beams that fill
  The world with glory, wastes away,
Till, parting from the mountain's brow,
  It vanishes from human eye,
And that which sprung of earth is now
  A portion of the glorious sky.

～～～～＊＊＊＊＊＊～～～～

THE HUNTER'S VISION.

Upon a rock that, high and sheer,
  Rose from the mountain's breast,
A weary hunter of the deer
  Had sat him down to rest,
And bared to the soft summer air
His hot red brow and sweaty hair.

138

All dim in haze the mountains lay,
  With dimmer vales between;
And rivers glimmered on their way
  By forests faintly seen;
While ever rose a murmuring sound
From brooks below and bees around.

He listened, till he seemed to hear
  A strain, so soft and low,
That whether in the mind or ear
  The listener scarce might know.
With such a tone, so sweet, so mild,
The watching mother lulls her child.

"Thou weary huntsman," thus it said,
  "Thou faint with toil and heat,
The pleasant land of rest is spread
  Before thy very feet,
And those whom thou wouldst gladly see
Are waiting there to welcome thee."

He looked, and 'twixt the earth and sky,
  Amid the noontide haze,
A shadowy region met his eye,
  And grew beneath his gaze,
As if the vapors of the air
Had gathered into shapes so fair.

Groves freshened as he looked, and flowers
  Showed bright on rocky bank,
And fountains welled beneath the bowers,
  Where deer and pheasant drank.
He saw the glittering streams, he heard
The rustling bough and twittering bird.

And friends, the dead, in boyhood dear
  There lived and walked again,
And there was one who many a year
  Within her grave had lain,
A fair young girl, the hamlet's pride—
His heart was breaking when she died:

Bounding, as was her wont, she came
  Right toward his resting-place,
And stretched her hand and called his name
  With that sweet smiling face.
Forward with fixed and eager eyes,
The hunter leaned in act to rise:

Forward he leaned, and headlong down
  Plunged from that craggy wall;
He saw the rocks, steep, stern, and brown,
  An instant, in his fall;
A frightful instant—and no more,
The dream and life at once were o'er.

THE GREEN MOUNTAIN BOYS. [27]

I.

Here halt we our march, and pitch our tent
  On the rugged forest-ground,
And light our fire with the branches rent
  By winds from the beeches round.
Wild storms have torn this ancient wood,
  But a wilder is at hand,
With hail of iron and rain of blood,
  To sweep and waste the land.

II.

How the dark wood rings with our voices shrill,
  That startle the sleeping bird!
To-morrow eve must the voice be still,
  And the step must fall unheard.
The Briton lies by the blue Champlain,
  In Ticonderoga's towers,
And ere the sun rise twice again,
  Must they and the lake be ours.

III.

Fill up the bowl from the brook that glides
  Where the fire-flies light the brake;
A ruddier juice the Briton hides
  In his fortress by the lake.
Build high the fire, till the panther leap
  From his lofty perch in flight,
And we'll strengthen our weary arms with sleep
For the deeds of to-morrow night.

~~~~~******~~~~~

A PRESENTIMENT.

"Oh father, let us hence—for hark,
  A fearful murmur shakes the air;
The clouds are coming swift and dark; —
  What horrid shapes they wear!
A winged giant sails the sky;
Oh father, father, let us fly!"

"Hush, child; it is a grateful sound,
  That beating of the summer shower;

---

[27] This song refers to the expedition of the Vermonters, commanded by Ethan Allen, by whom the British fort of Ticonderoga, c
Lake Champlain, was surprised and taken, in May, 1775.

Here, where the boughs hang close around,
　We'll pass a pleasant hour,
Till the fresh wind, that brings the rain,
Has swept the broad heaven clear again."

"Nay, father, let us haste—for see,
　That horrid thing with horned brow—
His wings o'erhang this very tree,
　He scowls upon us now;
His huge black arm is lifted high;
Oh father, father, let us fly!"

"Hush, child;" but, as the father spoke,
　Downward the livid firebolt came,
Close to his ear the thunder broke,
　And, blasted by the flame,
The child lay dead; while dark and still
Swept the grim cloud along the hill.

~~~~~~******~~~~~~

THE CHILD'S FUNERAL. [28]

Fair is thy sight, Sorrento, green thy shore,
　Black crags behind thee pierce the clear blue skies;
The sea, whose borderers ruled the world of yore,
　As clear and bluer still before thee lies.

Vesuvius smokes in sight, whose fount of fire,
　Outgushing, drowned the cities on his steeps;
And murmuring Naples, spire o'ertopping spire,
　Sits on the slope beyond where Virgil sleeps.

Here doth the earth, with flowers of every hue,
　Prank her green breast when April suns are bright;
Flowers of the morning-red, or ocean-blue,
　Or like the mountain-frost of silvery white.

Currents of fragrance, from the orange-tree,
　And sward of violets, breathing to and fro,
Mingle, and, wandering out upon the sea,
　Refresh the idle boatsman where they blow.

Yet even here, as under harsher climes,
　Tears for the loved and early lost are shed;
That soft air saddens with the funeral-chimes,
　Those shining flowers are gathered for the dead.

Here once a child, a smiling playful one,
　All the day long caressing and caressed,
Died when its little tongue had just begun

---

[28]　The incident on which this poem is founded was related to the author while in Europe, in a letter from an English lady. A child died in the south of Italy, and when they went to bury it they found it revived and playing with the flowers which, after the manner of that country, had been brought to grace his funeral.

To lisp the names of those it loved the best.

The father strove his struggling grief to quell,
  The mother wept as mothers use to weep,
Two little sisters wearied them to tell
  When their dear Carlo would awake from sleep.

Within an inner room his couch they spread,
  His funeral-couch; with mingled grief and love,
They laid a crown of roses on his head,
  And murmured, "Brighter is his crown above."

They scattered round him, on the snowy sheet,
  Laburnum's strings of sunny-colored gems,
Sad hyacinths, and violets dim and sweet,
  And orange-blossoms on their dark-green stems.

And now the hour is come, the priest is there;
  Torches are lit and bells are tolled; they go,
With solemn rites of blessing and of prayer,
  To lay the little one in earth below.

The door is opened; hark! that quick glad cry;
  Carlo has waked, has waked, and is at play;
The little sisters laugh and leap, and try
  To climb the bed on which the infant lay.

And there he sits alive, and gayly shakes
  In his full hands the blossoms red and white,
And smiles with winking eyes, like one who wakes
  From long deep slumbers at the morning light.

<div align="center">~~~~~~******~~~~~~</div>

THE BATTLE-FIELD.

Once this soft turf, this rivulet's sands,
  Were trampled by a hurrying crowd,
And fiery hearts and armed hands
  Encountered in the battle-cloud.

Ah! never shall the land forget
  How gushed the life-blood of her brave—
Gushed, warm with hope and courage yet,
  Upon the soil they fought to save.

Now all is calm, and fresh, and still;
  Alone the chirp of flitting bird,
And talk of children on the hill,
  And bell of wandering kine, are heard.

No solemn host goes trailing by
  The black-mouthed gun and staggering wain;
Men start not at the battle-cry,
  Oh, be it never heard again!

Soon rested those who fought; but thou
  Who minglest in the harder strife
For truths which men receive not now,
  Thy warfare only ends with life.

A friendless warfare! lingering long
  Through weary day and weary year,
A wild and many-weaponed throng
  Hang on thy front, and flank, and rear.

Yet nerve thy spirit to the proof,
  And blench not at thy chosen lot.
The timid good may stand aloof,
  The sage may frown—yet faint thou not.

Nor heed the shaft too surely cast,
  The foul and hissing bolt of scorn;
For with thy side shall dwell, at last,
  The victory of endurance born.

Truth, crushed to earth, shall rise again;
  Th' eternal years of God are hers;
But Error, wounded, writhes in pain,
  And dies among his worshippers.

Yea, though thou lie upon the dust,
  When they who helped thee flee in fear,
Die full of hope and manly trust,
  Like those who fell in battle here.

Another hand thy sword shall wield,
  Another hand the standard wave,
Till from the trumpet's mouth is pealed
  The blast of triumph o'er thy grave.

<div align="center">~~~~~******~~~~~</div>

THE FUTURE LIFE.

How shall I know thee in the sphere which keeps
  The disembodied spirits of the dead,
When all of thee that time could wither sleeps
  And perishes among the dust we tread?

For I shall feel the sting of ceaseless pain
  If there I meet thy gentle presence not;
Nor hear the voice I love, nor read again
  In thy serenest eyes the tender thought.

Will not thy own meek heart demand me there?
  That heart whose fondest throbs to me were given—
My name on earth was ever in thy prayer,
  And wilt thou never utter it in heaven?

In meadows fanned by heaven's life-breathing wind,
  In the resplendence of that glorious sphere,

And larger movements of the unfettered mind,
  Wilt thou forget the love that joined us here?

The love that lived through all the stormy past,
  And meekly with my harsher nature bore,
And deeper grew, and tenderer to the last,
  Shall it expire with life, and be no more?

A happier lot than mine, and larger light,
  Await thee there, for thou hast bowed thy will
In cheerful homage to the rule of right,
  And lovest all, and renderest good for ill.

For me, the sordid cares in which I dwell
  Shrink and consume my heart, as heat the scroll;
And wrath has left its scar—that fire of hell
  Has left its frightful scar upon my soul.

Yet, though thou wear'st the glory of the sky,
  Wilt thou not keep the same beloved name,
The same fair thoughtful brow, and gentle eye,
  Lovelier in heaven's sweet climate, yet the same?

Shalt thou not teach me, in that calmer home,
  The wisdom that I learned so ill in this—
The wisdom which is love—till I become
  Thy fit companion in that land of bliss?

~~~~~~******~~~~~~

THE DEATH OF SCHILLER. [29]

'Tis said, when Schiller's death drew nigh,
  The wish possessed his mighty mind,
To wander forth wherever lie
  The homes and haunts of humankind.

Then strayed the poet, in his dreams,
  By Rome and Egypt's ancient graves;
Went up the New World's forest-streams,
  Stood in the Hindoo's temple-caves;

Walked with the Pawnee, fierce and stark,
  The sallow Tartar, midst his herds,
The peering Chinese, and the dark
  False Malay, uttering gentle words.

How could he rest? even then he trod
  The threshold of the world unknown;
Already, from the seat of God,
  A ray upon his garments shone; —

---

[29] Shortly before the death of Schiller, he was seized with a strong desire to travel in foreign countries, as if his spirit had presentiment of its approaching enlargement, and already longed to expatiate in a wider and more varied sphere of existence.

144

Shone and awoke the strong desire
  For love and knowledge reached not here,
Till, freed by death, his soul of fire
  Sprang to a fairer, ampler sphere.

~~~~~******~~~~~

THE FOUNTAIN.

  Fountain, that springest on this grassy slope,
Thy quick cool murmur mingles pleasantly,
With the cool sound of breezes in the beech,
Above me in the noontide. Thou dost wear
No stain of thy dark birthplace; gushing up
From the red mould and slimy roots of earth
Thou flashest in the sun. The mountain-air,
In winter, is not clearer, nor the dew
That shines on mountain-blossom. Thus doth God
Bring, from the dark and foul, the pure and bright.

  This tangled thicket on the bank above
Thy basin, how thy waters keep it green!
For thou dost feed the roots of the wild-vine
That trails all over it, and to the twigs
Ties fast her clusters. There the spice-bush lifts
Her leafy lances; the viburnum there,
Paler of foliage, to the sun holds up
Her circlet of green berries. In and out
The chipping-sparrow, in her coat of brown,
Steals silently lest I should mark her nest.

  Not such thou wert of yore, ere yet the axe
Had smitten the old woods. Then hoary trunks
Of oak, and plane, and hickory, o'er thee held
A mighty canopy. When April winds
Grew soft, the maple burst into a flush
Of scarlet flowers. The tulip-tree, high up,
Opened, in airs of June, her multitude
Of golden chalices to humming-birds
And silken-winged insects of the sky.

  Frail wood-plants clustered round thy edge in spring;
The liver-leaf put forth her sister blooms
Of faintest blue. Here the quick-footed wolf,
Passing to lap thy waters, crushed the flower
Of sanguinaria, from whose brittle stem
The red drops fell like blood.[30] The deer, too, left
Her delicate footprint in the soft moist mould,
And on the fallen leaves. The slow-paced bear,
In such a sultry summer noon as this,

---

[30] The *Sanguinaria Canadensis*, or blood-root, as it is commonly called, bears a delicate white flower of a musky scent, the stem of which breaks easily, and distils a juice of a bright-red color.

Stopped at thy stream, and drank, and leaped across.

  But thou hast histories that stir the heart
With deeper feeling; while I look on thee
They rise before me. I behold the scene
Hoary again with forests; I behold
The Indian warrior, whom a hand unseen
Has smitten with his death-wound in the woods,
Creep slowly to thy well-known rivulet,
And slake his death-thirst. Hark, that quick fierce cry
That rends the utter silence! 'tis the whoop
Of battle, and a throng of savage men
With naked arms and faces stained like blood,
Fill the green wilderness; the long bare arms
Are heaved aloft, bows twang and arrows stream;
Each makes a tree his shield, and every tree
Sends forth its arrow. Fierce the fight and short,
As is the whirlwind. Soon the conquerors
And conquered vanish, and the dead remain
Mangled by tomahawks. The mighty woods
Are still again, the frighted bird comes back
And plumes her wings; but thy sweet waters run
Crimson with blood. Then, as the sun goes down,
Amid the deepening twilight I descry
Figures of men that crouch and creep unheard,
And bear away the dead. The next day's shower
Shall wash the tokens of the fight away.

  I look again—a hunter's lodge is built,
With poles and boughs, beside thy crystal well,
While the meek autumn stains the woods with gold,
And sheds his golden sunshine. To the door
The red-man slowly drags the enormous bear
Slain in the chestnut-thicket, or flings down
The deer from his strong shoulders. Shaggy fells
Of wolf and cougar hang upon the walls,
And loud the black-eyed Indian maidens laugh,
That gather, from the rustling heaps of leaves,
The hickory's white nuts, and the dark fruit
That falls from the gray butternut's long boughs.

  So centuries passed by, and still the woods
Blossomed in spring, and reddened when the year
Grew chill, and glistened in the frozen rains
Of winter, till the white man swung the axe
Beside thee—signal of a mighty change.
Then all around was heard the crash of trees,
Trembling awhile and rushing to the ground,
The low of ox, and shouts of men who fired
The brushwood, or who tore the earth with ploughs;
The grain sprang thick and tall, and hid in green
The blackened hill-side; ranks of spiky maize
Rose like a host embattled; the buckwheat
Whitened broad acres, sweetening with its flowers
The August wind. White cottages were seen
With rose-trees at the windows; barns from which

Came loud and shrill the crowing of the cock;
Pastures where rolled and neighed the lordly horse,
And white flocks browsed and bleated. A rich turf
Of grasses brought from far o'ercrept thy bank,
Spotted with the white clover. Blue-eyed girls
Brought pails, and dipped them in thy crystal pool;
And children, ruddy-cheeked and flaxen-haired,
Gathered the glistening cowslip from thy edge.

   Since then, what steps have trod thy border! Here
On thy green bank, the woodman of the swamp
Has laid his axe, the reaper of the hill
His sickle, as they stooped to taste thy stream.
The sportsman, tired with wandering in the still
September noon, has bathed his heated brow
In thy cool current. Shouting boys, let loose
For a wild holiday, have quaintly shaped
Into a cup the folded linden-leaf,
And dipped thy sliding crystal. From the wars
Returning, the plumed soldier by thy side
Has sat, and mused how pleasant 'twere to dwell
In such a spot, and be as free as thou,
And move for no man's bidding more. At eve
When thou wert crimson with the crimson sky,
Lovers have gazed upon thee, and have thought
Their mingled lives should flow as peacefully
And brightly as thy waters. Here the sage,
Gazing into thy self-replenished depth,
Has seen eternal order circumscribe
And bound the motions of eternal change,
And from the gushing of thy simple fount
Has reasoned to the mighty universe.

   Is there no other change for thee, that lurks
Among the future ages? Will not man
Seek out strange arts to wither and deform
The pleasant landscape which thou makest green?
Or shall the veins that feed thy constant stream
Be choked in middle earth, and flow no more
For ever, that the water-plants along
Thy channel perish, and the bird in vain
Alight to drink? Haply shall these green hills
Sink, with the lapse of years, into the gulf
Of ocean waters, and thy source be lost
Amidst the bitter brine? Or shall they rise,
Upheaved in broken cliffs and airy peaks,
Haunts of the eagle and the snake, and thou
Gush midway from the bare and barren steep?

~~~~~******~~~~~

THE WINDS.

I.

Ye winds, ye unseen currents of the air,

147

Softly ye played a few brief hours ago;
Ye bore the murmuring bee; ye tossed the air
  O'er maiden cheeks, that took a fresher glow;
Ye rolled the round white cloud through depths of blue;
Ye shook from shaded flowers the lingering dew;
Before you the catalpa's blossoms flew,
  Light blossoms, dropping on the grass like snow.

II.

What change is this! Ye take the cataract's sound;
  Ye take the whirlpool's fury and its might;
The mountain shudders as ye sweep the ground;
  The valley woods lie prone beneath your flight.
The clouds before you shoot like eagles past;
The homes of men are rocking in your blast;
Ye lift the roofs like autumn leaves, and cast,
  Skyward, the whirling fragments out of sight.

III.

The weary fowls of heaven make wing in vain,
  To escape your wrath; ye seize and dash them dead;
Against the earth ye drive the roaring rain;
  The harvest-field becomes a river's bed;
And torrents tumble from the hills around,
Plains turn to lakes, and villages are drowned,
And wailing voices, midst the tempest's sound,
  Rise, as the rushing waters swell and spread.

IV.

Ye dart upon the deep, and straight is heard
  A wilder roar, and men grow pale, and pray;
Ye fling its floods around you, as a bird
  Flings o'er his shivering plumes the fountain's spray.
See! to the breaking mast the sailor clings;
Ye scoop the ocean to its briny springs,
And take the mountain-billow on your wings,
  And pile the wreck of navies round the bay.

V.

Why rage ye thus? —no strife for liberty
  Has made you mad; no tyrant, strong through fear,
Has chained your pinions till ye wrenched them free,
  And rushed into the unmeasured atmosphere;
For ye were born in freedom where ye blow;
Free o'er the mighty deep to come and go;
Earth's solemn woods were yours, her wastes of snow,
  Her isles where summer blossoms all the year.

VI.

O ye wild winds! a mightier Power than yours
  In chains upon the shore of Europe lies;

The sceptred throng whose fetters he endures
　Watch his mute throes with terror in their eyes;
And armed warriors all around him stand,
And, as he struggles, tighten every band,
And lift the heavy spear, with threatening hand,
　To pierce the victim, should he strive to rise.

VII.

Yet oh, when that wronged Spirit of our race
　Shall break, as soon he must, his long-worn chains,
And leap in freedom from his prison-place,
　Lord of his ancient hills and fruitful plains,
Let him not rise, like these mad winds of air,
To waste the loveliness that time could spare,
To fill the earth with woe, and blot her fair
　Unconscious breast with blood from human veins.

VIII.

But may he like the spring-time come abroad,
　Who crumbles winter's gyves with gentle might,
When in the genial breeze, the breath of God,
　The unsealed springs come spouting up to light;
Flowers start from their dark prisons at his feet,
The woods, long dumb, awake to hymnings sweet,
And morn and eve, whose glimmerings almost meet,
　Crowd back to narrow bounds the ancient night.

<center>~~~~~~******~~~~~~</center>

THE OLD MAN'S COUNSEL.

　Among our hills and valleys, I have known
Wise and grave men, who, while their diligent hands
Tended or gathered in the fruits of earth,
Were reverent learners in the solemn school
Of Nature. Not in vain to them were sent
Seed-time and harvest, or the vernal shower
That darkened the brown tilth, or snow that beat
On the white winter hills. Each brought, in turn,
Some truth, some lesson on the life of man,
Or recognition of the Eternal mind
Who veils his glory with the elements.

　One such I knew long since, a white-haired man,
Pithy of speech, and merry when he would;
A genial optimist, who daily drew
From what he saw his quaint moralities.
Kindly he held communion, though so old,
With me a dreaming boy, and taught me much
That books tell not, and I shall ne'er forget.

　The sun of May was bright in middle heaven,
And steeped the sprouting forests, the green hills,
And emerald wheat-fields, in his yellow light.

149

Upon the apple-tree, where rosy buds
Stood clustered, ready to burst forth in bloom,
The robin warbled forth his full clear note
For hours, and wearied not. Within the woods,
Whose young and half transparent leaves scarce cast
A shade, gay circles of anemones
Danced on their stalks; the shad-bush, white with flowers,
Brightened the glens;[31] the new-leaved butternut
And quivering poplar to the roving breeze
Gave a balsamic fragrance. In the fields
I saw the pulses of the gentle wind
On the young grass. My heart was touched with joy
At so much beauty, flushing every hour
Into a fuller beauty; but my friend,
The thoughtful ancient, standing at my side,
Gazed on it mildly sad. I asked him why.

  "Well mayst thou join in gladness," he replied,
"With the glad earth, her springing plants and flowers,
And this soft wind, the herald of the green
Luxuriant summer. Thou art young like them,
And well mayst thou rejoice. But while the flight
Of seasons fills and knits thy spreading frame,
It withers mine, and thins my hair, and dims
These eyes, whose fading light shall soon be quenched
In utter darkness. Hearest thou that bird?"

  I listened, and from midst the depth of woods
Heard the love-signal of the grouse, that wears
A sable ruff around his mottled neck;
Partridge they call him by our northern streams,
And pheasant by the Delaware. He beat
His barred sides with his speckled wings, and made
A sound like distant thunder; slow the strokes
At first, then fast and faster, till at length
They passed into a murmur and were still.

  "There hast thou," said my friend, "a fitting type
Of human life.[32] 'Tis an old truth, I know,
But images like these revive the power
Of long familiar truths. Slow pass our days
In childhood, and the hours of light are long
Betwixt the morn and eve; with swifter lapse
They glide in manhood, and in age they fly;
Till days and seasons flit before the mind
As flit the snow-flakes in a winter storm,
Seen rather than distinguished. Ah! I seem
As if I sat within a helpless bark,

---

[31] The small tree, named by the botanists *Aronia Botyrapium*, is called, in some parts of our country, the shad-bush, from the circumstance that it flowers about the time that the shad ascend the rivers in early spring. Its delicate sprays, covered with white blossoms before the trees are yet in leaf, have a singularly beautiful appearance in the woods.

[32] I remember hearing an aged man, in the country, compare the slow movement of time in early life, and its swift flight as it approaches old age, to the drumming of a partridge or ruffed grouse in the woods—the strokes falling slow and distinct at first, and following each other more and more rapidly, till they end at last in a whirring sound.

By swiftly-running waters hurried on
To shoot some mighty cliff. Along the banks
Grove after grove, rock after frowning rock,
Bare sands and pleasant homes, and flowery nooks,
And isles and whirlpools in the stream, appear
Each after each, but the devoted skiff
Darts by so swiftly that their images
Dwell not upon the mind, or only dwell
In dim confusion; faster yet I sweep
By other banks, and the great gulf is near.

   "Wisely, my son, while yet thy days are long,
And this fair change of seasons passes slow,
Gather and treasure up the good they yield—
All that they teach of virtue, of pure thoughts
And kind affections, reverence for thy God
And for thy brethren; so when thou shalt come
Into these barren years, thou mayst not bring
A mind unfurnished and a withered heart."

   Long since that white-haired ancient slept—but still,
When the red flower-buds crowd the orchard-bough,
And the ruffed grouse is drumming far within
The woods, his venerable form again
Is at my side, his voice is in my ear.

******

IN MEMORY OF WILLIAM LEGGETT.

The earth may ring, from shore to shore,
  With echoes of a glorious name,
But he, whose loss our tears deplore,
  Has left behind him more than fame.

For when the death-frost came to lie
  On Leggett's warm and mighty heart,
And quench his bold and friendly eye,
  His spirit did not all depart.

The words of fire that from his pen
  Were flung upon the fervid page,
Still move, still shake the hearts of men,
  Amid a cold and coward age.

His love of truth, too warm, too strong
  For Hope or Fear to chain or chill,
His hate of tyranny and wrong,
  Burn in the breasts he kindled still.

******

AN EVENING REVERY. [33]

    The summer day is closed—the sun is set:
Well they have done their office, those bright hours,
The latest of whose train goes softly out
In the red west. The green blade of the ground
Has risen, and herds have cropped it; the young twig
Has spread its plaited tissues to the sun;
Flowers of the garden and the waste have blown
And withered; seeds have fallen upon the soil,
From bursting cells, and in their graves await
Their resurrection. Insects from the pools
Have filled the air awhile with humming wings,
That now are still for ever; painted moths
Have wandered the blue sky, and died again;
The mother-bird hath broken for her brood
Their prison shell, or shoved them from the nest,
Plumed for their earliest flight. In bright alcoves,
In woodland cottages with barky walls,
In noisome cells of the tumultuous town,
Mothers have clasped with joy the new-born babe.
Graves by the lonely forest, by the shore
Of rivers and of ocean, by the ways
Of the thronged city, have been hollowed out
And filled, and closed. This day hath parted friends
That ne'er before were parted; it hath knit
New friendships; it hath seen the maiden plight
Her faith, and trust her peace to him who long
Had wooed; and it hath heard, from lips which late
Were eloquent of love, the first harsh word,
That told the wedded one her peace was flown.
Farewell to the sweet sunshine! One glad day
Is added now to Childhood's merry days,
And one calm day to those of quiet Age.
Still the fleet hours run on; and as I lean,
Amid the thickening darkness, lamps are lit,
By those who watch the dead, and those who twine
Flowers for the bride. The mother from the eyes
Of her sick infant shades the painful light,
And sadly listens to his quick-drawn breath.

    O thou great Movement of the Universe,
Or Change, or Flight of Time—for ye are one!
That bearest, silently, this visible scene
Into night's shadow and the streaming rays
Of starlight, whither art thou bearing me?
I feel the mighty current sweep me on,
Yet know not whither. Man foretells afar
The courses of the stars; the very hour
He knows when they shall darken or grow bright;
Yet doth the eclipse of Sorrow and of Death

---

[33] This poem and that entitled "The Fountain," with one or two others in blank verse, were intended by the author as portions of larger poem.

Come unforewarned. Who next, of those I love,
Shall pass from life, or, sadder yet, shall fall
From virtue? Strife with foes, or bitterer strife
With friends, or shame and general scorn of men—
Which who can bear?—or the fierce rack of pain—
Lie within my path? Or shall the years
Push me, with soft and inoffensive pace,
Into the stilly twilight of my age?
Or do the portals of another life
Even now, while I am glorying in my strength,
Impend around me? Oh! beyond that bourne,
In the vast cycle of being which begins
At that dread threshold, with what fairer forms
Shall the great law of change and progress clothe
Its workings? Gently—so have good men taught—
Gently, and without grief, the old shall glide
Into the new; the eternal flow of things,
Like a bright river of the fields of heaven,
Shall journey onward in perpetual peace.

<center>~~~~~~******~~~~~~</center>

THE PAINTED CUP.

   The fresh savannas of the Sangamon
Here rise in gentle swells, and the long grass
Is mixed with rustling hazels. Scarlet tufts
Are glowing in the green, like flakes of fire;[34]
The wanderers of the prairie know them well,
And call that brilliant flower the Painted Cup.

   Now, if thou art a poet, tell me not
That these bright chalices were tinted thus
To hold the dew for fairies, when they meet
On moonlight evenings in the hazel-bowers,
And dance till they are thirsty. Call not up,
Amid this fresh and virgin solitude,
The faded fancies of an elder world;
But leave these scarlet cups to spotted moths
Of June, and glistening flies, and humming-birds,
To drink from, when on all these boundless lawns
The morning sun looks hot. Or let the wind
O'erturn in sport their ruddy brims, and pour
A sudden shower upon the strawberry-plant,
To swell the reddening fruit that even now
Breathes a slight fragrance from the sunny slope.

   But thou art of a gayer fancy. Well—
Let then the gentle Manitou of flowers,
Lingering amid the bloomy waste he loves,
Though all his swarthy worshippers are gone—

---

[34] The Painted Cup, *Euchroma coccinea*, or *Bartsia coccinea*, grows in great abundance in the hazel prairies of the Western States, where its scarlet tufts make a brilliant appearance in the midst of the verdure. The Sangamon is a beautiful river, tributary to the Ilinois, bordered with rich prairies.

Slender and small, his rounded cheek all brown
And ruddy with the sunshine; let him come
On summer mornings, when the blossoms wake,
And part with little hands the spiky grass,
And touching, with his cherry lips, the edge
Of these bright beakers, drain the gathered dew.

<center>~~~~~******~~~~~</center>

A DREAM.

I had a dream—a strange, wild dream—
  Said a dear voice at early light;
And even yet its shadows seem
  To linger in my waking sight.

Earth, green with spring, and fresh with dew,
  And bright with morn, before me stood;
And airs just wakened softly blew
  On the young blossoms of the wood.

Birds sang within the sprouting shade,
  Bees hummed amid the whispering grass,
And children prattled as they played
  Beside the rivulet's dimpling glass.

Fast climbed the sun: the flowers were flown,
  There played no children in the glen;
For some were gone, and some were grown
  To blooming dames and bearded men.

'Twas noon, 'twas summer: I beheld
  Woods darkening in the flush of day,
And that bright rivulet spread and swelled,
  A mighty stream, with creek and bay.

And here was love, and there was strife,
  And mirthful shouts, and wrathful cries,
And strong men, struggling as for life,
  With knotted limbs and angry eyes.

Now stooped the sun—the shades grew thin;
  The rustling paths were piled with leaves,
And sunburnt groups were gathering in,
  From the shorn field, its fruits and sheaves.

The river heaved with sullen sounds;
  The chilly wind was sad with moans;
Black hearses passed, and burial-grounds
  Grew thick with monumental stones.

Still waned the day; the wind that chased
  The jagged clouds blew chiller yet;
The woods were stripped, the fields were waste;
  The wintry sun was near his set.

And of the young, and strong, and fair,
  A lonely remnant, gray and weak,
Lingered, and shivered to the air
  Of that bleak shore and water bleak.

Ah! age is drear, and death is cold!
  I turned to thee, for thou wert near,
And saw thee withered, bowed, and old,
  And woke all faint with sudden fear.

'Twas thus I heard the dreamer say,
  And bade her clear her clouded brow;
"For thou and I, since childhood's day,
  Have walked in such a dream till now.

"Watch we in calmness, as they rise,
  The changes of that rapid dream,
And note its lessons, till our eyes
  Shall open in the morning beam."

~~~~~******~~~~~

THE ANTIQUITY OF FREEDOM.

Here are old trees, tall oaks and gnarled pines,
That stream with gray-green mosses; here the ground
Was never trenched by spade, and flowers spring up
Unsown, and die ungathered. It is sweet
To linger here, among the flitting birds
And leaping squirrels, wandering brooks, and winds
That shake the leaves, and scatter, as they pass,
A fragrance from the cedars, thickly set
With pale blue berries. In these peaceful shades—
Peaceful, unpruned, immeasurably old—
My thoughts go up the long dim path of years,
Back to the earliest days of liberty.

Oh FREEDOM! thou art not, as poets dream,
A fair young girl, with light and delicate limbs,
And wavy tresses gushing from the cap
With which the Roman master crowned his slave
When he took off the gyves. A bearded man,
Armed to the teeth, art thou; one mailed hand
Grasps the broad shield, and one the sword; thy brow,
Glorious in beauty though it be, is scarred
With tokens of old wars; thy massive limbs
Are strong with struggling. Power at thee has launched
His bolts, and with his lightnings smitten thee;
They could not quench the life thou hast from heaven.
Merciless power has dug thy dungeon deep,
And his swart armorers, by a thousand fires,
Have forged thy chain; yet, while he deems thee bound,
The links are shivered, and the prison walls
Fall outward; terribly thou springest forth,
As springs the flame above a burning pile,
And shoutest to the nations, who return

155

Thy shoutings, while the pale oppressor flies.

Thy birthright was not given by human hands:
Thou wert twin-born with man. In pleasant fields,
While yet our race was few, thou sat'st with him,
To tend the quiet flock and watch the stars,
And teach the reed to utter simple airs.
Thou by his side, amid the tangled wood,
Didst war upon the panther and the wolf,
His only foes; and thou with him didst draw
The earliest furrows on the mountain side,
Soft with the deluge. Tyranny himself,
Thy enemy, although of reverend look,
Hoary with many years, and far obeyed,
Is later born than thou; and as he meets
The grave defiance of thine elder eye,
The usurper trembles in his fastnesses.

Thou shalt wax stronger with the lapse of years,
But he shall fade into a feebler age;
Feebler, yet subtler. He shall weave his snares,
And spring them on thy careless steps, and clap
His withered hands, and from their ambush call
His hordes to fall upon thee. He shall send
Quaint maskers, wearing fair and gallant forms,
To catch thy gaze, and uttering graceful words
To charm thy ear; while his sly imps, by stealth,
Twine round thee threads of steel, light thread on thread
That grow to fetters; or bind down thy arms
With chains concealed in chaplets. Oh! not yet
Mayst thou unbrace thy corslet, nor lay by
Thy sword; nor yet, O Freedom! close thy lids
In slumber; for thine enemy never sleeps,
And thou must watch and combat till the day
Of the new earth and heaven. But wouldst thou rest
Awhile from tumult and the frauds of men,
These old and friendly solitudes invite
Thy visit. They, while yet the forest trees
Were young upon the unviolated earth,
And yet the moss-stains on the rock were new,
Beheld thy glorious childhood, and rejoiced.

******

THE MAIDEN'S SORROW.

Seven long years has the desert rain
  Dropped on the clods that hide thy face;
Seven long years of sorrow and pain
  I have thought of thy burial-place;

Thought of thy fate in the distant West,
  Dying with none that loved thee near,
They who flung the earth on thy breast
  Turned from the spot without a tear.

There, I think, on that lonely grave,
  Violets spring in the soft May shower;
There, in the summer breezes, wave
  Crimson phlox and moccasin-flower.

There the turtles alight, and there
  Feeds with her fawn the timid doe;
There, when the winter woods are bare,
  Walks the wolf on the crackling snow.

Soon wilt thou wipe my tears away;
  All my task upon earth is done;
My poor father, old and gray,
  Slumbers beneath the churchyard stone.

In the dreams of my lonely bed,
  Ever thy form before me seems,
All night long I talk with the dead,
  All day long I think of my dreams.

This deep wound that bleeds and aches,
  This long pain, a sleepless pain—
When the Father my spirit takes,
  I shall feel it no more again.

<center>~~~~~******~~~~~</center>

THE RETURN OF YOUTH.

My friend, thou sorrowest for thy golden prime,
  For thy fair youthful years too swift of flight;
Thou musest, with wet eyes, upon the time
  Of cheerful hopes that filled the world with light—

Years when thy heart was bold, thy hand was strong,
  And quick the thought that moved thy tongue to speak,
And willing faith was thine, and scorn of wrong
  Summoned the sudden crimson to thy cheek.

Thou lookest forward on the coming days,
  Shuddering to feel their shadow o'er thee creep;
A path, thick-set with changes and decays,
  Slopes downward to the place of common sleep;
And they who walked with thee in life's first stage,
  Leave one by one thy side, and, waiting near,
Thou seest the sad companions of thy age—
  Dull love of rest, and weariness and fear.

Yet grieve thou not, nor think thy youth is gone,
  Nor deem that glorious season e'er could die.
Thy pleasant youth, a little while withdrawn,
  Waits on the horizon of a brighter sky;
Waits, like the morn, that folds her wings and hides
  Till the slow stars bring back her dawning hour;
Waits, like the vanished spring, that slumbering bides
  Her own sweet time to waken bud and flower.

157

There shall he welcome thee, when thou shalt stand
  On his bright morning hills, with smiles more sweet
Than when at first he took thee by the hand,
  Through the fair earth to lead thy tender feet.
He shall bring back, but brighter, broader still,
  Life's early glory to thine eyes again,
Shall clothe thy spirit with new strength, and fill
  Thy leaping heart with warmer love than then.

Hast thou not glimpses, in the twilight here,
  Of mountains where immortal morn prevails?
Comes there not, through the silence, to thine ear
  A gentle rustling of the morning gales;
A murmur, wafted from that glorious shore,
  Of streams that water banks forever fair,
And voices of the loved ones gone before,
  More musical in that celestial air?

———******———

A HYMN OF THE SEA.

  The sea is mighty, but a mightier sways
His restless billows. Thou, whose hands have scooped
His boundless gulfs and built his shore, thy breath,
That moved in the beginning o'er his face,
Moves o'er it evermore. The obedient waves
To its strong motion roll, and rise and fall.
Still from that realm of rain thy cloud goes up,
As at the first, to water the great earth,
And keep her valleys green. A hundred realms
Watch its broad shadow warping on the wind,
And in the dropping shower, with gladness hear
Thy promise of the harvest. I look forth
Over the boundless blue, where joyously
The bright crests of innumerable waves
Glance to the sun at once, as when the hands
Of a great multitude are upward flung
In acclamation. I behold the ships
Gliding from cape to cape, from isle to isle,
Or stemming toward far lands, or hastening home
From the Old World. It is thy friendly breeze
That bears them, with the riches of the land,
And treasure of dear lives, till, in the port,
The shouting seaman climbs and furls the sail.

  But who shall bide thy tempest, who shall face
The blast that wakes the fury of the sea?
O God! thy justice makes the world turn pale,
When on the armed fleet, that royally
Bears down the surges, carrying war, to smite
Some city, or invade some thoughtless realm,
Descends the fierce tornado. The vast hulks
Are whirled like chaff upon the waves; the sails
Fly, rent like webs of gossamer; the masts

158

Are snapped asunder; downward from the decks,
Downward are slung, into the fathomless gulf,
Their cruel engines; and their hosts, arrayed
In trappings of the battle-field, are whelmed
By whirlpools, or dashed dead upon the rocks.
Then stand the nations still with awe, and pause
A moment, from the bloody work of war.

These restless surges eat away the shores
Of earth's old continents; the fertile plain
Welters in shallows, headlands crumble down,
And the tide drifts the sea-sand in the streets
Of the drowned city. Thou, meanwhile, afar
In the green chambers of the middle sea,
Where broadest spread the waters and the line
Sinks deepest, while no eye beholds thy work,
Creator! thou dost teach the coral-worm
To lay his mighty reefs. From age to age,
He builds beneath the waters, till, at last,
His bulwarks overtop the brine, and check
The long wave rolling from the southern pole
To break upon Japan.[35] Thou bidd'st the fires,
That smoulder under ocean, heave on high
The new-made mountains, and uplift their peaks,
A place of refuge for the storm-driven bird.
The birds and wafting billows plant the rifts
With herb and tree; sweet fountains gush; sweet airs
Ripple the living lakes that, fringed with flowers,
Are gathered in the hollows. Thou dost look
On thy creation and pronounce it good.
Its valleys, glorious in their summer green,
Praise thee in silent beauty, and its woods,
Swept by the murmuring winds of ocean, join
The murmuring shores in a perpetual hymn.

~~~~~******~~~~~

NOON.

FROM AN UNFINISHED POEM.

'Tis noon. At noon the Hebrew bowed the knee
And worshipped,[36] while the husbandmen withdrew
From the scorched field, and the wayfaring man
Grew faint, and turned aside by bubbling fount,
Or rested in the shadow of the palm.

I, too, amid the overflow of day,
Behold the power which wields and cherishes
The frame of Nature. From this brow of rock
That overlooks the Hudson's western marge,

---

[35] "Breaks the long wave that at the pole began." —TENNENT'S *Anster Fair*.

[36] "Evening and morning, and at noon, will I pray and cry aloud, and he shall hear my voice." —*Psalm* iv. 17.

159

I gaze upon the long array of groves,
The piles and gulfs of verdure drinking in
The grateful heats. They love the fiery sun;
Their broadening leaves grow glossier, and their sprays
Climb as he looks upon them. In the midst,
The swelling river, into his green gulfs,
Unshadowed save by passing sails above,
Takes the redundant glory, and enjoys
The summer in his chilly bed. Coy flowers,
That would not open in the early light,
Push back their plaited sheaths. The rivulet's pool,
That darkly quivered all the morning long
In the cool shade, now glimmers in the sun;
And o'er its surface shoots, and shoots again,
The glittering dragon-fly, and deep within
Run the brown water-beetles to and fro.

   A silence, the brief sabbath of an hour,
Reigns o'er the fields; the laborer sits within
His dwelling; he has left his steers awhile,
Unyoked, to bite the herbage, and his dog
Sleeps stretched beside the door-stone in the shade.
Now the gray marmot, with uplifted paws,
No more sits listening by his den, but steals
Abroad, in safety, to the clover-field,
And crops its juicy blossoms. All the while
A ceaseless murmur from the populous town
Swells o'er these solitudes: a mingled sound
Of jarring wheels, and iron hoofs that clash
Upon the stony ways, and hammer-clang,
And creak of engines lifting ponderous bulks,
And calls and cries, and tread of eager feet,
Innumerable, hurrying to and fro.
Noon, in that mighty mart of nations, brings
No pause to toil and care. With early day
Began the tumult, and shall only cease
When midnight, hushing one by one the sounds
Of bustle, gathers the tired brood to rest.

   Thus, in this feverish time, when love of gain
And luxury possess the hearts of men,
Thus is it with the noon of human life.
We, in our fervid manhood, in our strength
Of reason, we, with hurry, noise, and care,
Plan, toil, and strive, and pause not to refresh
Our spirits with the calm and beautiful
Of God's harmonious universe, that won
Our youthful wonder; pause not to inquire
Why we are here; and what the reverence
Man owes to man, and what the mystery
That links us to the greater world, beside
Whose borders we but hover for a space.

<div align="center">~~~~~~******~~~~~~</div>

THE CROWDED STREET.

Let me move slowly through the street,
  Filled with an ever-shifting train,
Amid the sound of steps that beat
  The murmuring walks like autumn rain.

How fast the flitting figures come!
  The mild, the fierce, the stony face;
Some bright with thoughtless smiles, and some
  Where secret tears have left their trace.

They pass—to toil, to strife, to rest;
  To halls in which the feast is spread;
To chambers where the funeral guest
  In silence sits beside the dead.

And some to happy homes repair,
  Where children, pressing cheek to cheek,
With mute caresses shall declare
  The tenderness they cannot speak.

And some, who walk in calmness here,
  Shall shudder as they reach the door
Where one who made their dwelling dear,
  Its flower, its light, is seen no more.

Youth, with pale cheek and slender frame,
  And dreams of greatness in thine eye!
Go'st thou to build an early name,
  Or early in the task to die?

Keen son of trade, with eager brow!
  Who is now fluttering in thy snare?
Thy golden fortunes, tower they now,
  Or melt the glittering spires in air?

Who of this crowd to-night shall tread
  The dance till daylight gleam again?
Who sorrow o'er the untimely dead?
  Who writhe in throes of mortal pain?

Some, famine-struck, shall think how long
  The cold dark hours, how slow the light;
And some, who flaunt amid the throng,
  Shall hide in dens of shame to-night.

Each, where his tasks or pleasures call,
  They pass, and heed each other not.
There is who heeds, who holds them all,
  In His large love and boundless thought.

These struggling tides of life that seem
  In wayward, aimless course to tend,
Are eddies of the mighty stream
  That rolls to its appointed end.

THE WHITE-FOOTED DEER. [37]

It was a hundred years ago,
  When, by the woodland ways,
The traveller saw the wild-deer drink,
  Or crop the birchen sprays.

Beneath a hill, whose rocky side
  O'erbrowed a grassy mead,
And fenced a cottage from the wind,
  A deer was wont to feed.

She only came when on the cliffs
  The evening moonlight lay,
And no man knew the secret haunts
  In which she walked by day.

White were her feet, her forehead showed
  A spot of silvery white,
That seemed to glimmer like a star
  In autumn's hazy night.

And here, when sang the whippoorwill,
  She cropped the sprouting leaves,
And here her rustling steps were heard
  On still October eves.

But when the broad midsummer moon
  Rose o'er that grassy lawn,
Beside the silver-footed deer
  There grazed a spotted fawn.

The cottage dame forbade her son
  To aim the rifle here;
"It were a sin," she said, "to harm
  Or fright that friendly deer.

"This spot has been my pleasant home
  Ten peaceful years and more;
And ever, when the moonlight shines,
  She feeds before our door.

"The red-men say that here she walked
  A thousand moons ago;
They never raise the war-whoop here,
  And never twang the bow.

---

[37] "During the stay of Long's Expedition at Engineer Cantonment, three specimens of a variety of the common deer were brought i▮ having all the feet white near the hoofs, and extending to those on the hind-feet from a little above the spurious hoofs. This whit▮ extremity was divided, upon the sides of the foot, by the general color of the leg, which extends down near to the hoofs, leaving white triangle in front, of which the point was elevated rather higher than the spurious hoofs." —GODMAN'S *Natural History*, vo▮ ii., p. 314.

"I love to watch her as she feeds,
  And think that all is well
While such a gentle creature haunts
  The place in which we dwell."

The youth obeyed, and sought for game
  In forests far away,
Where, deep in silence and in moss,
  The ancient woodland lay.

But once, in autumn's golden time
  He ranged the wild in vain,
Nor roused the pheasant nor the deer,
  And wandered home again.

The crescent moon and crimson eve
  Shone with a mingling light;
The deer, upon the grassy mead,
  Was feeding full in sight.

He raised the rifle to his eye,
  And from the cliffs around
A sudden echo, shrill and sharp,
  Gave back its deadly sound.

Away, into the neighboring wood,
  The startled creature flew,
And crimson drops at morning lay
  Amid the glimmering dew.

Next evening shone the waxing moon
  As brightly as before;
The deer upon the grassy mead
  Was seen again no more.

But ere that crescent moon was old,
  By night the red-men came,
And burnt the cottage to the ground,
  And slew the youth and dame.

Now woods have overgrown the mead,
  And hid the cliffs from sight;
There shrieks the hovering hawk at noon,
  And prowls the fox at night.

~~~~~******~~~~~

THE WANING MOON.

I've watched too late; the morn is near;
  One look at God's broad silent sky!
Oh, hopes and wishes vainly dear,
  How in your very strength ye die!

Even while your glow is on the cheek,

163

And scarce the high pursuit begun,
The heart grows faint, the hand grows weak,
The task of life is left undone.

See where, upon the horizon's brim,
Lies the still cloud in gloomy bars;
The waning moon, all pale and dim,
Goes up amid the eternal stars.

Late, in a flood of tender light,
She floated through the ethereal blue,
A softer sun, that shone all night
Upon the gathering beads of dew.

And still thou wanest, pallid moon!
The encroaching shadow grows apace;
Heaven's everlasting watchers soon
Shall see thee blotted from thy place.

Oh, Night's dethroned and crownless queen!
Well may thy sad, expiring ray
Be shed on those whose eyes have seen
Hope's glorious visions fade away.

Shine thou for forms that once were bright,
For sages in the mind's eclipse,
For those whose words were spells of might,
But falter now on stammering lips!

In thy decaying beam there lies
Full many a grave on hill and plain,
Of those who closed their dying eyes
In grief that they had lived in vain.

Another night, and thou among
The spheres of heaven shalt cease to shine,
All rayless in the glittering throng
Whose lustre late was quenched in thine.

Yet soon a new and tender light
From out thy darkened orb shall beam,
And broaden till it shines all night
On glistening dew and glimmering stream.

******

THE STREAM OF LIFE.

Oh silvery streamlet of the fields,
That flowest full and free,
For thee the rains of spring return,
The summer dews for thee;
And when thy latest blossoms die
In autumn's chilly showers,
The winter fountains gush for thee,
Till May brings back the flowers.

Oh Stream of Life! the violet springs
　But once beside thy bed;
But one brief summer, on thy path,
　The dews of heaven are shed.
Thy parent fountains shrink away,
　And close their crystal veins,
And where thy glittering current flowed
　The dust alone remains.

<center>~~~~******~~~~</center>

THE UNKNOWN WAY.

A burning sky is o'er me,
　The sands beneath me glow,
As onward, onward, wearily,
　In the sultry morn I go.

From the dusty path there opens,
　Eastward, an unknown way;
Above its windings, pleasantly,
　The woodland branches play.

A silvery brook comes stealing
　From the shadow of its trees,
Where slender herbs of the forest stoop
　Before the entering breeze.

Along those pleasant windings
　I would my journey lay,
Where the shade is cool and the dew of night
　Is not yet dried away.

Path of the flowery woodland!
　Oh whither dost thou lead,
Wandering by grassy orchard-grounds,
　Or by the open mead?

Goest thou by nestling cottage?
　Goest thou by stately hall,
Where the broad elm droops, a leafy dome,
　And woodbines flaunt on the wall?

By steeps where children gather
　Flowers of the yet fresh year?
By lonely walks where lovers stray
　Till the tender stars appear?

Or haply dost thou linger
　On barren plains and bare,
Or clamber the bald mountain-side
　Into the thinner air?—

Where they who journey upward
　Walk in a weary track,

165

And oft upon the shady vale
  With longing eyes look back?

I hear a solemn murmur,
  And, listening to the sound,
I know the voice of the mighty Sea,
  Beating his pebbly bound.

Dost thou, oh path of the woodland!
  End where those waters roar,
Like human life, on a trackless beach,
  With a boundless Sea before?

<div align="center">~~~*******~~~</div>

"OH MOTHER OF A MIGHTY RACE."

Oh mother of a mighty race,
Yet lovely in thy youthful grace!
The elder dames, thy haughty peers,
Admire and hate thy blooming years.
    With words of shame
And taunts of scorn they join thy name.

For on thy cheeks the glow is spread
That tints thy morning hills with red;
Thy step—the wild-deer's rustling feet
Within thy woods are not more fleet;
    Thy hopeful eye
Is bright as thine own sunny sky.

Ay, let them rail—those haughty ones,
While safe thou dwellest with thy sons.
They do not know how loved thou art,
How many a fond and fearless heart
    Would rise to throw
Its life between thee and the foe.

They know not, in their hate and pride,
What virtues with thy children bide;
How true, how good, thy graceful maids
Make bright, like flowers, the valley-shades;
    What generous men
Spring, like thine oaks, by hill and glen; —

What cordial welcomes greet the guest
By thy lone rivers of the West;
How faith is kept, and truth revered,
And man is loved, and God is feared,
    In woodland homes,
And where the ocean border foams.

There's freedom at thy gates and rest
For Earth's down-trodden and opprest,
A shelter for the hunted head,
For the starved laborer toil and bread.

Power, at thy bounds,
Stops and calls back his baffled hounds.

Oh, fair young mother! on thy brow
Shall sit a nobler grace than now.
Deep in the brightness of the skies
The thronging years in glory rise,
   And, as they fleet,
Drop strength and riches at thy feet.

Thine eye, with every coming hour,
Shall brighten, and thy form shall tower;
And when thy sisters, elder born,
Would brand thy name with words of scorn,
   Before thine eye,
Upon their lips the taunt shall die.

~~~~~******~~~~~

</div>

THE BURIAL OF LOVE.

Two dark-eyed maids, at shut of day,
Sat where a river rolled away,
With calm sad brows and raven hair,
And one was pale and both were fair.

Bring flowers, they sang, bring flowers unblown,
Bring forest-blooms of name unknown;
Bring budding sprays from wood and wild,
To strew the bier of Love, the child.

Close softly, fondly, while ye weep,
His eyes, that death may seem like sleep,
And fold his hands in sign of rest,
His waxen hands, across his breast.

And make his grave where violets hide,
Where star-flowers strew the rivulet's side,
And bluebirds in the misty spring
Of cloudless skies and summer sing.

Place near him, as ye lay him low,
His idle shafts, his loosened bow,
The silken fillet that around
His waggish eyes in sport he wound.

But we shall mourn him long, and miss
His ready smile, his ready kiss,
The patter of his little feet,
Sweet frowns and stammered phrases sweet;

And graver looks, serene and high,
A light of heaven in that young eye,
All these shall haunt us till the heart
Shall ache and ache—and tears will start.

The bow, the band shall fall to dust,
The shining arrows waste with rust,
And all of Love that earth can claim,
Be but a memory and a name.

Not thus his nobler part shall dwell
A prisoner in this narrow cell;
But he whom now we hide from men,
In the dark ground, shall live again:

Shall break these clods, a form of light,
With nobler mien and purer sight,
And in the eternal glory stand,
Highest and nearest God's right hand.

<center>~~~~~******~~~~~</center>

"THE MAY SUN SHEDS AN AMBER LIGHT."

The May sun sheds an amber light
On new-leaved woods and lawns between;
But she who, with a smile more bright,
Welcomed and watched the springing green,
Is in her grave,
Low in her grave.

The fair white blossoms of the wood
In groups beside the pathway stand;
But one, the gentle and the good,
Who cropped them with a fairer hand,
Is in her grave,
Low in her grave.

Upon the woodland's morning airs
The small birds' mingled notes are flung;
But she, whose voice, more sweet than theirs,
Once bade me listen while they sung,
Is in her grave,
Low in her grave.

That music of the early year
Brings tears of anguish to my eyes;
My heart aches when the flowers appear;
For then I think of her who lies
Within her grave,
Low in her grave.

<center>~~~~~******~~~~~</center>

THE VOICE OF AUTUMN.

There comes, from yonder height,
  A soft repining sound,
Where forest-leaves are bright,
And fall, like flakes of light,
        To the ground.

168

It is the autumn breeze,
  That, lightly floating on,
Just skims the weedy leas,
Just stirs the glowing trees,
      And is gone.

He moans by sedgy brook,
  And visits, with a sigh,
The last pale flowers that look,
From out their sunny nook,
      At the sky.

O'er shouting children flies
  That light October wind,
And, kissing cheeks and eyes,
He leaves their merry cries
      Far behind,

And wanders on to make
  That soft uneasy sound
By distant wood and lake,
Where distant fountains break
      From the ground.

No bower where maidens dwell
  Can win a moment's stay;
Nor fair untrodden dell;
He sweeps the upland swell,
      And away!

Mourn'st thou thy homeless state?
  O soft, repining wind!
That early seek'st and late
The rest it is thy fate
      Not to find.

Not on the mountain's breast,
  Not on the ocean's shore,
In all the East and West:
The wind that stops to rest
      Is no more.

By valleys, woods, and springs,
  No wonder thou shouldst grieve
For all the glorious things
Thou touchest with thy wings
      And must leave.

~~~~~******~~~~~

THE CONQUEROR'S GRAVE.

Within this lowly grave a Conqueror lies,
  And yet the monument proclaims it not,
Nor round the sleeper's name hath chisel wrought

169

The emblems of a fame that never dies, —
Ivy and amaranth, in a graceful sheaf,
Twined with the laurel's fair, imperial leaf.
    A simple name alone,
    To the great world unknown,
Is graven here, and wild-flowers, rising round,
Meek meadow-sweet and violets of the ground,
  Lean lovingly against the humble stone.
Here, in the quiet earth, they laid apart
  No man of iron mould and bloody hands,
Who sought to wreak upon the cowering lands
  The passions that consumed his restless heart;
But one of tender spirit and delicate frame,
    Gentlest, in mien and mind,
    Of gentle womankind,
Timidly shrinking from the breath of blame:
One in whose eyes the smile of kindness made
  Its haunt, like flowers by sunny brooks in May,
Yet at the thought of others' pain, a shade
Of sweeter sadness chased the smile away.

Nor deem that when the hand that moulders here
Was raised in menace, realms were chilled with fear,
  And armies mustered at the sign, as when
Clouds rise on clouds before the rainy East—
  Gray captains leading bands of veteran men
And fiery youths to be the vulture's feast.
Not thus were waged the mighty wars that gave
The victory to her who fills this grave:
    Alone her task was wrought,
    Alone the battle fought;
Through that long strife her constant hope was staid
On God alone, nor looked for other aid.

She met the hosts of Sorrow with a look
  That altered not beneath the frown they wore,
And soon the lowering brood were tamed, and took,
  Meekly, her gentle rule, and frowned no more.
Her soft hand put aside the assaults of wrath,
    And calmly broke in twain
    The fiery shafts of pain,
And rent the nets of passion from her path.
  By that victorious hand despair was slain.
With love she vanquished hate and overcame
Evil with good, in her Great Master's name.
Her glory is not of this shadowy state,
  Glory that with the fleeting season dies;
But when she entered at the sapphire gate
  What joy was radiant in celestial eyes!
How heaven's bright depths with sounding welcome rung,
And flowers of heaven by shining hands were flung!
    And He who, long before,
    Pain, scorn, and sorrow bore,
The Mighty Sufferer, with aspect sweet,
Smiled on the timid stranger from his seat;
He who returning, glorious, from the grave,

Dragged Death, disarmed, in chains, a crouching slave.

See, as I linger here, the sun grows low;
  Cool airs are murmuring that the night is near.
Oh, gentle sleeper, from thy grave I go
  Consoled though sad, in hope and yet in fear.
    Brief is the time, I know,
    The warfare scarce begun;
Yet all may win the triumphs thou hast won.
Still flows the fount whose waters strengthened thee,
  The victors' names are yet too few to fill
Heaven's mighty roll; the glorious armory,
  That ministered to thee, is open still.

<center>~~~~~~******~~~~~~</center>

THE PLANTING OF THE APPLE-TREE.

  Come, let us plant the apple-tree.
Cleave the tough greensward with the spade;
Wide let its hollow bed be made;
There gently lay the roots, and there
Sift the dark mould with kindly care,
  And press it o'er them tenderly,
As, round the sleeping infant's feet,
We softly fold the cradle-sheet:
  So plant we the apple-tree.

  What plant we in this apple-tree?
Buds, which the breath of summer days
Shall lengthen into leafy sprays;
Boughs where the thrush, with crimson breast,
Shall haunt and sing and hide her nest;
  We plant, upon the sunny lea,
A shadow for the noontide hour,
A shelter from the summer shower,
  When we plant the apple-tree.

  What plant we in this apple-tree?
Sweets for a hundred flowery springs
To load the May-wind's restless wings,
When, from the orchard-row, he pours
Its fragrance through our open doors;
  A world of blossoms for the bee,
Flowers for the sick girl's silent room,
For the glad infant sprigs of bloom,
  We plant with the apple-tree.

  What plant we in this apple-tree?
Fruits that shall swell in sunny June,
And redden in the August noon,
And drop, when gentle airs come by,
That fan the blue September sky,
  While children come, with cries of glee,
And seek them where the fragrant grass
Betrays their bed to those who pass,

171

At the foot of the apple-tree.

And when, above this apple-tree,
The winter stars are quivering bright,
And winds go howling through the night,
Girls, whose young eyes o'erflow with mirth,
Shall peel its fruit by cottage-hearth,
  And guests in prouder homes shall see,
Heaped with the grape of Cintra's vine
And golden orange of the line,
  The fruit of the apple-tree.

The fruitage of this apple-tree
Winds and our flag of stripe and star
Shall bear to coasts that lie afar,
Where men shall wonder at the view,
And ask in what fair groves they grew;
  And sojourners beyond the sea
Shall think of childhood's careless day,
And long, long hours of summer play,
  In the shade of the apple-tree.

Each year shall give this apple-tree
A broader flush of roseate bloom,
A deeper maze of verdurous gloom,
And loosen, when the frost-clouds lower,
The crisp brown leaves in thicker shower.
  The years shall come and pass, but we
Shall hear no longer, where we lie,
The summer's songs, the autumn's sigh,
  In the boughs of the apple-tree.

And time shall waste this apple-tree.
Oh, when its aged branches throw
Thin shadows on the ground below,
Shall fraud and force and iron will
Oppress the weak and helpless still?
  What shall the tasks of mercy be,
Amid the toils, the strifes, the tears
Of those who live when length of years
  Is wasting this little apple-tree?

"Who planted this old apple-tree?"
The children of that distant day
Thus to some aged man shall say;
And, gazing on its mossy stem,
The gray-haired man shall answer them:
  "A poet of the land was he,
Born in the rude but good old times;
'Tis said he made some quaint old rhymes,
  On planting the apple-tree."

~~~~~******~~~~~

172

THE SNOW-SHOWER.

Stand here by my side and turn, I pray,
  On the lake below thy gentle eyes;
The clouds hang over it, heavy and gray,
  And dark and silent the water lies;
And out of that frozen mist the snow
In wavering flakes begins to flow;
      Flake after flake
They sink in the dark and silent lake.

See how in a living swarm they come
  From the chambers beyond that misty veil;
Some hover awhile in air, and some
  Rush prone from the sky like summer hail.
All, dropping swiftly or settling slow,
Meet, and are still in the depths below;
      Flake after flake
Dissolved in the dark and silent lake.

Here delicate snow-stars, out of the cloud,
  Come floating downward in airy play,
Like spangles dropped from the glistening crowd
  That whiten by night the milky way;
There broader and burlier masses fall;
The sullen water buries them all—
      Flake after flake—
All drowned in the dark and silent lake.

And some, as on tender wings they glide
  From their chilly birth-cloud, dim and gray,
Are joined in their fall, and, side by side,
  Come clinging along their unsteady way;
As friend with friend, or husband with wife,
Makes hand in hand the passage of life;
      Each mated flake
Soon sinks in the dark and silent lake.

Lo! while we are gazing, in swifter haste
  Stream down the snows, till the air is white
As, myriads by myriads madly chased,
  They fling themselves from their shadowy height.
The fair, frail creatures of middle sky,
What speed they make, with their grave so nigh;
      Flake after flake,
To lie in the dark and silent lake!

I see in thy gentle eyes a tear;
  They turn to me in sorrowful thought;
Thou thinkest of friends, the good and dear,
  Who were for a time, and now are not;
Like these fair children of cloud and frost,
That glisten a moment and then are lost,
      Flake after flake—
All lost in the dark and silent lake.

Yet look again, for the clouds divide;
  A gleam of blue on the water lies;
And far away, on the mountain-side,
  A sunbeam falls from the opening skies,
But the hurrying host that flew between
The cloud and the water, no more is seen;
        Flake after flake,
At rest in the dark and silent lake.

<div align="center">~~~~~******~~~~~</div>

A RAIN-DREAM.

These strifes, these tumults of the noisy world,
Where Fraud, the coward, tracks his prey by stealth,
And Strength, the ruffian, glories in his guilt,
Oppress the heart with sadness. Oh, my friend,
In what serener mood we look upon
The gloomiest aspects of the elements
Among the woods and fields! Let us awhile,
As the slow wind is rolling up the storm,
In fancy leave this maze of dusty streets,
Forever shaken by the importunate jar
Of commerce, and upon the darkening air
Look from the shelter of our rural home.
  Who is not awed that listens to the Rain,
Sending his voice before him? Mighty Rain!
The upland steeps are shrouded by thy mists;
Thy shadow fills the hollow vale; the pools
No longer glimmer, and the silvery streams
Darken to veins of lead at thy approach.
O mighty Rain! already thou art here;
And every roof is beaten by thy streams,
And, as thou passest, every glassy spring
Grows rough, and every leaf in all the woods
Is struck, and quivers. All the hill-tops slake
Their thirst from thee; a thousand languishing fields,
A thousand fainting gardens, are refreshed;
A thousand idle rivulets start to speed,
And with the graver murmur of the storm
Blend their light voices as they hurry on.
  Thou fill'st the circle of the atmosphere
Alone; there is no living thing abroad,
No bird to wing the air nor beast to walk
The field; the squirrel in the forest seeks
His hollow tree; the marmot of the field
Has scampered to his den; the butterfly
Hides under her broad leaf; the insect crowds,
That made the sunshine populous, lie close
In their mysterious shelters, whence the sun
Will summon them again. The mighty Rain
Holds the vast empire of the sky alone.
  I shut my eyes, and see, as in a dream,
The friendly clouds drop down spring violets
And summer columbines, and all the flowers
That tuft the woodland floor, or overarch

174

The streamlet:—spiky grass for genial June,
Brown harvests for the waiting husbandman,
And for the woods a deluge of fresh leaves.
  I see these myriad drops that slake the dust,
Gathered in glorious streams, or rolling blue
In billows on the lake or on the deep,
And bearing navies. I behold them change
To threads of crystal as they sink in earth
And leave its stains behind, to rise again
In pleasant nooks of verdure, where the child,
Thirsty with play, in both his little hands
Shall take the cool, clear water, raising it
To wet his pretty lips. To-morrow noon
How proudly will the water-lily ride
The brimming pool, o'erlooking, like a queen,
Her circle of broad leaves! In lonely wastes,
When next the sunshine makes them beautiful,
Gay troops of butterflies shall light to drink
At the replenished hollows of the rock.
  Now slowly falls the dull blank night, and still,
All through the starless hours, the mighty Rain
Smites with perpetual sound the forest-leaves,
And beats the matted grass, and still the earth
Drinks the unstinted bounty of the clouds—
Drinks for her cottage wells, her woodland brooks—
Drinks for the springing trout, the toiling bee,
And brooding bird—drinks for her tender flowers,
Tall oaks, and all the herbage of her hills.
  A melancholy sound is in the air,
A deep sigh in the distance, a shrill wail
Around my dwelling. 'Tis the Wind of night;
A lonely wanderer between earth and cloud,
In the black shadow and the chilly mist,
Along the streaming mountain-side, and through
The dripping woods, and o'er the plashy fields,
Roaming and sorrowing still, like one who makes
The journey of life alone, and nowhere meets
A welcome or a friend, and still goes on
In darkness. Yet a while, a little while,
And he shall toss the glittering leaves in play,
And dally with the flowers, and gayly lift
The slender herbs, pressed low by weight of rain,
And drive, in joyous triumph, through the sky,
White clouds, the laggard remnants of the storm.

******

ROBERT OF LINCOLN.

Merrily swinging on brier and weed,
  Near to the nest of his little dame,
Over the mountain-side or mead,
  Robert of Lincoln is telling his name:
    Bob-o'-link, bob-o'-link,
    Spink, spank, spink;
Snug and safe is that nest of ours,

Hidden among the summer flowers.
          Chee, chee, chee.

Robert of Lincoln is gayly drest,
  Wearing a bright black wedding-coat;
White are his shoulders and white his crest.
  Hear him call in his merry note:
    Bob-o'-link, bob-o'-link,
    Spink, spank, spink;
Look, what a nice new coat is mine,
Sure there was never a bird so fine.
          Chee, chee, chee.

Robert of Lincoln's Quaker wife,
  Pretty and quiet, with plain brown wings,
Passing at home a patient life,
  Broods in the grass while her husband sings:
    Bob-o'-link, bob-o'-link,
    Spink, spank, spink;
Brood, kind creature; you need not fear
Thieves and robbers while I am here.
          Chee, chee, chee.

Modest and shy as a nun is she;
  One weak chirp is her only note.
Braggart and prince of braggarts is he,
  Pouring boasts from his little throat:
    Bob-o'-link, bob-o'-link,
    Spink, spank, spink;
Never was I afraid of man;
Catch me, cowardly knaves, if you can!
          Chee, chee, chee.

Six white eggs on a bed of hay,
  Flecked with purple, a pretty sight!
There as the mother sits all day,
  Robert is singing with all his might:
    Bob-o'-link, bob-o'-link,
    Spink, spank, spink;
Nice good wife, that never goes out,
Keeping house while I frolic about.
          Chee, chee, chee.

Soon as the little ones chip the shell,
  Six wide mouths are open for food;
Robert of Lincoln bestirs him well,
  Gathering seeds for the hungry brood.
    Bob-o'-link, bob-o'-link,
    Spink, spank, spink;
This new life is likely to be
Hard for a gay young fellow like me.
          Chee, chee, chee.

Robert of Lincoln at length is made
  Sober with work, and silent with care;
Off is his holiday garment laid,

Half forgotten that merry air:
  Bob-o'-link, bob-o'-link,
    Spink, spank, spink;
Nobody knows but my mate and I
Where our nest and our nestlings lie.
        Chee, chee, chee.

Summer wanes; the children are grown;
  Fun and frolic no more he knows;
Robert of Lincoln's a humdrum crone;
  Off he flies, and we sing as he goes:
    Bob-o'-link, bob-o'-link,
      Spink, spank, spink;
When you can pipe that merry old strain,
Robert of Lincoln, come back again.
        Chee, chee, chee.

~~~~~******~~~~~

THE TWENTY-SEVENTH OF MARCH.

Oh, gentle one, thy birthday sun should rise
Amid a chorus of the merriest birds
That ever sang the stars out of the sky
In a June morning. Rivulets should send
A voice of gladness from their winding paths,
Deep in o'erarching grass, where playful winds,
Stirring the loaded stems, should shower the dew
Upon the grassy water. Newly-blown
Roses, by thousands, to the garden-walks
Should tempt the loitering moth and diligent bee.
The longest, brightest day in all the year
Should be the day on which thy cheerful eyes
First opened on the earth, to make thy haunts
Fairer and gladder for thy kindly looks.
Thus might a poet say; but I must bring
A birthday offering of an humbler strain,
And yet it may not please thee less. I hold
That 'twas the fitting season for thy birth
When March, just ready to depart, begins
To soften into April. Then we have
The delicatest and most welcome flowers,
And yet they take least heed of bitter wind
And lowering sky. The periwinkle then,
In an hour's sunshine, lifts her azure blooms
Beside the cottage-door; within the woods
Tufts of ground-laurel, creeping underneath
The leaves of the last summer, send their sweets
Up to the chilly air, and, by the oak,
The squirrel-cups, a graceful company,
Hide in their bells, a soft aerial blue—
Sweet flowers, that nestle in the humblest nooks
And yet within whose smallest bud is wrapped
A world of promise! Still the north wind breathes
His frost, and still the sky sheds snow and sleet;
Yet ever, when the sun looks forth again,

177

The flowers smile up to him from their low seats.
   Well hast thou borne the bleak March day of life.
Its storms and its keen winds to thee have been
Most kindly tempered, and through all its gloom
There has been warmth and sunshine in thy heart;
The griefs of life to thee have been like snows,
That light upon the fields in early spring,
Making them greener. In its milder hours,
The smile of this pale season, thou hast seen
The glorious bloom of June, and in the note
Of early bird, that comes a messenger
From climes of endless verdure, thou hast heard
The choir that fills the summer woods with song.
   Now be the hours that yet remain to thee
Stormy or sunny, sympathy and love,
That inextinguishably dwell within
Thy heart, shall give a beauty and a light
To the most desolate moments, like the glow
Of a bright fireside in the wildest day;
And kindly words and offices of good
Shall wait upon thy steps, as thou goest on,
Where God shall lead thee, till thou reach the gates
Of a more genial season, and thy path
Be lost to human eye among the bowers
And living fountains of a brighter land.

March, 1855.

~~~~~******~~~~~

AN INVITATION TO THE COUNTRY.

Already, close by our summer dwelling,
   The Easter sparrow repeats her song;
A merry warbler, she chides the blossoms—
   The idle blossoms that sleep so long.

The bluebird chants, from the elm's long branches,
   A hymn to welcome the budding year.
The south wind wanders from field to forest,
   And softly whispers, "The Spring is here."

Come, daughter mine, from the gloomy city,
   Before those lays from the elm have ceased;
The violet breathes, by our door, as sweetly
   As in the air of her native East.

Though many a flower in the wood is waking,
   The daffodil is our doorside queen;
She pushes upward the sward already,
   To spot with sunshine the early green.

No lays so joyous as these are warbled
   From wiry prison in maiden's bower;
No pampered bloom of the green-house chamber
   Has half the charm of the lawn's first flower.

178

Yet these sweet sounds of the early season,
  And these fair sights of its sunny days,
Are only sweet when we fondly listen,
  And only fair when we fondly gaze.

There is no glory in star or blossom
  Till looked upon by a loving eye;
There is no fragrance in April breezes
  Till breathed with joy as they wander by.

Come, Julia dear, for the sprouting willows,
  The opening flowers, and the gleaming brooks,
And hollows, green in the sun, are waiting
  Their dower of beauty from thy glad looks.

******

A SONG FOR NEW-YEAR'S EVE.

Stay yet, my friends, a moment stay—
  Stay till the good old year,
So long companion of our way,
  Shakes hands, and leaves us here.
    Oh stay, oh stay,
One little hour, and then away.

The year, whose hopes were high and strong,
  Has now no hopes to wake;
Yet one hour more of jest and song
  For his familiar sake.
    Oh stay, oh stay,
One mirthful hour, and then away.

The kindly year, his liberal hands
  Have lavished all his store.
And shall we turn from where he stands,
  Because he gives no more?
    Oh stay, oh stay,
One grateful hour, and then away.

Days brightly came and calmly went,
  While yet he was our guest;
How cheerfully the week was spent!
  How sweet the seventh day's rest!
    Oh stay, oh stay,
One golden hour, and then away.

Dear friends were with us, some who sleep
  Beneath the coffin-lid:
What pleasant memories we keep
  Of all they said and did!
    Oh stay, oh stay,
One tender hour, and then away.

Even while we sing, he smiles his last,

179

And leaves our sphere behind.
The good old year is with the past;
  Oh be the new as kind!
    Oh stay, oh stay,
One parting strain, and then away.

~~~~~******~~~~~

THE WIND AND STREAM.

A brook came stealing from the ground;
  You scarcely saw its silvery gleam
Among the herbs that hung around
  The borders of the winding stream,
The pretty stream, the placid stream,
The softly-gliding, bashful stream.

A breeze came wandering from the sky,
  Light as the whispers of a dream;
He put the o'erhanging grasses by,
  And softly stooped to kiss the stream,
The pretty stream, the flattered stream,
The shy, yet unreluctant stream.

The water, as the wind passed o'er,
  Shot upward many a glancing beam,
Dimpled and quivered more and more,
  And tripped along, a livelier stream,
The flattered stream, the simpering stream,
The fond, delighted, silly stream.

Away the airy wanderer flew
  To where the fields with blossoms teem,
To sparkling springs and rivers blue,
  And left alone that little stream,
The flattered stream, the cheated stream,
The sad, forsaken, lonely stream.

That careless wind came never back;
  He wanders yet the fields, I deem,
But, on its melancholy track,
  Complaining went that little stream,
The cheated stream, the hopeless stream,
The ever-murmuring, mourning stream.

~~~~~******~~~~~

THE LOST BIRD.

FROM THE SPANISH OF CAROLINA CORONADO DE PERRY. [38]

---

[38] Readers who are acquainted with the Spanish language, may not be displeased at seeing the original of this little poem:

EL PAJARO PERDIDO.

Huyo con vuelo incierto,

Y de mis ojos ha desparecido.
Mirad, si, a vuestro huerto,
 Mi pajaro querido,
 Ninas hermosas, por acaso ha huido.

Sus ojos relucientes
 Son como los del aguila orgullosa;
Plumas resplandecientes,
 En la cabeza airosa,
 Lleva; y su voz es tierna y armoniosa.

Mirad, si cuidadoso
 Junto a las flores se escondio en la grama.
Ese laurel frondoso
 Mirad, rama por rama,
 Que el los laureles y los flores ama.

Si le hallais, por ventura,
 No os enamore su amoroso acento;
No os prende su hermosura;
 Volvedmele al momento;
 O dejadle, si no, libre en el viento.

Por que su pico de oro
 Solo en mi mano toma la semilla;
Y no enjugare el lloro
 Que veis en mi mejilla,
 Hasta encontrar mi profugo avecilla.

Mi vista se oscurece,
 Si sus ojos no ve, que son mi dia
Mi anima desfallece
 Con la melancolia
 De no escucharle ya su melodia.

The literature of Spain at the present day has this peculiarity, that female writers have, in considerable number, entered into competition with the other sex. One of the most remarkable of these, as a writer of both prose and poetry, is Carolina Coronado de Perry, the author of the little poem here given. The poetical literature of Spain has felt the influence of the female mind in the infusion of a certain delicacy and tenderness, and the more frequent choice of subjects which interest the domestic affections. Concerning the verses of the lady already mentioned, Don Juan Eugenio Hartzenbusch, one of the most accomplished Spanish critics of the present day, and himself a successful dramatic writer, says:

* * * *

"If Carolina Coronado had, through modesty, sent her productions from Estremadura to Madrid under the name of a person of the other sex, itwould still have been difficult for intelligent readers to persuade themselves that they were written by a man, or at least, considering their graceful sweetness, purity of tone, simplicity of conception, brevity of development, and delicate and particular choice of subject, we should be constrained to attribute them to one yet in his early youth, whom the imagination would represent as ingenuous, innocent, and gay, who had scarce ever wandered beyond the flowery grove or pleasant valley where his cradle was rocked, and where he has been lulled to sleep by the sweetest songs of Francisea de la Torre, Garcilaso, and Melendez."

* * * *

The author of the *Pajaro Perdido*, according to a memoir of her by Angel Fernandez de los Rios, was born at Almendralejo, in Estremadura, in 1823. At the age of nine years she began to steal from sleep, after a day passed in various lessons, and in domestic occupations, several hours every night to read the poets of her country, and other books belonging to the library of the household, among which are mentioned, as a proof of her vehement love of reading, the "Critical History of Spain," by the Abbe Masuden, "and other works equally dry and prolix." She was afterward sent to Badajoz, where she received the best education which the state of the country, then on fire with a civil war, would admit. Here the intensity of her application to her studies caused a severe malady, which has frequently recurred in after-life. At the age of thirteen years she wrote a poem entitled *La Palma*, which the author of her biography declares to be worthy of Herrera, and which led Espronceda, a poet of Estremadura, a man of genius, and the author of several translations from Byron, whom he resembled both in mental and personal characteristics, to address her an eulogistic sonnet. In 1843,when she was but twenty years old, a volume of her poems was published at Madrid, in which were included both that entitled *La Palma* and the one I have given in this note. To this volume Hartzenbusch, in his admiration for her genius, prefaced an ntroduction.

The task of writing verses in Spanish is not difficult. Rhymes are readily found, and the language is easily moulded into metrical forms. Those who have distinguished themselves in this literature have generally made their first essays in verse. What is remarkable enough, the men who afterward figured in political life mostly began their career as the authors of madrigals. A poem introduces the future statesman to the public, as a speech at a popular meeting introduces the candidate for political distinctions in this country. I have heard of but one of the eminent Spanish politicians of the present time, who made a boast that he was innocent of poetry; and if ll that his enemies say of him be true, it would have been well both for his country and his own fame, if he had been equally innocent

My bird has flown away,
Far out of sight has flown, I know not where.
  Look in your lawn, I pray,
  Ye maidens, kind and fair,
And see if my beloved bird be there.

  His eyes are full of light;
The eagle of the rock has such an eye;
  And plumes, exceeding bright,
  Round his smooth temples lie,
And sweet his voice and tender as a sigh.

  Look where the grass is gay
With summer blossoms, haply there he cowers;
  And search, from spray to spray,
  The leafy laurel-bowers,
For well he loves the laurels and the flowers.

  Find him, but do not dwell,
With eyes too fond, on the fair form you see,
  Nor love his song too well;
  Send him, at once, to me,
Or leave him to the air and liberty.

  For only from my hand
He takes the seed into his golden beak,
  And all unwiped shall stand
  The tears that wet my cheek,
Till I have found the wanderer I seek.

  My sight is darkened o'er,
Whene'er I miss his eyes, which are my day,
  And when I hear no more
  The music of his lay,
My heart in utter sadness faints away.

---

of corrupt practices. The compositions of Carolina Coronado, even her earliest, do not deserve to be classed with the productions of which I have spoken, and which are simply the effect of inclination and facility. They possess the *mens divinior*.

In 1852 a collection of poems of Carolina Coronado was brought out at Madrid, including those which were first published. The subjects are of larger variety than those which prompted her earlier productions; some of them are of a religious cast, others refer to political matters. One of them, which appears among the "Improvisations," is an energetic protest against erecting a new amphitheatre for bull-fights. The spirit in all her poetry is humane and friendly to the best interests of mankind.

Her writings in prose must not be overlooked. Among them is a novel entitled *Sigea*, founded on the adventures of Camoens; another entitled *Jarilla*, a beautiful story, full of pictures of rural life in Estremadura, which deserves, if it could find a competent translator, to be transferred to our language. Besides these there are two other novels from her pen, *Paquita* and *La Luz del Tejo*. A few years since appeared, in a Madrid periodical, the *Semanario*, a series of letters written by her, giving an account of the impressions received in a journey from the Tagus to the Rhine, including a visit to England. Among the subjects on which she has written, is the idea, still warmly cherished in Spain, of uniting the entire peninsula under one government. In an ably-conducted journal of Madrid, she has given accounts of the poetesses of Spain, her contemporaries, with extracts from their writings, and a kindly estimate of their respective merits.

Her biographer speaks of her activity and efficiency in charitable enterprises, her interest in the cause of education, her visits to the primary schools of Madrid, encouraging and rewarding the pupils, and her patronage of the *escuela de parvules*, or infant school at Badajoz, established by a society of that city, with the design of improving the education of the laboring class.

It must have been not long after the publication of her poems, in 1852, that Carolina Coronado became the wife of an American gentleman, Mr. Horatio J. Perry, at one time our Secretary of Legation at the Court of Madrid, afterward our *Charge d'Affaires*, and now, in 1863, again Secretary of Legation. Amid the duties of a wife and mother, which she fulfils with exemplary fidelity and grace, she has neither forgotten nor forsaken the literary pursuits which have given her so high a reputation.

THE NIGHT JOURNEY OF A RIVER.

Oh River, gentle River! gliding on
In silence underneath the starless sky!
Thine is a ministry that never rests
Even while the living slumber. For a time
The meddler, man, hath left the elements
In peace; the ploughman breaks the clods no more;
The miner labors not, with steel and fire,
To rend the rock, and he that hews the stone,
And he that fells the forest, he that guides
The loaded wain, and the poor animal
That drags it, have forgotten, for a time,
Their toils, and share the quiet of the earth.
  Thou pausest not in thine allotted task,
Oh darkling River! Through the night I hear
Thy wavelets rippling on the pebbly beach;
I hear thy current stir the rustling sedge,
That skirts thy bed; thou intermittest not
Thine everlasting journey, drawing on
A silvery train from many a woodland spring
And mountain-brook. The dweller by thy side,
Who moored his little boat upon thy beach,
Though all the waters that upbore it then
Have slid away o'er night, shall find, at morn,
Thy channel filled with waters freshly drawn
From distant cliffs, and hollows where the rill
Comes up amid the water-flags. All night
Thou givest moisture to the thirsty roots
Of the lithe willow and o'erhanging plane,
And cherishest the herbage of thy bank,
Spotted with little flowers, and sendest up
Perpetually the vapors from thy face,
To steep the hills with dew, or darken heaven
With drifting clouds, that trail the shadowy shower.
  Oh River! darkling River! what a voice
Is that thou utterest while all else is still—
The ancient voice that, centuries ago,
Sounded between thy hills, while Rome was yet
A weedy solitude by Tiber's stream!
How many, at this hour, along thy course,
Slumber to thine eternal murmurings,
That mingle with the utterance of their dreams!
At dead of night the child awakes and hears
Thy soft, familiar dashings, and is soothed,
And sleeps again. An airy multitude
Of little echoes, all unheard by day,
Faintly repeat, till morning, after thee,
The story of thine endless goings forth.
  Yet there are those who lie beside thy bed
For whom thou once didst rear the bowers that screen
Thy margin, and didst water the green fields;
And now there is no night so still that they
Can hear thy lapse; their slumbers, were thy voice

Louder than Ocean's, it could never break.
For them the early violet no more
Opens upon thy bank, nor, for their eyes,
Glitter the crimson pictures of the clouds,
Upon thy bosom, when the sun goes down.
Their memories are abroad, the memories
Of those who last were gathered to the earth,
Lingering within the homes in which they sat,
Hovering above the paths in which they walked,
Haunting them like a presence. Even now
They visit many a dreamer in the forms
They walked in, ere at last they wore the shroud.
And eyes there are which will not close to dream,
For weeping and for thinking of the grave,
The new-made grave, and the pale one within.
These memories and these sorrows all shall fade,
And pass away, and fresher memories
And newer sorrows come and dwell awhile
Beside thy borders, and, in turn, depart.
  On glide thy waters, till at last they flow
Beneath the windows of the populous town,
And all night long give back the gleam of lamps,
And glimmer with the trains of light that stream
From halls where dancers whirl. A dimmer ray
Touches thy surface from the silent room
In which they tend the sick, or gather round
The dying; and a slender, steady beam
Comes from the little chamber, in the roof
Where, with a feverous crimson on her cheek,
The solitary damsel, dying, too,
Plies the quick needle till the stars grow pale.
There, close beside the haunts of revel, stand
The blank, unlighted windows, where the poor,
In hunger and in darkness, wake till morn.
There, drowsily, on the half-conscious ear
Of the dull watchman, pacing on the wharf,
Falls the soft ripple of the waves that strike
On the moored bark; but guiltier listeners
Are nigh, the prowlers of the night, who steal
From shadowy nook to shadowy nook, and start
If other sounds than thine are in the air.
  Oh, glide away from those abodes, that bring
Pollution to thy channel and make foul
Thy once clear current; summon thy quick waves
And dimpling eddies; linger not, but haste,
With all thy waters, haste thee to the deep,
There to be tossed by shifting winds and rocked
By that mysterious force which lives within
The sea's immensity, and wields the weight
Of its abysses, swaying to and fro
The billowy mass, until the stain, at length,
Shall wholly pass away, and thou regain
The crystal brightness of thy mountain-springs.

<center>~~~~~******~~~~~</center>

THE LIFE THAT IS.

Thou, who so long hast pressed the couch of pain,
  Oh welcome, welcome back to life's free breath—
To life's free breath and day's sweet light again,
  From the chill shadows of the gate of death!

For thou hadst reached the twilight bound between
  The world of spirits and this grosser sphere;
Dimly by thee the things of earth were seen,
  And faintly fell earth's voices on thine ear.

And now, how gladly we behold, at last,
  The wonted smile returning to thy brow!
The very wind's low whisper, breathing past,
  In the light leaves, is music to thee now.

Thou wert not weary of thy lot; the earth
  Was ever good and pleasant in thy sight;
Still clung thy loves about the household hearth,
  And sweet was every day's returning light.

Then welcome back to all thou wouldst not leave,
  To this grand march of seasons, days, and hours;
The glory of the morn, the glow of eve,
  The beauty of the streams, and stars, and flowers;

To eyes on which thine own delight to rest;
  To voices which it is thy joy to hear;
To the kind toils that ever pleased thee best,
  The willing tasks of love, that made life dear.

Welcome to grasp of friendly hands; to prayers
  Offered where crowds in reverent worship come,
Or softly breathed amid the tender cares
  And loving inmates of thy quiet home.

Thou bring'st no tidings of the better land,
  Even from its verge; the mysteries opened there
Are what the faithful heart may understand
  In its still depths, yet words may not declare.

And well I deem, that, from the brighter side
  Of life's dim border, some o'erflowing rays
Streamed from the inner glory, shall abide
  Upon thy spirit through the coming days.

Twice wert thou given me; once in thy fair prime,
  Fresh from the fields of youth, when first we met,
And all the blossoms of that hopeful time
  Clustered and glowed where'er thy steps were set.

And now, in thy ripe autumn, once again
  Given back to fervent prayers and yearnings strong,
From the drear realm of sickness and of pain
  When we had watched, and feared, and trembled long.

Now may we keep thee from the balmy air
  And radiant walks of heaven a little space,
Where He, who went before thee to prepare
  For His meek followers, shall assign thy place.

CASTELLAMARE, *May*, 1858.

~~~~~******~~~~~

SONG.

"THESE PRAIRIES GLOW WITH FLOWERS."

These prairies glow with flowers,
  These groves are tall and fair,
The sweet lay of the mocking-bird
  Rings in the morning air;
And yet I pine to see
  My native hill once more,
And hear the sparrow's friendly chirp
  Beside its cottage-door.

And he, for whom I left
  My native hill and brook,
Alas, I sometimes think I trace
  A coldness in his look!
If I have lost his love,
  I know my heart will break;
And haply, they I left for him
  Will sorrow for my sake.

~~~~~******~~~~~

THE SONG OF THE SOWER.

I.

The maples redden in the sun;
  In autumn gold the beeches stand;
Rest, faithful plough, thy work is done
  Upon the teeming land.
Bordered with trees whose gay leaves fly
On every breath that sweeps the sky,
The fresh dark acres furrowed lie,
  And ask the sower's hand.
Loose the tired steer and let him go
To pasture where the gentians blow,
And we, who till the grateful ground,
Fling we the golden shower around.

II.

Fling wide the generous grain; we fling
O'er the dark mould the green of spring.
For thick the emerald blades shall grow,

When first the March winds melt the snow,
And to the sleeping flowery below,
  The early bluebirds sing.
Fling wide the grain; we give the fields
  The ears that nod in summer's gale,
The shining stems that summer gilds,
  The harvest that o'erflows the vale,
And swells, an amber sea, between
The full-leaved woods, its shores of green.
Hark! from the murmuring clods I hear
Glad voices of the coming year;
The song of him who binds the grain,
The shout of those that load the wain,
And from the distant grange there comes
  The clatter of the thresher's flail,
And steadily the millstone hums
  Down in the willowy vale.

III.

Fling wide the golden shower; we trust
The strength of armies to the dust.
This peaceful lea may haply yield
Its harvest for the tented field.
Ha! feel ye not your fingers thrill,
  As o'er them, in the yellow grains,
Glide the warm drops of blood that fill,
  For mortal strife, the warrior's veins;
Such as, on Solferino's day,
Slaked the brown sand and flowed away—
Flowed till the herds, on Mincio's brink,
Snuffed the red stream and feared to drink;—
Blood that in deeper pools shall lie,
  On the sad earth, as time grows gray,
When men by deadlier arts shall die,
And deeper darkness blot the sky
  Above the thundering fray;
And realms, that hear the battle-cry,
  Shall sicken with dismay;
And chieftains to the war shall lead
Whole nations, with the tempest's speed,
  To perish in a day; —
Till man, by love and mercy taught,
Shall rue the wreck his fury wrought,
  And lay the sword away!
Oh strew, with pausing, shuddering hand,
The seed upon the helpless land,
As if, at every step, ye cast
The pelting hail and riving blast.

IV.

Nay, strew, with free and joyous sweep,
  The seed upon the expecting soil;
For hence the plenteous year shall heap
  The garners of the men who toil.

Strew the bright seed for those who tear
The matted sward with spade and share,
And those whose sounding axes gleam
Beside the lonely forest-stream,
   Till its broad banks lie bare;
And him who breaks the quarry-ledge,
  With hammer-blows, plied quick and strong,
And him who, with the steady sledge,
  Smites the shrill anvil all day long.
Sprinkle the furrow's even trace
  For those whose toiling hands uprear
The roof-trees of our swarming race,
  By grove and plain, by stream and mere;
Who forth, from crowded city, lead
  The lengthening street, and overlay
Green orchard-plot and grassy mead
  With pavement of the murmuring way.
Cast, with full hands the harvest cast,
For the brave men that climb the mast,
When to the billow and the blast
  It swings and stoops, with fearful strain,
And bind the fluttering mainsail fast,
  Till the tossed bark shall sit, again,
  Safe as a sea-bird on the main.

V.

Fling wide the grain for those who throw
The clanking shuttle to and fro,
In the long row of humming rooms,
  And into ponderous masses wind
The web that, from a thousand looms,
  Comes forth to clothe mankind.
Strew, with free sweep, the grain for them,
  By whom the busy thread
Along the garment's even hem
  And winding seam is led;
A pallid sisterhood, that keep
  The lonely lamp alight,
In strife with weariness and sleep,
  Beyond the middle night.
Large part be theirs in what the year
Shall ripen for the reaper here.

VI.

Still, strew, with joyous hand, the wheat
On the soft mould beneath our feet,
  For even now I seem
To hear a sound that lightly rings
From murmuring harp and viol's strings,
  As in a summer dream.
The welcome of the wedding-guest,
  The bridegroom's look of bashful pride,
  The faint smile of the pallid bride,
And bridemaid's blush at matron's jest,

And dance and song and generous dower,
Are in the shining grains we shower.

VII.

Scatter the wheat for shipwrecked men,
Who, hunger-worn, rejoice again
  In the sweet safety of the shore,
And wanderers, lost in woodlands drear,
Whose pulses bound with joy to hear
  The herd's light bell once more.
  Freely the golden spray be shed
For him whose heart, when night comes down
On the close alleys of the town,
  Is faint for lack of bread.
In chill roof-chambers, bleak and bare,
Or the damp cellar's stifling air,
She who now sees, in mute despair,
    Her children pine for food,
Shall feel the dews of gladness start
To lids long tearless, and shall part
The sweet loaf with a grateful heart,
    Among her thin pale brood.
Dear, kindly Earth, whose breast we till!
Oh, for thy famished children, fill,
    Where'er the sower walks,
Fill the rich ears that shade the mould
With grain for grain, a hundredfold,
    To bend the sturdy stalks.

VIII.

Strew silently the fruitful seed,
  As softly o'er the tilth ye tread,
For hands that delicately knead
  The consecrated bread—
The mystic loaf that crowns the board.
When, round the table of their Lord,
    Within a thousand temples set,
In memory of the bitter death
Of Him who taught at Nazareth,
    His followers are met,
And thoughtful eyes with tears are wet,
  As of the Holy One they think,
The glory of whose rising yet
  Makes bright the grave's mysterious brink.

IX.

  Brethren, the sower's task is done.
The seed is in its winter bed.
Now let the dark-brown mould be spread,
  To hide it from the sun,
And leave it to the kindly care
Of the still earth and brooding air,
As when the mother, from her breast,

Lays the hushed babe apart to rest,
And shades its eyes, and waits to see
How sweet its waking smile will be.
The tempest now may smite, the sleet
All night on the drowned furrow beat,
And winds that, from the cloudy hold,
Of winter breathe the bitter cold,
Stiffen to stone the mellow mould,
   Yet safe shall lie the wheat;
Till, out of heaven's unmeasured blue,
  Shall walk again the genial year,
To wake with warmth and nurse with dew
  The germs we lay to slumber here.

X.

Oh blessed harvest yet to be!
  Abide thou with the Love that keeps,
In its warm bosom, tenderly,
  The Life which wakes and that which sleeps.
The Love that leads the willing spheres
Along the unending track of years,
And watches o'er the sparrow's nest,
Shall brood above thy winter rest,
And raise thee from the dust, to hold
  Light whisperings with the winds of May,
And fill thy spikes with living gold,
  From summer's yellow ray;
Then, as thy garners give thee forth,
  On what glad errands shalt thou go,
Wherever, o'er the waiting earth,
  Roads wind and rivers flow!
The ancient East shall welcome thee
To mighty marts beyond the sea,
And they who dwell where palm-groves sound
To summer winds the whole year round,
Shall watch, in gladness, from the shore,
The sails that bring thy glistening store.

******

THE NEW AND THE OLD.

New are the leaves on the oaken spray,
  New the blades of the silky grass;
Flowers, that were buds but yesterday,
  Peep from the ground where'er I pass.

These gay idlers, the butterflies,
  Broke, to-day, from their winter shroud;
These light airs, that winnow the skies,
  Blow, just born, from the soft, white cloud.

Gushing fresh in the little streams,
  What a prattle the waters make!
Even the sun, with his tender beams,

Seems as young as the flowers they wake.

Children are wading, with cheerful cries,
  In the shoals of the sparkling brook;
Laughing maidens, with soft, young eyes,
  Walk or sit in the shady nook.

What am I doing, thus alone,
  In the glory of Nature here,
Silver-haired, like a snow-flake thrown
  On the greens of the springing year?

Only for brows unploughed by care,
  Eyes that glisten with hope and mirth,
Cheeks unwrinkled, and unblanched hair,
  Shines this holiday of the earth.

Under the grass, with the clammy clay,
  Lie in darkness the last year's flowers,
Born of a light that has passed away,
  Dews long dried and forgotten showers.

"Under the grass is the fitting home,"
  So they whisper, "for such as thou,
When the winter of life is come,
  Chilling the blood, and frosting the brow."

~~~~~~******~~~~~~

THE CLOUD ON THE WAY.

See, before us, in our journey, broods a mist upon the ground;
Thither leads the path we walk in, blending with that gloomy bound.
Never eye hath pierced its shadows to the mystery they screen;
Those who once have passed within it never more on earth are seen.
Now it seems to stoop beside us, now at seeming distance lowers,
Leaving banks that tempt us onward bright with summer-green and flowers.
Yet it blots the way forever; there our journey ends at last;
Into that dark cloud we enter, and are gathered to the past.
Thou who, in this flinty pathway, leading through a stranger-land,
Passest down the rocky valley, walking with me hand in hand,
Which of us shall be the soonest folded to that dim Unknown?
Which shall leave the other walking in this flinty path alone?
Even now I see thee shudder, and thy cheek is white with fear,
And thou clingest to my side as comes that darkness sweeping near.
"Here," thou sayst, "the path is rugged, sown with thorns that wound the feet;
But the sheltered glens are lovely, and the rivulet's song is sweet;
Roses breathe from tangled thickets; lilies bend from ledges brown;
Pleasantly between the pelting showers the sunshine gushes down;
Dear are those who walk beside us, they whose looks and voices make
All this rugged region cheerful, till I love it for their sake.
Far be yet the hour that takes me where that chilly shadow lies,
From the things I know and love, and from the sight of loving eyes!"
So thou murmurest, fearful one; but see, we tread a rougher way;
Fainter glow the gleams of sunshine that upon the dark rocks play;
Rude winds strew the faded flowers upon the crags o'er which we pass;

Banks of verdure, when we reach them, hiss with tufts of withered grass.
One by one we miss the voices which we loved so well to hear;
One by one the kindly faces in that shadow disappear.
Yet upon the mist before us fix thine eyes with closer view;
See, beneath its sullen skirts, the rosy morning glimmers through.
One whose feet the thorns have wounded passed that barrier and came back,
With a glory on His footsteps lighting yet the dreary track.
Boldly enter where He entered; all that seems but darkness here,
When thou once hast passed beyond it, haply shall be crystal-clear.
Viewed from that serener realm, the walks of human life may lie,
Like the page of some familiar volume, open to thine eye;
Haply, from the o'erhanging shadow, thou mayst stretch an unseen hand,
To support the wavering steps that print with blood the rugged land.
Haply, leaning o'er the pilgrim, all unweeting thou art near,
Thou mayst whisper words of warning or of comfort in his ear
Till, beyond the border where that brooding mystery bars the sight,
Those whom thou hast fondly cherished stand with thee in peace and light.

~~~~******~~~~

THE TIDES.

The moon is at her full, and, riding high,
  Floods the calm fields with light;
The airs that hover in the summer-sky
  Are all asleep to-night.

There comes no voice from the great woodlands round
  That murmured all the day;
Beneath the shadow of their boughs the ground
  Is not more still than they.

But ever heaves and moans the restless Deep;
  His rising tides I hear,
Afar I see the glimmering billows leap;
  I see them breaking near.

Each wave springs upward, climbing toward the fair
  Pure light that sits on high—
Springs eagerly, and faintly sinks, to where
  The mother-waters lie.

Upward again it swells; the moonbeams show
  Again its glimmering crest;
Again it feels the fatal weight below,
  And sinks, but not to rest.

Again and yet again; until the Deep
  Recalls his brood of waves;
And, with a sullen moan, abashed, they creep
  Back to his inner caves.

Brief respite! they shall rush from that recess
  With noise and tumult soon,
And fling themselves, with unavailing stress,
  Up toward the placid moon.

O restless Sea, that, in thy prison here,
    Dost struggle and complain;
Through the slow centuries yearning to be near
    To that fair orb in vain;

The glorious source of light and heat must warm
    Thy billows from on high,
And change them to the cloudy trains that form
    The curtain of the sky.

Then only may they leave the waste of brine
    In which they welter here,
And rise above the hills of earth, and shine
    In a serener sphere.

******

ITALY.

Voices from the mountains speak,
  Apennines to Alps reply;
Vale to vale and peak to peak
  Toss an old-remembered cry:
      "Italy
      Shall be free!"
Such the mighty shout that fills
All the passes of her hills.

All the old Italian lakes
  Quiver at that quickening word;
Como with a thrill awakes;
  Garda to her depths is stirred;
      Mid the steeps
      Where he sleeps,
Dreaming of the elder years,
Startled Thrasymenus hears.

Sweeping Arno, swelling Po,
  Murmur freedom to their meads.
Tiber swift and Liris slow
  Send strange whispers from their reeds.
      "Italy
      Shall be free!"
Sing the glittering brooks that slide,
Toward the sea, from Etna's side.

Long ago was Gracchus slain;
  Brutus perished long ago;
Yet the living roots remain
  Whence the shoots of greatness grow;
      Yet again,
      Godlike men,
Sprung from that heroic stem,
Call the land to rise with them.

They who haunt the swarming street,
  They who chase the mountain-boar,
Or, where cliff and billow meet,
  Prune the vine or pull the oar,
      With a stroke
      Break their yoke;
Slaves but yestereve were they—
Freemen with the dawning day.

Looking in his children's eyes,
  While his own with gladness flash,
"These," the Umbrian father cries,
  "Ne'er shall crouch beneath the lash!
      These shall ne'er
      Brook to wear
Chains whose cruel links are twined
Round the crushed and withering mind."

Monarchs! ye whose armies stand
  Harnessed for the battle-field!
Pause, and from the lifted hand
  Drop the bolts of war ye wield.
      Stand aloof
      While the proof
Of the people's might is given;
Leave their kings to them and Heaven!

Stand aloof, and see the oppressed
  Chase the oppressor, pale with fear,
As the fresh winds of the west
  Blow the misty valleys clear.
      Stand and see
      Italy
Cast the gyves she wears no more
To the gulfs that steep her shore.

~~~~~******~~~~~

A DAY-DREAM.

A day-dream by the dark-blue deep;
  Was it a dream, or something more?
I sat where Posilippo's steep,
  With its gray shelves, o'erhung the shore.

On ruined Roman walls around
  The poppy flaunted, for 'twas May;
And at my feet, with gentle sound,
  Broke the light billows of the bay.

I sat and watched the eternal flow
  Of those smooth billows toward the shore,
While quivering lines of light below
  Ran with them on the ocean-floor:

Till, from the deep, there seemed to rise

194

White arms upon the waves outspread,
 Young faces, lit with soft blue eyes,
And smooth, round cheeks, just touched with red.

Their long, fair tresses, tinged with gold,
 Lay floating on the ocean-streams,
And such their brows as bards behold—
 Love-stricken bards—in morning dreams.

Then moved their coral lips; a strain
 Low, sweet and sorrowful, I heard,
As if the murmurs of the main
 Were shaped to syllable and word.

"The sight thou dimly dost behold,
 Oh, stranger from a distant sky!
Was often, in the days of old,
 Seen by the clear, believing eye.

"Then danced we on the wrinkled sand,
 Sat in cool caverns by the sea,
Or wandered up the bloomy land,
 To talk with shepherds on the lea.

"To us, in storms, the seaman prayed,
 And where our rustic altars stood,
His little children came and laid
 The fairest flowers of field and wood.

"Oh woe, a long, unending woe!
 For who shall knit the ties again
That linked the sea-nymphs, long ago,
 In kindly fellowship with men?

"Earth rears her flowers for us no more;
 A half-remembered dream are we;
Unseen we haunt the sunny shore,
 And swim, unmarked, the glassy sea.

"And we have none to love or aid,
 But wander, heedless of mankind,
With shadows by the cloud-rack made,
 With moaning wave and sighing wind.

"Yet sometimes, as in elder days,
 We come before the painter's eye,
Or fix the sculptor's eager gaze,
 With no profaner witness nigh.

"And then the words of men grow warm
 With praise and wonder, asking where
The artist saw the perfect form
 He copied forth in lines so fair."

As thus they spoke, with wavering sweep
 Floated the graceful forms away;

Dimmer and dimmer, through the deep,
  I saw the white arms gleam and play.

Fainter and fainter, on mine ear,
  Fell the soft accents of their speech,
Till I, at last, could only hear
  The waves run murmuring up the beach.

<div align="center">~~~~~******~~~~~</div>

THE RUINS OF ITALICA. [39]

FROM THE SPANISH OF RIOJA.

I.

Fabius, this region, desolate and drear,
  These solitary fields, this shapeless mound,
  Were once Italica, the far-renowned;
For Scipio, the mighty, planted here
His conquering colony, and now, o'erthrown,
Lie its once-dreaded walls of massive stone,
    Sad relics, sad and vain,
    Of those invincible men
    Who held the region then.
Funereal memories alone remain
  Where forms of high example walked of yore.
Here lay the forum, there arose the fane—
  The eye beholds their places, and no more.
Their proud gymnasium and their sumptuous baths
Resolved to dust and cinders, strew the paths;
Their towers, that looked defiance at the sky,
Fallen by their own vast weight, in fragments lie.

II.

This broken circus, where the rock-weeds climb,
  Flaunting with yellow blossoms, and defy
  The gods to whom its walls were piled so high,
Is now a tragic theatre, where Time
Acts his great fable, spreads a stage that shows
Past grandeur's story and its dreary close.
    Why, round this desert pit,
    Shout not the applauding rows
    Where the great people sit?
Wild beasts are here, but where the combatant;
  With his bare arms, the strong athleta where?
All have departed from this once gay haunt
  Of noisy crowds, and silence holds the air.

---

[39] The poems of the Spanish author, Francisco de Rioja, who lived in the first half of the seventeenth century, are few in number, but much esteemed. His ode on the Ruins of Italica is one of the most admired of these, but in the only collection of his poems which have seen, it is said that the concluding stanza, in the original copy, was deemed so little worthy of the rest that it was purposely omitted in the publication. Italica was a city founded by the Romans in the south of Spain, the remains of which are still an object of interest.

Yet, on this spot, Time gives us to behold
A spectacle as stern as those of old.
As dreamily I gaze, there seem to rise,
From all the mighty ruin, wailing cries.

III.

The terrible in war, the pride of Spain,
  Trajan, his country's father, here was born;
Good, fortunate, triumphant, to whose reign
  Submitted the far regions, where the morn
Rose from her cradle, and the shore whose steeps
O'erlooked the conquered Gaditanian deeps.
    Of mighty Adrian here,
    Of Theodosius, saint,
    Of Silius, Virgil's peer,
Were rocked the cradles, rich with gold, and quaint
With ivory carvings; here were laurel-boughs
And sprays of jasmine gathered for their brows,
  From gardens now a marshy, thorny waste.
Where rose the palace, reared for Caesar, yawn
  Foul rifts to which the scudding lizards haste.
Palaces, gardens, Caesars, all are gone,
And even the stones their names were graven on.

IV.

Fabius, if tears prevent thee not, survey
  The long-dismantled streets, so thronged of old,
The broken marbles, arches in decay,
  Proud statues, toppled from their place and rolled
In dust, when Nemesis, the avenger, came,
  And buried, in forgetfulness profound,
    The owners and their fame.
    Thus Troy, I deem, must be,
    With many a mouldering mound;
And thou, whose name alone remains to thee,
Rome, of old gods and kings the native ground;
And thou, sage Athens, built by Pallas, whom
Just laws redeemed not from the appointed doom.
The envy of earth's cities once wert thou—
A weary solitude and ashes now!
For Fate and Death respect ye not; they strike
The mighty city and the wise alike.

V.

But why goes forth the wandering thought to frame
  New themes of sorrow, sought in distant lands?
  Enough the example that before me stands;
For here are smoke-wreaths seen, and glimmering flame,
And hoarse lamentings on the breezes die;
So doth the mighty ruin cast its spell
    On those who near it dwell.
    And under night's still sky,
    As awe-struck peasants tell,

A melancholy voice is heard to cry,
  "Italica is fallen!" the echoes then
  Mournfully shout "Italica" again.
The leafy alleys of the forest nigh
  Murmur "Italica," and all around,
  A troop of mighty shadows, at the sound
Of that illustrious name, repeat the call,
"Italica!" from ruined tower and wall.

~~~~~~******~~~~~~

WAITING BY THE GATE

Beside a massive gateway built up in years gone by,
Upon whose top the clouds in eternal shadow lie,
While streams the evening sunshine on quiet wood and lea,
I stand and calmly wait till the hinges turn for me.

The tree-tops faintly rustle beneath the breeze's flight,
A soft and soothing sound, yet it whispers of the night;
I hear the wood-thrush piping one mellow descant more,
And scent the flowers that blow when the heat of day is o'er.

Behold, the portals open, and o'er the threshold, now,
There steps a weary one with a pale and furrowed brow;
His count of years is full, his allotted task is wrought;
He passes to his rest from a place that needs him not.

In sadness then I ponder how quickly fleets the hour
Of human strength and action, man's courage and his power.
I muse while still the wood-thrush sings down the golden day,
And as I look and listen the sadness wears away.

Again the hinges turn, and a youth, departing, throws
A look of longing backward, and sorrowfully goes;
A blooming maid, unbinding the roses from her hair,
Moves mournfully away from amid the young and fair.

O glory of our race that so suddenly decays!
O crimson flush of morning that darkens as we gaze!
O breath of summer blossoms that on the restless air
Scatters a moment's sweetness, and flies we know not where!

I grieve for life's bright promise, just shown and then withdrawn;
But still the sun shines round me: the evening bird sings on,
And I again am soothed, and, beside the ancient gate,
In this soft evening sunlight, I calmly stand and wait.

Once more the gates are opened; an infant group go out,
The sweet smile quenched forever, and stilled the sprightly shout.
O frail, frail tree of Life, that upon the greensward strows
Its fair young buds unopened, with every wind that blows!

So come from every region, so enter, side by side,
The strong and faint of spirit, the meek and men of pride.
Steps of earth's great and mighty, between those pillars gray,

And prints of little feet, mark the dust along the way.

And some approach the threshold whose looks are blank with fear,
And some whose temples brighten with joy in drawing near,
As if they saw dear faces, and caught the gracious eye
Of Him, the Sinless Teacher, who came for us to die.

I mark the joy, the terror; yet these, within my heart,
Can neither wake the dread nor the longing to depart;
And, in the sunshine streaming on quiet wood and lea,
I stand and calmly wait till the hinges turn for me.

******

NOT YET.

Oh country, marvel of the earth!
  Oh realm to sudden greatness grown!
The age that gloried in thy birth,
  Shall it behold thee overthrown?
Shall traitors lay that greatness low?
No, land of Hope and Blessing, No!

And we, who wear thy glorious name,
  Shall we, like cravens, stand apart,
When those whom thou hast trusted aim
  The death-blow at thy generous heart?
Forth goes the battle-cry, and lo!
Hosts rise in harness, shouting, No!

And they who founded, in our land,
  The power that rules from sea to sea,
Bled they in vain, or vainly planned
  To leave their country great and free?
Their sleeping ashes, from below,
Send up the thrilling murmur, No!

Knit they the gentle ties which long
  These sister States were proud to wear,
And forged the kindly links so strong
  For idle hands in sport to tear?
For scornful hands aside to throw?
No, by our fathers' memory, No!

Our humming marts, our iron ways,
  Our wind-tossed woods on mountain-crest,
The hoarse Atlantic, with its bays,
  The calm, broad Ocean of the West,
And Mississippi's torrent-flow,
And loud Niagara, answer, No!

Not yet the hour is nigh when they
  Who deep in Eld's dim twilight sit,
Earth's ancient kings, shall rise and say,
  "Proud country, welcome to the pit!
So soon art thou, like us, brought low!"

No, sullen group of shadows, No!

For now, behold, the arm that gave
  The victory in our fathers' day,
Strong, as of old, to guard and save—
  That mighty arm which none can stay--
On clouds above and fields below,
Writes, in men's sight, the answer, No!

July, 1861.

~~~~********~~~~

OUR COUNTRY'S CALL.

Lay down the axe; fling by the spade;
  Leave in its track the toiling plough;
The rifle and the bayonet-blade
  For arms like yours were fitter now;
And let the hands that ply the pen
  Quit the light task, and learn to wield
The horseman's crooked brand, and rein
  The charger on the battle-field.

Our country calls; away! away!
  To where the blood-stream blots the green.
Strike to defend the gentlest sway
  That Time in all his course has seen.
See, from a thousand coverts—see,
  Spring the armed foes that haunt her track;
They rush to smite her down, and we
  Must beat the banded traitors back.

Ho! sturdy as the oaks ye cleave,
  And moved as soon to fear and flight,
Men of the glade and forest! leave
  Your woodcraft for the field of fight.
The arms that wield the axe must pour
  An iron tempest on the foe;
His serried ranks shall reel before
  The arm that lays the panther low.

And ye, who breast the mountain-storm
  By grassy steep or highland lake,
Come, for the land ye love, to form
  A bulwark that no foe can break.
Stand, like your own gray cliffs that mock
  The whirlwind, stand in her defence;
The blast as soon shall move the rock
  As rushing squadrons bear ye thence.

And ye, whose homes are by her grand
  Swift rivers, rising far away,
Come from the depth of her green land,
  As mighty in your march as they;
As terrible as when the rains

Have swelled them over bank and bourne
With sudden floods to drown the plains
 And sweep along the woods uptorn.

And ye, who throng, beside the deep,
 Her ports and hamlets of the strand,
In number like the waves that leap
 On his long-murmuring marge of sand—
Come like that deep, when, o'er his brim,
 He rises, all his floods to pour,
And flings the proudest barks that swim,
 A helpless wreck, against the shore!

Few, few were they whose swords of old
 Won the fair land in which we dwell;
But we are many, we who hold
 The grim resolve to guard it well.
Strike, for that broad and goodly land,
 Blow after blow, till men shall see
That Might and Right move hand in hand,
 And glorious must their triumph be!

September, 1861.

～～～～＊＊＊＊＊＊～～～～

THE CONSTELLATIONS.

O Constellations of the early night,
That sparkled brighter as the twilight died,
And made the darkness glorious! I have seen
Your rays grow dim upon the horizon's edge,
And sink behind the mountains. I have seen
The great Orion, with his jewelled belt,
That large-limbed warrior of the skies, go down
Into the gloom. Beside him sank a crowd
Of shining ones. I look in vain to find
The group of sister-stars, which mothers love
To show their wondering babes, the gentle Seven.
Along the desert space mine eyes in vain
Seek the resplendent cressets which the Twins
Uplifted in their ever-youthful hands.
The streaming tresses of the Egyptian Queen
Spangle the heavens no more. The Virgin trails
No more her glittering garments through the blue.
Gone! all are gone! and the forsaken Night,
With all her winds, in all her dreary wastes,
Sighs that they shine upon her face no more
 Now only here and there a little star
Looks forth alone. Ah me! I know them not,
Those dim successors of the numberless host
That filled the heavenly fields, and flung to earth
Their quivering fires. And now the middle watch
Betwixt the eve and morn is past, and still
The darkness gains upon the sky, and still
It closes round my way. Shall, then, the Night

Grow starless in her later hours? Have these
No train of flaming watchers, that shall mark
Their coming and farewell? O Sons of Light!
Have ye then left me ere the dawn of day
To grope along my journey sad and faint?
  Thus I complained, and from the darkness round
A voice replied—was it indeed a voice,
Or seeming accents of a waking dream
Heard by the inner ear? But thus it said:
O Traveller of the Night! thine eyes are dim
With watching; and the mists, that chill the vale
Down which thy feet are passing, hide from view
The ever-burning stars. It is thy sight
That is so dark, and not the heavens. Thine eyes,
Were they but clear, would see a fiery host
Above thee; Hercules, with flashing mace,
The Lyre with silver chords, the Swan uppoised
On gleaming wings, the Dolphin gliding on
With glistening scales, and that poetic steed,
With beamy mane, whose hoof struck out from earth
The fount of Hippocrene, and many more,
Fair clustered splendors, with whose rays the Night
Shall close her march in glory, ere she yield,
To the young Day, the great earth steeped in dew.
  So spake the monitor, and I perceived
How vain were my repinings, and my thought
Went backward to the vanished years and all
The good and great who came and passed with them,
And knew that ever would the years to come
Bring with them, in their course, the good and great,
Lights of the world, though, to my clouded sight,
Their rays might seem but dim, or reach me not.

<center>~~~~~~******~~~~~~</center>

THE THIRD OF NOVEMBER, 1861.

Softly breathes the west-wind beside the ruddy forest,
  Taking leaf by leaf from the branches where he flies.
Sweetly streams the sunshine, this third day of November,
  Through the golden haze of the quiet autumn skies.

Tenderly the season has spared the grassy meadows,
  Spared the potted flowers that the old world gave the new.
Spared the autumn-rose and the garden's group of pansies,
  Late-blown dandelions and periwinkles blue.

On my cornice linger the ripe black grapes ungathered;
  Children fill the groves with the echoes of their glee,
Gathering tawny chestnuts, and shouting when beside them
  Drops the heavy fruit of the tall black-walnut tree.

Glorious are the woods in their latest gold and crimson,
  Yet our full-leaved willows are in their freshest green.
Such a kindly autumn, so mercifully dealing
  With the growths of summer, I never yet have seen.

Like this kindly season may life's decline come o'er me;
  Past is manhood's summer, the frosty months are here;
Yet be genial airs and a pleasant sunshine left me,
  Leaf, and fruit, and blossom, to mark the closing year!

Dreary is the time when the flowers of earth are withered;
  Dreary is the time when the woodland leaves are cast—
When, upon the hillside, all hardened into iron,
  Howling, like a wolf, flies the famished northern blast.

Dreary are the years when the eye can look no longer
  With delight on Nature, or hope on human kind;
Oh, may those that whiten my temples, as they pass me,
  Leave the heart unfrozen, and spare the cheerful mind!

******

THE MOTHER'S HYMN.

Lord, who ordainest for mankind
  Benignant toils and tender cares!
We thank Thee for the ties that bind
  The mother to the child she bears.

We thank Thee for the hopes that rise,
  Within her heart, as, day by day,
The dawning soul, from those young eyes,
  Looks, with a clearer, steadier ray.

And grateful for the blessing given
  With that dear infant on her knee,
She trains the eye to look to heaven,
  The voice to lisp a prayer to Thee.

Such thanks the blessed Mary gave,
  When, from her lap, the Holy Child,
Sent from on high to seek and save
  The lost of earth, looked up and smiled.

All-Gracious! grant, to those that bear
  A mother's charge, the strength and light
To lead the steps that own their care
  In ways of Love, and Truth, and Right.

******

SELLA. [40]

Hear now a legend of the days of old—
The days when there were goodly marvels yet,

---

[40] Sella is the name given by the Vulgate to one of the wives of Lamech, mentioned in the fourth chapter of the Book of Genesis, and called Zillah in the corn-won English version of the Bible.

203

When man to man gave willing faith, and loved
A tale the better that 'twas wild and strange.
  Beside a pleasant dwelling ran a brook
Scudding along a narrow channel, paved
With green and yellow pebbles; yet full clear
Its waters were, and colorless and cool,
As fresh from granite rocks. A maiden oft
Stood at the open window, leaning out,
And listening to the sound the water made,
A sweet, eternal murmur, still the same,
And not the same; and oft, as spring came on,
She gathered violets from its fresh moist bank,
To place within her bower, and when the herbs
Of summer drooped beneath the mid-day sun,
She sat within the shade of a great rock,
Dreamily listening to the streamlet's song.
  Ripe were the maiden's years; her stature showed
Womanly beauty, and her clear, calm eye
Was bright with venturous spirit, yet her face
Was passionless, like those by sculptor graved
For niches in a temple. Lovers oft
Had wooed her, but she only laughed at love,
And wondered at the silly things they said.
'Twas her delight to wander where wild-vines
O'erhang the river's brim, to climb the path
Of woodland streamlet to its mountain-springs,
To sit by gleaming wells and mark below
The image of the rushes on its edge,
And, deep beyond, the trailing clouds that slid
Across the fair blue space. No little fount
Stole forth from hanging rock, or in the side
Of hollow dell, or under roots of oak;
No rill came trickling, with a stripe of green,
Down the bare hill, that to this maiden's eye
Was not familiar. Often did the banks
Of river or of sylvan lakelet hear
The dip of oars with which the maiden rowed
Her shallop, pushing ever from the prow
A crowd of long, light ripples toward the shore.
  Two brothers had the maiden, and she thought,
Within herself: "I would I were like them;
For then I might go forth alone, to trace
The mighty rivers downward to the sea,
And upward to the brooks that, through the year,
Prattle to the cool valleys. I would know
What races drink their waters; how their chiefs
Bear rule, and how men worship there, and how
They build, and to what quaint device they frame,
Where sea and river meet, their stately ships;
What flowers are in their gardens, and what trees
Bear fruit within their orchards; in what garb
Their bowmen meet on holidays, and how
Their maidens bind the waist and braid the hair.
Here, on these hills, my father's house o'erlooks
Broad pastures grazed by flocks and herds, but there
I hear they sprinkle the great plains with corn

And watch its springing up, and when the green
Is changed to gold, they cut the stems and bring
The harvest in, and give the nations bread.
And there they hew the quarry into shafts,
And pile up glorious temples from the rock,
And chisel the rude stones to shapes of men.
All this I pine to see, and would have seen,
But that I am a woman, long ago."
  Thus in her wanderings did the maiden dream,
Until, at length, one morn in early spring,
When all the glistening fields lay white with frost,
She came half breathless where her mother sat:
"See, mother dear," she said, "what I have found,
Upon our rivulet's bank; two slippers, white
As the midwinter snow, and spangled o'er
With twinkling points, like stars, and on the edge
My name is wrought in silver; read, I pray,
Sella, the name thy mother, now in heaven,
Gave at my birth; and sure, they fit my feet!"
"A dainty pair," the prudent matron said,
"But thine they are not. We must lay them by
For those whose careless hands have left them here;
Or haply they were placed beside the brook
To be a snare. I cannot see thy name
Upon the border—only characters
Of mystic look and dim are there, like signs
Of some strange art; nay, daughter, wear them not."
  Then Sella hung the slippers in the porch
Of that broad rustic lodge, and all who passed
Admired their fair contexture, but none knew
Who left them by the brook. And now, at length,
May, with her flowers and singing birds, had gone,
And on bright streams and into deep wells shone
The high, midsummer sun. One day, at noon,
Sella was missed from the accustomed meal.
They sought her in her favorite haunts, they looked
By the great rock and far along the stream,
And shouted in the sounding woods her name.
Night came, and forth the sorrowing household went
With torches over the wide pasture-grounds,
To pool and thicket, marsh and briery dell,
And solitary valley far away.
The morning came, and Sella was not found.
The sun climbed high; they sought her still; the noon,
The hot and silent noon, heard Sella's name,
Uttered with a despairing cry, to wastes
O'er which the eagle hovered. As the sun
Stooped toward the amber west to bring the close
Of that sad second day, and, with red eyes,
The mother sat within her home alone,
Sella was at her side. A shriek of joy
Broke the sad silence; glad, warm tears were shed,
And words of gladness uttered. "Oh, forgive,"
The maiden said, "that I could e'er forget
Thy wishes for a moment. I just tried
The slippers on, amazed to see them shaped

So fairly to my feet, when, all at once,
I felt my steps upborne and hurried on
Almost as if with wings. A strange delight,
Blent with a thrill of fear, o'er mastered me,
And, ere I knew, my splashing steps were set
Within the rivulet's pebbly bed, and I
Was rushing down the current. By my side
Tripped one as beautiful as ever looked
From white clouds in a dream; and, as we ran,
She talked with musical voice and sweetly laughed.
Gayly we leaped the crag and swam the pool,
And swept with dimpling eddies round the rock,
And glided between shady meadow-banks.
The streamlet, broadening as we went, became
A swelling river, and we shot along
By stately towns, and under leaning masts
Of gallant barks, nor lingered by the shore
Of blooming gardens; onward, onward still,
The same strong impulse bore me, till, at last,
We entered the great deep, and passed below
His billows, into boundless spaces, lit
With a green sunshine. Here were mighty groves
Far down the ocean-valleys, and between
Lay what might seem fair meadows, softly tinged
With orange and with crimson. Here arose
Tall stems, that, rooted in the depths below,
Swung idly with the motions of the sea;
And here were shrubberies in whose mazy screen
The creatures of the deep made haunt. My friend
Named the strange growths, the pretty coralline,
The dulse with crimson leaves, and, streaming far,
Sea-thong and sea-lace. Here the tangle spread
Its broad, thick fronds, with pleasant bowers beneath;
And oft we trod a waste of pearly sands,
Spotted with rosy shells, and thence looked in
At caverns of the sea whose rock-roofed halls
Lay in blue twilight. As we moved along,
The dwellers of the deep, in mighty herds,
Passed by us, reverently they passed us by,
Long trains of dolphins rolling through the brine,
Huge whales, that drew the waters after them,
A torrent-stream, and hideous hammer-sharks,
Chasing their prey. I shuddered as they came;
Gently they turned aside and gave us room."
  Hereat broke in the mother: "Sella dear,
This is a dream, the idlest, vainest dream."
  "Nay, mother, nay; behold this sea-green scarf,
Woven of such threads as never human hand
Twined from the distaff. She who led my way
Through the great waters, bade me wear it home,
A token that my tale is true. 'And keep,'
She said, 'the slippers thou hast found, for thou,
When shod with them, shalt be like one of us,
With power to walk at will the ocean-floor,
Among its monstrous creatures, unafraid,
And feel no longing for the air of heaven

To fill thy lungs, and send the warm, red blood
Along thy veins. But thou shalt pass the hours
In dances with the sea-nymphs, or go forth,
To look into the mysteries of the abyss
Where never plummet reached. And thou shalt sleep
Thy weariness away on downy banks
Of sea-moss, where the pulses of the tide
Shall gently lift thy hair, or thou shalt float
On the soft currents that go forth and wind
From isle to isle, and wander through the sea.'
   "So spake my fellow-voyager, her words
Sounding like wavelets on a summer shore,
And then we stopped beside a hanging rock,
With a smooth beach of white sands at its foot,
Where three fair creatures like herself were set
At their sea-banquet, crisp and juicy stalks,
Culled from the ocean's meadows, and the sweet
Midrib of pleasant leaves, and golden fruits
Dropped from the trees that edge the southern isles,
And gathered on the waves. Kindly they prayed
That I would share their meal, and *I* partook
With eager appetite, for long had been
My journey, and I left the spot refreshed.
   "And then we wandered off amid the groves
Of coral loftier than the growths of earth;
The mightiest cedar lifts no trunk like theirs,
So huge, so high toward heaven, nor overhangs
Alleys and bowers so dim. We moved between
Pinnacles of black rock, which, from beneath,
Molten by inner fires, so said my guide,
Gushed long ago into the hissing brine,
That quenched and hardened them, and now they stand
Motionless in the currents of the sea
That part and flow around them. As we went,
We looked into the hollows of the abyss,
To which the never-resting waters sweep
The skeletons of sharks, the long white spines
Of narwhal and of dolphin, bones of men
Shipwrecked, and mighty ribs of foundered barks.
Down the blue pits we looked, and hastened on.
   "But beautiful the fountains of the sea
Sprang upward from its bed: the silvery jets
Shot branching far into the azure brine,
And where they mingled with it, the great deep
Quivered and shook, as shakes the glimmering air
Above a furnace. So we wandered through
The mighty world of waters, till at length
I wearied of its wonders, and my heart
Began to yearn for my dear mountain-home.
I prayed my gentle guide to lead me back
To the upper air. 'A glorious realm,' I said,
'Is this thou openest to me; but I stray
Bewildered in its vastness; these strange sights
And this strange light oppress me. I must see
The faces that I love, or I shall die.'
   "She took my hand, and, darting through the waves

Brought me to where the stream, by which we came,
Rushed into the main ocean. Then began
A slower journey upward. Wearily
We breasted the strong current, climbing through
The rapids, tossing high their foam. The night
Came down, and in the clear depth of a pool,
Edged with o'erhanging rock, we took our rest
Till morning; and I slept, and dreamed of home
And thee. A pleasant sight the morning showed;
The green fields of this upper world, the herds
That grazed the bank, the light on the red clouds,
The trees, with all their host of trembling leaves,
Lifting and lowering to the restless wind
Their branches. As I woke, I saw them all
From the clear stream; yet strangely was my heart
Parted between the watery world and this,
And as we journeyed upward, oft I thought
Of marvels I had seen, and stopped and turned,
And lingered, till I thought of thee again;
And then again I turned and clambered up
The rivulet's murmuring path, until we came
Beside the cottage-door. There tenderly
My fair conductor kissed me, and I saw
Her face no more. I took the slippers off.
Oh! with what deep delight my lungs drew in
The air of heaven again, and with what joy
I felt my blood bound with its former glow;
And now I never leave thy side again!"
    So spoke the maiden Sella, with large tears
Standing in her mild eyes, and in the porch
Replaced the slippers. Autumn came and went;
The winter passed; another summer warmed
The quiet pools; another autumn tinged
The grape with red, yet while it hung unplucked,
The mother ere her time was carried forth
To sleep among the solitary hills.
    A long, still sadness settled on that home
Among the mountains. The stern father there
Wept with his children, and grew soft of heart,
And Sella, and the brothers twain, and one
Younger than they, a sister fair and shy,
Strewed the new grave with flowers, and round it set
Shrubs that all winter held their lively green.
Time passed; the grief with which their hearts were wrung
Waned to a gentle sorrow. Sella, now,
Was often absent from the patriarch's board;
The slippers hung no longer in the porch;
And sometimes after summer nights her couch
Was found unpressed at dawn, and well they knew
That she was wandering with the race who make
Their dwelling in the waters. Oft her looks
Fixed on blank space, and oft the ill-suited word
Told that her thoughts were far away. In vain
Her brothers reasoned with her tenderly:
"Oh leave not thus thy kindred!" so they prayed;
"Dear Sella, now that she who gave us birth

Is in her grave, oh go not hence, to seek
Companions in that strange cold realm below,
For which God made not us nor thee, but stay
To be the grace and glory of our home."
She looked at them with those mild eyes and wept,
But said no word in answer, nor refrained
From those mysterious wanderings that filled
Their loving hearts with a perpetual pain.

   And now the younger sister, fair and shy,
Had grown to early womanhood, and one
Who loved her well had wooed her for his bride,
And she had named the wedding-day. The herd
Had given its fatlings for the marriage-feast;
The roadside garden and the secret glen
Were rifled of their sweetest flowers to twine
The door-posts, and to lie among the locks
Of maids, the wedding-guests, and from the boughs
Of mountain-orchards had the fairest fruit
Been plucked to glisten in the canisters.

   Then, trooping over hill and valley, came
Matron and maid, grave men and smiling youths,
Like swallows gathering for their autumn flight,
In costumes of that simpler age they came,
That gave the limbs large play, and wrapped the form
In easy folds, yet bright with glowing hues
As suited holidays. All hastened on
To that glad bridal. There already stood
The priest prepared to say the spousal rite,
And there the harpers in due order sat,
And there the singers. Sella, midst them all,
Moved strangely and serenely beautiful,
With clear blue eyes, fair locks, and brow and cheek
Colorless as the lily of the lakes,
Yet moulded to such shape as artists give
To beings of immortal youth. Her hands
Had decked her sister for the bridal hour
With chosen flowers, and lawn whose delicate threads
Vied with the spider's spinning. There she stood
With such a gentle pleasure in her looks
As might beseem a river-nymph's soft eyes
Gracing a bridal of the race whose flocks
Were pastured on the borders of her stream.

   She smiled, but from that calm sweet face the smile
Was soon to pass away. That very morn
The elder of the brothers, as he stood
Upon the hillside, had beheld the maid,
Emerging from the channel of the brook,
With three fresh water-lilies in her hand,
Wring dry her dripping locks, and in a cleft
Of hanging rock, beside a screen of boughs,
Bestow the spangled slippers. None before
Had known where Sella hid them. Then she laid
The light-brown tresses smooth, and in them twined
The lily-buds, and hastily drew forth
And threw across her shoulders a light robe
Wrought for the bridal, and with bounding steps

Ran toward the lodge. The youth beheld and marked
The spot and slowly followed from afar.
  Now had the marriage-rite been said; the bride
Stood in the blush that from her burning cheek
Glowed down the alabaster neck, as morn
Crimsons the pearly heaven half-way to the west.
At once the harpers struck their chords; a gush
Of music broke upon the air; the youths
All started to the dance. Among them moved
The queenly Sella with a grace that seemed
Caught from the swaying of the summer sea.
The young drew forth the elders to the dance,
Who joined it half abashed, but when they felt
The joyous music tingling in their veins,
They called for quaint old measures, which they trod
As gayly as in youth, and far abroad
Came through the open windows cheerful shouts
And bursts of laughter. They who heard the sound
Upon the mountain footpaths paused and said,
"A merry wedding." Lovers stole away
That sunny afternoon to bowers that edged
The garden-walks, and what was whispered there
The lovers of these later times can guess.
  Meanwhile the brothers, when the merry din
Was loudest, stole to where the slippers lay,
And took them thence, and followed down the brook
To where a little rapid rushed between
Its borders of smooth rock, and dropped them in.
The rivulet, as they touched its face, flung up
Its small bright waves like hands, and seemed to take
The prize with eagerness and draw it down.
They, gleaming through the waters as they went,
And striking with light sound the shining stones,
Slid down the stream. The brothers looked and watched,
And listened with full beating hearts, till now
The sight and sound had passed, and silently
And half repentant hastened to the lodge.
  The sun was near his set; the music rang
Within the dwelling still, but the mirth waned;
For groups of guests were sauntering toward their homes
Across the fields, and far, on hillside paths,
Gleamed the white robes of maidens. Sella grew
Weary of the long merriment; she thought
Of her still haunts beneath the soundless sea,
And all unseen withdrew and sought the cleft
Where she had laid the slippers. They were gone!
She searched the brookside near, yet found them not.
Then her heart sank within her, and she ran
Wildly from place to place, and once again
She searched the secret cleft, and next she stooped
And with spread palms felt carefully beneath
The tufted herbs and bushes, and again,
And yet again, she searched the rocky cleft.
"Who could have taken them?" That question cleared
The mystery. She remembered suddenly
That when the dance was in its gayest whirl,

Her brothers were not seen, and when, at length,
They reappeared, the elder joined the sports
With shouts of boisterous mirth, and from her eye
The younger shrank in silence. "Now, I know
The guilty ones," she said, and left the spot,
And stood before the youths with such a look
Of anguish and reproach that well they knew
Her thought, and almost wished the deed undone.
   Frankly they owned the charge: "And pardon us;
We did it all in love; we could not bear
That the cold world of waters and the strange
Beings that dwell within it should beguile
Our sister from us." Then they told her all;
How they had seen her stealthily bestow
The slippers in the cleft, and how by stealth
They took them thence and bore them down the brook,
And dropped them in, and how the eager waves
Gathered and drew them down; but at that word
The maiden shrieked—a broken-hearted shriek—
And all who heard it shuddered and turned pale
At the despairing cry, and "They are gone,"
She said, "gone—gone forever! Cruel ones!
'Tis you who shut me out eternally
From that serener world which I had learned
To love so well. Why took ye not my life?
Ye cannot know what ye have done!" She spake
And hurried to her chamber, and the guests
Who yet had lingered silently withdrew.
   The brothers followed to the maiden's bower,
But with a calm demeanor, as they came,
She met them at the door. "The wrong is great,"
She said, "that ye have done me, but no power
Have ye to make it less, nor yet to soothe
My sorrow; I shall bear it as I may,
The better for the hours that I have passed
In the calm region of the middle sea.
Go, then. I need you not." They, overawed,
Withdrew from that grave presence. Then her tears
Broke forth a flood, as when the August cloud,
Darkening beside the mountain, suddenly
Melts into streams of rain. That weary night
She paced her chamber, murmuring as she walked,
"O peaceful region of the middle sea!
O azure bowers and grots, in which I loved
To roam and rest! Am I to long for you,
And think how strangely beautiful ye are,
Yet never see you more? And dearer yet,
Ye gentle ones in whose sweet company
I trod the shelly pavements of the deep,
And swam its currents, creatures with calm eyes
Looking the tenderest love, and voices soft
As ripple of light waves along the shore,
Uttering the tenderest words! Oh! ne'er again
Shall I, in your mild aspects, read the peace
That dwells within, and vainly shall I pine
To hear your sweet low voices. Haply now

Ye miss me in your deep-sea home, and think
Of me with pity, as of one condemned
To haunt this upper world, with its harsh sounds
And glaring lights, its withering heats, its frosts,
Cruel and killing, its delirious strifes,
And all its feverish passions, till I die."
  So mourned she the long night, and when the morn
Brightened the mountains, from her lattice looked
The maiden on a world that was to her
A desolate and dreary waste. That day
She passed in wandering by the brook that oft
Had been her pathway to the sea, and still
Seemed, with its cheerful murmur, to invite
Her footsteps thither. "Well mayst thou rejoice,
Fortunate stream!" she said, "and dance along
Thy bed, and make thy course one ceaseless strain
Of music, for thou journeyest toward the deep,
To which I shall return no more." The night
Brought her to her lone chamber, and she knelt
And prayed, with many tears, to Him whose hand
Touches the wounded heart and it is healed.
With prayer there came new thoughts and new desires.
She asked for patience and a deeper love
For those with whom her lot was henceforth cast,
And that in acts of mercy she might lose
The sense of her own sorrow. When she rose
A weight was lifted from her heart. She sought
Her couch, and slept a long and peaceful sleep.
At morn she woke to a new life. Her days
Henceforth were given to quiet tasks of good
In the great world. Men hearkened to her words,
And wondered at their wisdom and obeyed,
And saw how beautiful the law of love
Can make the cares and toils of daily life.
  Still did she love to haunt the springs and brooks
As in her cheerful childhood, and she taught
The skill to pierce the soil and meet the veins
Of clear cold water winding underneath,
And call them forth to daylight. From afar
She bade men bring the rivers on long rows
Of pillared arches to the sultry town,
And on the hot air of the summer fling
The spray of dashing fountains. To relieve
Their weary hands, she showed them how to tame
The rushing stream, and make him drive the wheel
That whirls the humming millstone and that wields
The ponderous sledge. The waters of the cloud,
That drench the hillside in the time of rains,
Were gathered, at her bidding, into pools,
And in the months of drought led forth again,
In glimmering rivulets, to refresh the vales,
Till the sky darkened with returning showers.
  So passed her life, a long and blameless life,
And far and near her name was named with love
And reverence. Still she kept, as age came on,
Her stately presence; still her eyes looked forth

From under their calm brows as brightly clear
As the transparent wells by which she sat
So oft in childhood. Still she kept her fair
Unwrinkled features, though her locks were white.
A hundred times had summer, since her birth,
Opened the water-lily on the lakes,
So old traditions tell, before she died.
A hundred cities mourned her, and her death
Saddened the pastoral valleys. By the brook,
That bickering ran beside the cottage-door
Where she was born, they reared her monument.
Ere long the current parted and flowed round
The marble base, forming a little isle,
And there the flowers that love the running stream,
Iris and orchis, and the cardinal-flower,
Crowded and hung caressingly around
The stone engraved with Sella's honored name.

~~~~~~******~~~~~~

THE FIFTH BOOK OF HOMER'S ODYSSEY. [41]

TRANSLATED.

Aurora, rising from her couch beside
The famed Tithonus, brought the light of day
To men and to immortals. Then the gods
Came to their seats in council. With them came
High-thundering Jupiter, among them all
The mightiest. Pallas, mindful of the past,
Spoke of Ulysses and his many woes,
Grieved that he still was with the island-nymph.
    "Oh, father Jove, and all ye blessed ones
Who live forever! let not sceptred king,
Henceforth, be gracious, mild, and merciful,
And righteous; rather be he deaf to prayer,
And prone to deeds of wrong, since no one now
Remembers the divine Ulysses more
Among the people over whom he ruled,
Benignly, like a father. Still he lies,
Weighed down by many sorrows, in the isle
And dwelling of Calypso, who so long
Constrains his stay. To his dear native land

---

[41]
    It may be esteemed presumptuous in the author of this volume to attempt a translation of any part of Homer in blank verse after that of Cowper. It has always seemed to him, however, that Cowper's version had very great defects. The style of Homer is simple, and he has been praised for fire and rapidity of narrative. Does anybody find these qualities in Cowper's Homer? If Cowper had rendered him into such English as he employed in his "Task," there would be no reason to complain; but in translating Homer he seems to have thought it necessary to use a different style from that of his original work. Almost every sentence is stiffened by some clumsy inversion; stately phrases are used when simpler ones were at hand, and would have rendered the meaning of the original better. The entire version has the appearance of being hammered out with great labor, and as a whole it is cold and constrained; scarce any thing seems spontaneous; it is only now and then that the translator has caught the fervor of his author. Homer, of course, wrote in idiomatic Greek, and, in order to produce either a true copy of the original, or an agreeable poem, should have been translated into idiomatic English.
    I am almost ashamed, after this censure of an author whom, in the main, I admire as much as I do Cowper, to refer to my own translation of the Fifth Book of the Odyssey. I desire barely to say that I have endeavored to give the verses of the old Greek poet at least a simpler presentation in English, and one more conformable to the genius of our language.

Depart he cannot; ship, arrayed with oars,
And seamen has he none, to bear him o'er
The breast of the broad ocean. Nay, even now,
Against his well-beloved son a plot
Is laid, to slay him as he journeys home
From Pylos the divine, and from the walls
Of famous Sparta, whither he had gone
To gather tidings of his father's fate."
   Then answered her the ruler of the storms:
"My child, what words are these that pass thy lips?
Was not thy long-determined counsel this,
That, in good time, Ulysses should return,
To be avenged? Guide, then, Telemachus,
Wisely, for thou canst, that, all unharmed,
He reach his native land, and, in their barks,
Homeward the suitor-train retrace their way."
   He spake, and turned to Hermes, his dear son:
"Hermes, for thou, in this, my messenger
Art, as in all things, to the bright-haired nymph
Make known my steadfast purpose, the return
Of suffering Ulysses. Neither gods
Nor men shall guide his voyage. On a raft,
Made firm with bands, he shall depart and reach,
After long hardships, on the twentieth day,
The fertile shore of Scheria, on whose isle
Dwell the Pheacians, kinsmen of the gods.
They like a god shall honor him, and thence
Send him to his loved country in a ship,
With ample gifts of brass and gold, and store
Of raiment—wealth like which he ne'er had brought
From conquered Ilion, had he reached his home
Safely, with all his portion of the spoil.
So is it preordained, that he behold
His friends again, and stand once more within
His high-roofed palace, on his native soil."
   He spake; the herald Argicide obeyed,
And hastily beneath his feet he bound
The fair, ambrosial, golden sandals, worn
To bear him over ocean like the wind,
And o'er the boundless land. His wand he took,
Wherewith he softly seals the eyes of men,
And opens them at will from sleep. With this
In hand, the mighty Argos-queller flew,
And lighting on Pieria, from the sky
Plunged downward to the deep, and skimmed its face
Like hovering sea-mew, that on the broad gulfs
Of the unfruitful ocean seeks her prey,
And often dips her pinions in the brine.
So Hermes flew along the waste of waves.
   But when he reached that island, far away,
Forth from the dark-blue ocean-swell he stepped
Upon the sea-beach, walking till he came
To the vast cave in which the bright-haired nymph
Made her abode. He found the nymph within.
A fire blazed brightly on the hearth, and far
Was wafted o'er the isle the fragrant smoke

214

Of cloven cedar, burning in the flame,
And cypress-wood. Meanwhile, in her recess,
She sweetly sang, as busily she threw
The golden shuttle through the *web* she wove.
And all about the grotto alders grew,
And poplars, and sweet-smelling cypresses,
In a green forest, high among whose boughs
Birds of broad wing, wood-owls and falcons, built
Their nests, and crows, with voices sounding far,
All haunting for their food the ocean-side.
A vine, with downy leaves and clustering grapes,
Crept over all the cavern-rock. Four springs
Poured forth their glittering waters in a row,
And here and there went wandering side by side.
Around were meadows of soft green, o'ergrown
With violets and parsley. 'Twas a spot
Where even an Immortal might, awhile,
Linger, and gaze with wonder and delight.
The herald Argos-queller stood, and saw,
And marvelled: but as soon as he had viewed
The wonders of the place, he turned his steps,
Entering the broad-roofed cave. Calypso there,
The glorious goddess, saw him as he came,
And knew him, for the ever-living gods
Are to each other known, though one may dwell
Far from the rest. Ulysses, large of heart,
Was not within. Apart, upon the shore,
He sat and sorrowed, where he oft, in tears
And sighs and vain repinings, passed the hours,
Gazing with wet eyes on the barren deep.
Now, placing Hermes on a shining seat
Of state, Calypso, glorious goddess, said:
  "Thou of the golden wand, revered and loved,
What, Hermes, brings thee hither? Passing few
Have been thy visits. Make thy pleasure known,
My heart enjoins me to obey, if aught
That thou commandest be within my power.
But first accept the offerings due a guest."
  The goddess, speaking thus, before him placed
A table where the heaped ambrosia lay,
And mingled the red nectar. Ate and drank
The herald Argos-queller, and, refreshed,
Answered the nymph, and made his message known:
  "Art thou a goddess, and dost ask of me,
A god, why came I hither? Yet, since thou
Requirest, I will truly tell the cause.
I came unwillingly at Jove's command,
For who, of choice, would traverse the wide waste
Of the salt ocean, with no city near,
Where men adore the gods with solemn rites
And chosen hecatombs? No god has power
To elude or to resist the purposes
Of aegis-bearing Jove. With thee abides,
He bids me say, the most unhappy man
Of all who round the city of Priam waged
The battle through nine years, and, in the tenth,

Laying it waste, departed for their homes.
But in their voyage, they provoked the wrath
Of Pallas, who called up the furious winds
And angry waves against them. By his side
Sank all his gallant comrades in the deep.
Him did the winds and waves drive hither. Him
Jove bids thee send away with speed, for here
He must not perish, far from all he loves.
So is it preordained that he behold
His friends again, and stand once more within
His high-roofed palace, on his native soil."
  He spoke; Calypso, glorious goddess, heard,
And shuddered, and with winged words replied:
  "Ye are unjust, ye gods, and, envious far
Beyond all other beings, cannot bear
That ever goddess openly should make
A mortal man her consort. Thus it was
When once Aurora, rosy-fingered, took
Orion for her husband; ye were stung,
Amid your blissful lives, with envious hate,
Till chaste Diana, of the golden throne,
Smote him with silent arrows from her bow,
And slew him in Ortygia. Thus, again,
When bright-haired Ceres, swayed by her own heart,
In fields which bore three yearly harvests, met
Iasion as a lover, this was known
Ere long to Jupiter, who flung from high
A flaming thunderbolt, and laid him dead.
And now ye envy me, that with me dwells
A mortal man. I saved him, as he clung,
Alone, upon his floating keel, for Jove
Had cloven, with a bolt of fire from heaven,
His galley in the midst of the black sea,
And all his gallant comrades perished there.
Him kindly I received; I cherished him,
And promised him a life that ne'er should know
Decay or death. But, since no god has power
To elude or to withstand the purposes
Of aegis-bearing Jove, let him depart,
If so the sovereign moves him and commands,
Over the barren deep. I send him not;
For neither ship arrayed with oars have I,
Nor seamen, o'er the boundless waste of waves
To bear him hence. My counsel I will give,
And nothing will I hide that he should know,
To place him safely on his native shore."
  The herald Argos-queller answered her:
"Dismiss him thus, and bear in mind the wrath
Of Jove, lest it be kindled against thee."
  Thus having said, the mighty Argicide
Departed, and the nymph, who now had heard
The doom of Jove, sought the great-hearted man,
Ulysses. Him she found beside the deep,
Seated alone, with eyes from which the tears
Were never dried, for now no more the nymph
Delighted him; he wasted his sweet life

In yearning for his home. Night after night
He slept constrained within the hollow cave,
The unwilling by the fond, and, day by day,
He sat upon the rocks that edged the shore,
And in continual weeping and in sighs
And vain repinings, wore the hours away,
Gazing through tears upon the barren deep.
The glorious goddess stood by him and spoke:
  "Unhappy! sit no longer sorrowing here,
Nor waste life thus. Lo! I most willingly
Dismiss thee hence. Rise, hew down trees, and bind
Their trunks, with brazen clamps, into a raft,
And fasten planks above, a lofty floor,
That it may bear thee o'er the dark-blue deep.
Bread will I put on board, water, and wine,
Red wine, that cheers the heart, and wrap thee well
In garments, and send after thee the wind,
That safely thou attain thy native shore;
If so the gods permit thee, who abide
In the broad heaven above, and better know
By far than I, and far more wisely judge."
  Ulysses, the great sufferer, as she spoke,
Shuddered, and thus with winged words replied:
"Some other purpose than to send me home
Is in thy heart, oh goddess, bidding me
To cross this frightful sea upon a raft,
This perilous sea, where never even ships
Pass with their rapid keels, though Jove bestow
The wind that glads the seamen. Nay, I climb
No raft, against thy wish, unless thou swear
The great oath of the gods, that thou, in this,
Dost meditate no other harm to me."
  He spake; Calypso, glorious goddess, smiled,
And smoothed his forehead with her hand, and said:
  "Perverse! and slow to see where guile is not!
How could thy heart permit thee thus to speak?
Now bear me witness, Earth, and ye broad Heavens
Above us, and ye waters of the Styx
That flow beneath us, mightiest oath of all,
And most revered by all the blessed gods,
That I design no other harm to thee;
But that I plan for thee and counsel thee
What I would do were I in need like thine.
I bear a juster mind; my bosom holds
A pitying heart, and not a heart of steel."
  Thus having said, the glorious goddess moved
Away with hasty steps, and where she trod
He followed, till they reached the vaulted cave,
The goddess and the hero. There he took
The seat whence Hermes had just risen. The nymph
Brought forth whatever mortals eat and drink
To set before him. She, right opposite
To that of Ulysses, took her seat,
Ambrosia there her maidens laid, and there
Poured nectar. Both put forth their hands, and took
The ready viands, till at length the calls

Of hunger and of thirst were satisfied;
Calypso, glorious goddess, then began:
  "Son of Laertes, man of many wiles,
High-born Ulysses! Thus wilt thou depart
Home to thy native country? Then farewell;
But, couldst thou know the sufferings Fate ordains
For thee ere yet thou landest on its shore,
Thou wouldst remain to keep this home with me,
And be immortal, strong as is thy wish
To see thy wife—a wish that, day by day,
Possesses thee. I cannot deem myself
In form or face less beautiful than she;
For never with immortals can the race
Of mortal dames in form or face compare."
  Ulysses, the sagacious, answered her:
"Bear with me, gracious goddess; well I know
All thou couldst say. The sage Penelope
In feature and in stature comes not nigh
To thee; for she is mortal, deathless thou
And ever young; yet, day by day, I long
To be at home once more, and pine to see
The hour of my return. Even though some god
Smite me on the black ocean, I shall bear
The stroke, for in my bosom dwells a mind
Patient of suffering; much have I endured,
And much survived, in tempests on the deep,
And in the battle; let this happen too."
  He spoke; the sun went down; the night came on,
And now the twain withdrew to a recess
Deep in the vaulted cave, where, side by side,
They took their rest. But when the child of dawn,
Aurora, rosy-fingered, looked abroad,
Ulysses put his vest and mantle on;
The nymph too, in a robe of silver white,
Ample, and delicate, and beautiful,
Arrayed herself, and round about her loins
Wound a fair golden girdle, drew a veil
Over her head, and planned to send away
Magnanimous Ulysses. She bestowed
A heavy axe, of steel, and double-edged,
Well fitted to the hand, the handle wrought
Of olive-wood, firm set and beautiful.
A polished adze she gave him next, and led
The way to a far corner of the isle,
Where lofty trees, alders and poplars, stood,
And firs that reach the clouds, sapless and dry
Long since, and fitter thus to ride the waves.
Then, having shown where grew the tallest trees,
Calypso, glorious goddess, sought her home.
  Trees then he felled, and soon the task was done.
Twenty in all he brought to earth, and squared
Their trunks with the sharp steel, and carefully
He smoothed their sides, and wrought them by a line.
Calypso, gracious goddess, having brought
Wimbles, he bored the beams, and, fitting them
Together, made them fast with nails and clamps.

As when some builder, skillful in his art,
Frames, for a ship of burden, the broad keel,
Such ample breadth Ulysses gave the raft.
Upon the massy beams he reared a deck,
And floored it with long planks from end to end.
On this a mast he raised, and to the mast
Fitted a yard; he shaped a rudder next,
To guide the raft along her course, and round
With woven work of willow-boughs he fenced
Her sides against the dashings of the sea.
Calypso, gracious goddess, brought him store
Of canvas, which he fitly shaped to sails,
And, rigging her with cords, and ropes, and stays,
Heaved her with levers into the great deep.
    'Twas the fourth day; his labors now were done,
And, on the fifth, the goddess from her isle
Dismissed him, newly from the bath, arrayed
In garments given by her, that shed perfumes.
A skin of dark-red wine she put on board,
A larger one of water, and for food
A basket, stored with viands such as please
The appetite. A friendly wind and soft
She sent before. The great Ulysses spread
His canvas joyfully, to catch the breeze,
And sat and guided with nice care the helm,
Gazing with fixed eye on the Pleiades,
Booetes setting late, and the Great Bear,
By others called the Wain, which, wheeling round,
Looks ever toward Orion, and alone
Dips not into the waters of the deep.
For so Calypso, glorious goddess, bade
That, on his ocean journey, he should keep
That constellation ever on his left.
Now seventeen days were in the voyage past,
And on the eighteenth shadowy heights appeared,
The nearest point of the Pheacian land,
Lying on the dark ocean like a shield.
    But mighty Neptune, coming from among
The Ethiopians, saw him. Far away
He saw, from mountain-heights of Solyma,
The voyager, and burned with fiercer wrath,
And shook his head, and said within himself:
    "Strange! now I see the gods have new designs
For this Ulysses, formed while I was yet
In Ethiopia. He draws near the land
Of the Pheacians, where it is decreed
He shall o'erpass the boundary of his woes;
But first, I think, he will have much to bear."
    He spoke, and round about him called the clouds
And roused the ocean, wielding in his hand
The trident, summoned all the hurricanes
Of all the winds, and covered earth and sky
At once with mists, while from above, the night
Fell suddenly. The east wind and the south
Rushed forth at once, with the strong-blowing west,
And the clear north rolled up his mighty waves.

Ulysses trembled in his knees and heart,
And thus to his great soul, lamenting, said:
  "What will become of me? unhappy man!
I fear that all the goddess said was true,
Foretelling what disasters should o'ertake
My voyage, ere I reach my native land.
Now are her words fulfilled. Now Jupiter
Wraps the great heaven in clouds and stirs the deep
To tumult! Wilder grow the hurricanes
Of all the winds, and now my fate is sure.
Thrice happy, four times happy they, who fell
On Troy's wide field, warring for Atreus' sons:
O, had I met my fate and perished there,
That very day on which the Trojan host,
Around the dead Achilles, hurled at me
Their brazen javelins! I had then received
Due burial and great glory with the Greeks;
Now must I die a miserable death."
  As thus he spoke, upon him, from on high,
A huge and frightful billow broke; it whirled
The raft around, and far from it he fell.
His hands let go the rudder; a fierce rush
Of all the winds together snapped in twain
The mast; far off the yard and canvas flew
Into the deep; the billow held him long
Beneath the waters, and he strove in vain
Quickly to rise to air from that huge swell
Of ocean, for the garments weighed him down
Which fair Calypso gave him. But, at length,
Emerging, he rejected from his throat
The bitter brine that down his forehead streamed.
Even then, though hopeless with dismay, his thought
Was on the raft, and, struggling through the waves,
He seized it, sprang on board, and seated there
Escaped the threatened death. Still to and fro
The rolling billows drove it. As the wind
In autumn sweeps the thistles o'er the field,
Clinging together, so the blasts of heaven
Hither and thither drove it o'er the sea.
And now the south wind flung it to the north
To buffet; now the east wind to the west.
  Ino Leucothea saw him clinging there,
The delicate-footed child of Cadmus, once
A mortal, speaking with a mortal voice;
Though now within the ocean-gulfs, she shares
The honors of the gods. With pity she
Beheld Ulysses struggling thus distressed,
And, rising from the abyss below, in form
A cormorant, the sea-nymph took her perch
On the well-banded raft, and thus she said:
  "Ah, luckless man, how hast thou angered thus
Earth-shaking Neptune, that he visits thee
With these disasters? Yet he cannot take,
Although he seek it earnestly, thy life.
Now do my bidding, for thou seemest wise.
Laying aside thy garments, let the raft

Drift with the winds, while thou, by strength of arm,
Makest thy way in swimming to the land
Of the Pheacians, where thy safety lies.
Receive this veil and bind its heavenly woof
Beneath thy breast, and have no further fear
Of hardship or of danger. But, as soon
As thou shalt touch the island, take it off,
And turn away thy face, and fling it far
From where thou standest, into the black deep."

  The goddess gave the veil as thus she spoke,
And to the tossing deep went down, in form
A cormorant; the black wave covered her.
But still Ulysses, mighty sufferer,
Pondered, and thus to his great soul he said:

  "Ah me! perhaps some god is planning here
Some other fraud against me, bidding me
Forsake my raft. I will not yet obey,
For still far off I see the land in which
'Tis said my refuge lies. This will I do,
For this seems wisest. While the fastenings last
That hold these timbers, I will keep my place
And bide the tempest here. But when the waves
Shall dash my raft in pieces, I will swim,
For nothing better will remain to do."

  As he revolved this purpose in his mind,
Earth-shaking Neptune sent a mighty wave,
Horrid, and huge, and high, and where he sat
It smote him. As a violent wind uplifts
The dry chaff heaped upon a threshing-floor,
And sends it scattered through the air abroad,
So did that wave fling loose the ponderous beams.
To one of these, Ulysses, clinging fast,
Bestrode it, like a horseman on his steed;
And now he took the garments off, bestowed
By fair Calypso, binding round his breast
The veil, and forward plunged into the deep,
With palms outspread, prepared to swim. Meanwhile,
Neptune beheld him, Neptune, mighty king,
And shook his head, and said within himself:

  "Go thus, and, laden with mischances, roam
The waters, till thou come among the race
Cherished by Jupiter; but well I deem
Thou wilt not find thy share of suffering light."

  Thus having spoke, he urged his coursers on,
With their fair-flowing manes, until he came
To AEgae, where his glorious palace stands.

  But Pallas, child of Jove, had other thoughts.
She stayed the course of every wind beside,
And bade them rest, and lulled them into sleep,
But summoned the swift north to break the waves,
That so Ulysses, the high-born, escaped
From death and from the fates, might be the guest
Of the Pheacians, men who love the sea.

  Two days and nights, among the mighty waves
He floated, oft his heart foreboding death,
But when the bright-haired Eos had fulfilled

The third day's course, and all the winds were laid,
And calm was on the watery waste, he saw
The land was near, as, lifted on the crest
Of a huge swell, he looked with sharpened sight;
And as a father's life preserved makes glad
His children's hearts, when long time he has lain
Sick, wrung with pain, and wasting by the power
Of some malignant genius, till, at length,
The gracious gods bestow a welcome cure;
So welcome to Ulysses was the sight
Of woods and fields. By swimming on he thought
To climb and tread the shore, but when he drew
So near that one who shouted could be heard
From land, the sound of ocean on the rocks
Came to his ear, for there huge breakers roared
And spouted fearfully, and all around
Was covered with the sea-foam. Haven here
Was none for ships, nor sheltering creek, but shores
Beetling from high, and crags and walls of rock.
Ulysses trembled both in knees and heart,
And thus, to his great soul, lamenting, said:
  "Now woe is me! as soon as Jove has shown
What I had little hoped to see, the land,
And I through all these waves have ploughed my way,
I find no issue from the hoary deep.
For sharp rocks border it, and all around
Roar the wild surges; slippery cliffs arise
Close to deep gulfs, and footing there is none,
Where I might plant my steps and thus escape.
All effort now were fruitless to resist
The mighty billow hurrying me away
To dash me on the pointed rocks. If yet
I strive, by swimming further, to descry
Some sloping shore or harbor of the isle,
I fear the tempest, lest it hurl me back,
Heavily groaning, to the fishy deep,
Or huge sea-monster, from the multitude
Which sovereign Amphitrite feeds, be sent
Against me by some god, for well I know
The power who shakes the shores is wroth with me."
  While he revolved these doubts within his mind,
A huge wave hurled him toward the rugged coast.
Then had his limbs been flayed, and all his bones
Broken at once, had not the blue-eyed maid,
Minerva, prompted him. Borne toward the rock,
He clutched it instantly, with both his hands,
And panting clung till that huge wave rolled by,
And so escaped its fury. But it came,
And smote him once again, and flung him far
Seaward. As to the claws of polypus,
Plucked from its bed, the pebbles thickly cling,
So flakes of skin, from off his powerful hands,
Were left upon the rock. The mighty surge
O'erwhelmed him; he had perished ere his time,
Hapless Ulysses, but the blue-eyed maid,
Pallas, informed his mind with forecast. Straight

Emerging from the wave that shoreward rolled,
He swam along the coast and eyed it well,
In hope of sloping beach or sheltered creek.
But when, in swimming, he had reached the mouth
Of a soft-flowing river, here appeared
The spot he wished for, smooth, without a rock,
And here was shelter from the wind. He felt
The current's flow, and thus devoutly prayed:
  "Hear me, oh sovereign power, whoe'er thou art!
To thee, the long-desired, I come. I seek
Escape from Neptune's threatenings on the sea.
The deathless gods respect the prayer of him
Who looks to them for help, a fugitive,
As I am now, when to thy stream I come,
And to thy knees, from many a hardship past,
Oh thou that here art ruler, I declare
Myself thy suppliant; be thou merciful."
  He spoke; the river stayed his current, checked
The billows, smoothed them, to a calm, and gave
The swimmer a safe landing at his mouth.
Then dropped his knees and sinewy arms, at once
Unstrung, for faint with struggling was his heart.
His body was all swoln; the brine gushed forth
From mouth and nostrils; all unnerved he lay,
Breathless and speechless; utter weariness
O'ermastered him. But when he breathed again,
And his flown senses had returned, he loosed
The veil that Ino gave him from his breast,
And to the salt flood cast it. A great wave
Bore it far down the stream; the goddess there
In her own hands received it. He, meanwhile,
Withdrawing from the brink, lay down among
The reeds, and kissed the harvest-bearing earth,
And thus to his great soul, lamenting, said:
  "Ah me! what must I suffer more! what yet
Will happen to me? If, by the river's side,
I pass the unfriendly watches of the night,
The cruel cold and dews that steep the bank
May, in this weakness, end me utterly,
For chilly blows the river-air at dawn.
But should I climb this hill, to sleep within
The shadowy wood, among their shrubs, if cold
And weariness allow me, then I fear,
That, while the pleasant slumbers o'er me steal,
I may become the prey of savage beasts."
  Yet, as he longer pondered, this seemed best.
He rose and sought the wood, and found it near
The water, on a height, o'erlooking far
The region round. Between two shrubs, that sprung
Both from one spot, he entered—olive-trees,
One wild, one fruitful. The damp-blowing wind
Ne'er pierced their covert; never blazing sun
Darted his beams within, nor pelting shower
Beat through, so closely intertwined they grew.
Here entering, Ulysses heaped a bed
Of leaves with his own hands; he made it broad

And high, for thick the leaves had fallen around.
Two men and three, in that abundant store,
Might bide the winter-storm, though keen the cold.
Ulysses, the great sufferer, on his couch
Looked and rejoiced, and placed himself within,
And heaped the leaves high o'er him and around.
As one who, dwelling in the distant fields,
Without a neighbor near him, hides a brand
In the dark ashes, keeping carefully
The seeds of fire alive, lest he, perforce,
To light his hearth must bring them from afar;
So did Ulysses, in that pile of leaves,
Bury himself, while Pallas o'er his eyes
Poured sleep and closed his lids, that he might take,
After his painful toils, the fitting rest.

<center>~~~~~******~~~~~</center>

THE LITTLE PEOPLE OF THE SNOW.

Alice. —One of your old-world stories, Uncle John,
Such as you tell us by the winter fire,
Till we all wonder it is grown so late.
Uncle John.—The story of the witch that ground to death
Two children in her mill, or will you have
The tale of Goody Cutpurse?
Alice.—Nay now, nay;
Those stories are too childish, Uncle John,
Too childish even for little Willy here,
And I am older, two good years, than he;
No, let us have a tale of elves that ride,
By night, with jingling reins, or gnomes of the mine,
Or water-fairies, such as you know how
To spin, till Willy's eyes forget to wink,
And good Aunt Mary, busy as she is,
Lays down her knitting.
Uncle John.—Listen to me, then.
'Twas in the olden time, long, long ago,
And long before the great oak at our door
Was yet an acorn, on a mountain's side
Lived, with his wife, a cottager. They dwelt
Beside a glen and near a clashing brook,
A pleasant spot in spring, where first the wren
Was heard to chatter, and, among the grass,
Flowers opened earliest; but when winter came,
That little brook was fringed with other flowers, —
White flowers, with crystal leaf and stem, that grew
In clear November nights. And, later still,
That mountain-glen was filled with drifted snows
From side to side, that one might walk across;
While, many a fathom deep, below, the brook
Sang to itself, and leaped and trotted on
Unfrozen, o'er its pebbles, toward the vale.
Alice.—A mountain-side, you said; the Alps, perhaps,
Or our own Alleghanies.
Uncle John.—*Not* so fast,

224

My young geographer, for then the Alps,
With their broad pastures, haply were untrod
Of herdsman's foot, and never human voice
Had sounded in the woods that overhang
Our Alleghany's streams. I think it was
Upon the slopes of the great Caucasus,
Or where the rivulets of Ararat
Seek the Armenian vales. That mountain rose
So high, that, on its top, the winter-snow
Was never melted, and the cottagers
Among the summer-blossoms, far below,
Saw its white peaks in August from their door.
  One little maiden, in that cottage-home,
Dwelt with her parents, light of heart and limb,
Bright, restless, thoughtless, flitting here and there,
Like sunshine on the uneasy ocean-waves,
And sometimes she forgot what she was bid,
As Alice does.
    Alice.—Or Willy, quite as oft.
    Uncle John.—But you are older, Alice, two good years,
And should be wiser. Eva was the name
Of this young maiden, now twelve summers old.
  Now you must know that, in those early times,
When autumn days grew pale, there came a troop
Of childlike forms from that cold mountain-top;
With trailing garments through the air they came,
Or walked the ground with girded loins, and threw
Spangles of silvery frost upon the grass,
And edged the brooks with glistening parapets,
And built it crystal bridges, touched the pool,
And turned its face to glass, or, rising thence,
They shook from their full laps the soft, light snow,
And buried the great earth, as autumn winds
Bury the forest-floor in heaps of leaves.
  A beautiful race were they, with baby brows,
And fair, bright locks, and voices like the sound
Of steps on the crisp snow, in which they talked
With man, as friend with friend. A merry sight
It was, when, crowding round the traveller,
They smote him with their heaviest snow-flakes, flung
Needles of frost in handfuls at his cheeks,
And, of the light wreaths of his smoking breath,
Wove a white fringe for his brown beard, and laughed
Their slender laugh to see him wink and grin
And make grim faces as he floundered on.
  But, when the spring came on, what terror reigned
Among these Little People of the Snow!
To them the sun's warm beams were shafts of fire,
And the soft south-wind was the wind of death.
Away they flew, all with a pretty scowl
Upon their childish faces, to the north,
Or scampered upward to the mountain's top,
And there defied their enemy, the Spring;
Skipping and dancing on the frozen peaks,
And moulding little snow-balls in their palms,
And rolling them, to crush her flowers below,

225

Down the steep snow-fields.

   Alice.—That, too, must have been
A merry sight to look at.

   Uncle John.—You are right,
But I must speak of graver matters now.

  Midwinter was the time, and Eva stood,
Within the cottage, all prepared to dare
The outer cold, with ample furry robe
Close-belted round her waist, and boots of fur,
And a broad kerchief, which her mother's hand
Had closely drawn about her ruddy cheek.
"Now, stay not long abroad," said the good dame,
"For sharp is the outer air, and, mark me well,
Go not upon the snow beyond the spot
Where the great linden bounds the neighboring field."

  The little maiden promised, and went forth,
And climbed the rounded snow-swells firm with frost
Beneath her feet, and slid, with balancing arms,
Into the hollows. Once, as up a drift
She slowly rose, before her, in the way,
She saw a little creature, lily-cheeked,
With flowing flaxen locks, and faint blue eyes,
That gleamed like ice, and robe that only seemed
Of a more shadowy whiteness than her cheek.
On a smooth bank she sat.

   Alice.—She must have been
One of your Little People of the Snow.

   Uncle John.—She was so, and, as Eva now drew near,
The tiny creature bounded from her seat;
"And come," she said, "my pretty friend; to-day
We will be playmates. I have watched thee long,
And seen how well thou lov'st to walk these drifts,
And scoop their fair sides into little cells,
And carve them with quaint figures, huge-limbed men,
Lions, and griffins. We will have, to-day,
A merry ramble over these bright fields,
And thou shalt see what thou hast never seen."
On went the pair, until they reached the bound
Where the great linden stood, set deep in snow,
Up to the lower branches. "Here we stop,"
Said Eva, "for my mother has my word
That I will go no farther than this tree."
Then the snow-maiden laughed: "And what is this?
This fear of the pure snow, the innocent snow,
That never harmed aught living? Thou mayst roam
For leagues beyond this garden, and return
In safety; here the grim wolf never prowls,
And here the eagle of our mountain-crags
Preys not in winter. I will show the way,
And bring thee safely home. Thy mother, sure,
Counselled thee thus because thou hadst no guide."

  By such smooth words was Eva won to break
Her promise, and went on with her new friend,
Over the glistening snow and down a bank
Where a white shelf, wrought by the eddying wind,
Like to a billow's crest in the great sea,

Curtained an opening. "Look, we enter here."
And straight, beneath the fair o'erhanging fold,
Entered the little pair that hill of snow,
Walking along a passage with white walls,
And a white vault above where snow-stars shed
A wintry twilight. Eva moved in awe,
And held her peace, but the snow-maiden smiled,
And talked and tripped along, as down the way,
Deeper they went into that mountainous drift.
    And now the white walls widened, and the vault
Swelled upward, like some vast cathedral-dome,
Such as the Florentine, who bore the name
Of heaven's most potent angel, reared, long since,
Or the unknown builder of that wondrous fane,
The glory of Burgos. Here a garden lay,
In which the Little People of the Snow
Were wont to take their pastime when their tasks
Upon the mountain's side and in the clouds
Were ended. Here they taught the silent frost
To mock, in stem and spray, and leaf and flower,
The growths of summer. Here the palm upreared
Its white columnar trunk and spotless sheaf
Of plume-like leaves; here cedars, huge as those
Of Lebanon, stretched far their level boughs,
Yet pale and shadowless; the sturdy oak
Stood, with its huge gnarled roots of seeming strength,
Fast anchored in the glistening bank; light sprays
Of myrtle, roses in their bud and bloom,
Drooped by the winding walks; yet all seemed wrought
Of stainless alabaster; up the trees
Ran the lithe jessamine, with stalk and leaf
Colorless as her flowers. "Go softly on,"
Said the snow-maiden; "touch not, with thy hand,
The frail creation round thee, and beware
To sweep it with thy skirts. Now look above.
How sumptuously these bowers are lighted up
With shifting gleams that softly come and go!
These are the northern lights, such as thou seest
In the midwinter nights, cold, wandering flames,
That float with our processions, through the air;
And here, within our winter palaces,
Mimic the glorious daybreak." Then she told
How, when the wind, in the long winter nights,
Swept the light snows into the hollow dell,
She and her comrades guided to its place
Each wandering flake, and piled them quaintly up,
In shapely colonnade and glistening arch,
With shadowy aisles between, or bade them grow,
Beneath their little hands, to bowery walks
In gardens such as these, and, o'er them all,
Built the broad roof. "But thou hast yet to see
A fairer sight," she said, and led the way
To where a window of pellucid ice
Stood in the wall of snow, beside their path.
"Look, but thou mayst not enter." Eva looked,
And lo! a glorious hall, from whose high vault

Stripes of soft light, ruddy and delicate green,
And tender blue, flowed downward to the floor
And far around, as if the aerial hosts,
That march on high by night, with beamy spears,
And streaming banners, to that place had brought
Their radiant flags to grace a festival.
  And in that hall a joyous multitude
Of these by whom its glistening walls were reared,
Whirled in a merry dance to silvery sounds,
That rang from cymbals of transparent ice,
And ice-cups, quivering to the skilful touch
Of little fingers. Round and round they flew,
As when, in spring, about a chimney-top,
A cloud of twittering swallows, just returned,
Wheel round and round, and turn and wheel again,
Unwinding their swift track. So rapidly
Flowed the meandering stream of that fair dance,
Beneath that dome of light. Bright eyes that looked
From under lily-brows, and gauzy scarfs
Sparkling like snow-wreaths in the early sun,
Shot by the window in their mazy whirl.
And there stood Eva, wondering at the sight
Of those bright revellers and that graceful sweep
Of motion as they passed her; —long she gazed,
And listened long to the sweet sounds that thrilled
The frosty air, till now the encroaching cold
Recalled her to herself. "Too long, too long
I linger here," she said, and then she sprang
Into the path, and with a hurried step
Followed it upward. Ever by her side
Her little guide kept pace. As on they went,
Eva bemoaned her fault: "What must they think—
The dear ones in the cottage, while so long,
Hour after hour, I stay without? I know
That they will seek me far and near, and weep
To find me not. How could I, wickedly,
Neglect the charge they gave me?" As she spoke,
The hot tears started to her eyes; she knelt
In the mid-path. "Father! forgive this sin;
Forgive myself I cannot"—thus she prayed,
And rose and hastened onward. When, at last,
They reached the outer air, the clear north breathed
A bitter cold, from which she shrank with dread,
But the snow-maiden bounded as she felt
The cutting blast, and uttered shouts of joy,
And skipped, with boundless glee, from drift to drift,
And danced round Eva, as she labored up
The mounds of snow. "Ah me! I feel my eyes
Grow heavy," Eva said; "they swim with sleep;
I cannot walk for utter weariness,
And I must rest a moment on this bank,
But let it not be long." As thus she spoke,
In half formed words, she sank on the smooth snow,
With closing lids. Her guide composed the robe
About her limbs, and said: "A pleasant spot
Is this to slumber in; on such a couch

Oft have I slept away the winter night,
And had the sweetest dreams." So Eva slept,
But slept in death; for when the power of frost
Locks up the motions of the living frame,
The victim passes to the realm of Death
Through the dim porch of Sleep. The little guide,
Watching beside her, saw the hues of life
Fade from the fair smooth brow and rounded cheek,
As fades the crimson from a morning cloud,
Till they were white as marble, and the breath
Had ceased to come and go, yet knew she not
At first that this was death. But when she marked
How deep the paleness was, how motionless
That once lithe form, a fear came over her.
She strove to wake the sleeper, plucked her robe,
And shouted in her ear, but all in vain;
The life had passed away from those young limbs.
Then the snow-maiden raised a wailing cry,
Such as the dweller in some lonely wild,
Sleepless through all the long December night,
Hears when the mournful East begins to blow.
  But suddenly was heard the sound of steps,
Grating on the crisp snow; the cottagers
Were seeking Eva; from afar they saw
The twain, and hurried toward them. As they came
With gentle chidings ready on their lips,
And marked that deathlike sleep, and heard the tale
Of the snow-maiden, mortal anguish fell
Upon their hearts, and bitter words of grief
And blame were uttered: "Cruel, cruel one,
To tempt our daughter thus, and cruel we,
Who suffered her to wander forth alone
In this fierce cold!" They lifted the dear child,
And bore her home and chafed her tender limbs,
And strove, by all the simple arts they knew,
To make the chilled blood move, and win the breath
Back to her bosom; fruitlessly they strove;
The little maid was dead. In blank despair
They stood, and gazed at her who never more
Should look on them. "Why die we not with her?"
They said; "without her, life is bitterness."
  Now came the funeral-day; the simple folk
Of all that pastoral region gathered round
To share the sorrow of the cottagers.
They carved a way into the mound of snow
To the glen's side, and dug a little grave
In the smooth slope, and, following the bier,
In long procession from the silent door,
Chanted a sad and solemn melody:
  "Lay her away to rest within the ground.
Yea, lay her down whose pure and innocent life
Was spotless as these snows; for she was reared
In love, and passed in love life's pleasant spring,
And all that now our tenderest love can do
Is to give burial to her lifeless limbs."
  They paused. A thousand slender voices round,

Like echoes softly flung from rock and hill,
Took up the strain, and all the hollow air
Seemed mourning for the dead; for, on that day,
The Little People of the Snow had come,
From mountain-peak, and cloud, and icy hall,
To Eva's burial. As the murmur died,
The funeral-train renewed the solemn chant:
  "Thou, Lord, hast taken her to be with Eve,
Whose gentle name was given her. Even so,
For so Thy wisdom saw that it was best
For her and us. We bring our bleeding hearts,
And ask the touch of healing from Thy hand,
As, with submissive tears, we render back
The lovely and beloved to Him who gave."
  They ceased. Again the plaintive murmur rose.
From shadowy skirts of low-hung cloud it came,
And wide white fields, and fir-trees capped with snow,
Shivering to the sad sounds. They sank away
To silence in the dim-seen distant woods.
  The little grave was closed; the funeral-train
Departed; winter wore away; the Spring
Steeped, with her quickening rains, the violet-tufts,
By fond hands planted where the maiden slept.
But, after Eva's burial, never more
The Little People of the Snow were seen
By human eye, nor ever human ear
Heard from their lips articulate speech again;
For a decree went forth to cut them off,
Forever, from communion with mankind.
The winter-clouds, along the mountain-side,
Rolled downward toward the vale, but no fair form
Leaned from their folds, and, in the icy glens,
And aged woods, under snow-loaded pines,
Where once they made their haunt, was emptiness.
  But ever, when the wintry days drew near,
Around that little grave, in the long night,
Frost-wreaths were laid and tufts of silvery rime
In shape like blades and blossoms of the field,
As one would scatter flowers upon a bier.

<center>~~~~******~~~~</center>

THE POET.

Thou, who wouldst wear the name
  Of poet mid thy brethren of mankind,
And clothe in words of flame
  Thoughts that shall live within the general mind!
Deem not the framing of a deathless lay
The pastime of a drowsy summer day.

But gather all thy powers,
  And wreak them on the verse that thou dost weave,
And in thy lonely hours,
  At silent morning or at wakeful eve,
While the warm current tingles through thy veins,

230

Set forth the burning words in fluent strains.

No smooth array of phrase,
  Artfully sought and ordered though it be,
Which the cold rhymer lays
  Upon his page with languid industry,
Can wake the listless pulse to livelier speed,
Or fill with sudden tears the eyes that read.

The secret wouldst thou know
  To touch the heart or fire the blood at will?
Let thine own eyes o'erflow;
  Let thy lips quiver with the passionate thrill;
Seize the great thought, ere yet its power be past,
And bind, in words, the fleet emotion fast.

Then, should thy verse appear
  Halting and harsh, and all unaptly wrought,
Touch the crude line with fear,
  Save in the moment of impassioned thought;
Then summon back the original glow, and mend
The strain with rapture that with fire was penned.

Yet let no empty gust
  Of passion find an utterance in thy lay,
A blast that whirls the dust
  Along the howling street and dies away;
But feelings of calm power and mighty sweep,
Like currents journeying through the windless deep.

Seek'st thou, in living lays,
  To limn the beauty of the earth and sky?
Before thine inner gaze
  Let all that beauty in clear vision lie;
Look on it with exceeding love, and write
The words inspired by wonder and delight.

Of tempests wouldst thou sing,
  Or tell of battles—make thyself a part
Of the great tumult; cling
  To the tossed wreck with terror in thy heart;
Scale, with the assaulting host, the rampart's height,
And strike and struggle in the thickest fight.

So shalt thou frame a lay
  That haply may endure from age to age,
And they who read shall say:
  "What witchery hangs upon this poet's page!
What art is his the written spells to find
That sway from mood to mood the willing mind!"

~~~~~******~~~~~

THE PATH.

The path we planned beneath October's sky,

Along the hillside, through the woodland shade,
Is finished; thanks to thee, whose kindly eye
  Has watched me, as I plied the busy spade;
Else had I wearied, ere this path of ours
Had pierced the woodland to its inner bowers.

Yet, 'twas a pleasant toil to trace and beat,
  Among the glowing trees, this winding way,
While the sweet autumn sunshine, doubly sweet,
  Flushed with the ruddy foliage, round us lay,
As if some gorgeous cloud of morning stood,
In glory, mid the arches of the wood.

A path! what beauty does a path bestow
  Even on the dreariest wild! its savage nooks
Seem homelike where accustomed footsteps go,
  And the grim rock puts on familiar looks.
The tangled swamp, through which a pathway strays,
Becomes a garden with strange flowers and sprays.

See from the weedy earth a rivulet break
  And purl along the untrodden wilderness;
There the shy cuckoo comes his thirst to slake,
  There the shrill jay alights his plumes to dress;
And there the stealthy fox, when morn is gray,
Laps the clear stream and lightly moves away.

But let a path approach that fountain's brink,
  And nobler forms of life, behold! are there:
Boys kneeling with protruded lips to drink,
  And slender maids that homeward slowly bear
The brimming pail, and busy dames that lay
Their webs to whiten in the summer ray.

Then know we that for herd and flock are poured
  Those pleasant streams that o'er the pebbles slip;
Those pure sweet waters sparkle on the board;
  Those fresh cool waters wet the sick man's lip;
Those clear bright waters from the font are shed,
In dews of baptism, on the infant's head.

What different steps the rural footway trace!
  The laborer afield at early day;
The schoolboy sauntering with uneven pace;
  The Sunday worshipper in fresh array;
And mourner in the weeds of sorrow drest;
And, smiling to himself, the wedding guest.

There he who cons a speech and he who hums
  His yet unfinished verses, musing walk.
There, with her little brood, the matron comes,
  To break the spring flower from its juicy stalk;
And lovers, loitering, wonder that the moon
Has risen upon their pleasant stroll so soon.

Bewildered in vast woods, the traveller feels

His heavy heart grow lighter, if he meet
The traces of a path, and straight he kneels,
　And kisses the dear print of human feet,
And thanks his God, and journeys without fear,
For now he knows the abodes of men are near.
Pursue the slenderest path across a lawn:
　Lo! on the broad highway it issues forth,
And, blended with the greater track, goes on,
　Over the surface of the mighty earth,
Climbs hills and crosses vales, and stretches far,
Through silent forests, toward the evening star—

And enters cities murmuring with the feet
　Of multitudes, and wanders forth again,
And joins the climes of frost to climes of heat,
　Binds East to West, and marries main to main,
Nor stays till at the long-resounding shore
Of the great deep, where paths are known no more.

Oh, mighty instinct, that dost thus unite
　Earth's neighborhoods and tribes with friendly bands,
What guilt is theirs who, in their greed or spite,
　Undo thy holy work with violent hands,
And post their squadrons, nursed in war's grim trade,
To bar the ways for mutual succor made!

~~~~~******~~~~~

THE RETURN OF THE BIRDS.

I hear, from many a little throat,
　A warble interrupted long;
I hear the robin's flute-like note,
　The bluebird's slenderer song.

Brown meadows and the russet hill,
　Not yet the haunt of grazing herds,
And thickets by the glimmering rill,
　Are all alive with birds.

Oh choir of spring, why come so soon?
　On leafless grove and herbless lawn
Warm lie the yellow beams of moon;
　Yet winter is not gone.

For frost shall sheet the pools again;
　Again the blustering East shall blow—
Whirl a white tempest through the glen,
　And load the pines with snow.

Yet, haply, from the region where,
　Waked by an earlier spring than here,
The blossomed wild-plum scents the air,
　Ye come in haste and fear.

For there is heard the bugle-blast,

The booming gun, the jarring drum,
And on their chargers, spurring fast,
  Armed warriors go and come.

There mighty hosts have pitched the camp
  In valleys that were yours till then,
And Earth has shuddered to the tramp
  Of half a million men!

In groves where once ye used to sing,
  In orchards where ye had your birth,
A thousand glittering axes swing
  To smite the trees to earth.

Ye love the fields by ploughmen trod;
  But there, when sprouts the beechen spray,
The soldier only breaks the sod
  To hide the slain away.

Stay, then, beneath our ruder sky;
  Heed not the storm-clouds rising black,
Nor yelling winds that with them fly;
  Nor let them fright you back,—

Back to the stifling battle-cloud,
  To burning towns that blot the day,
And trains of mounting dust that shroud
  The armies on their way.

Stay, for a tint of green shall creep
  Soon o'er the orchard's grassy floor,
And from its bed the crocus peep
  Beside the housewife's door.

Here build, and dread no harsher sound,
  To scare you from the sheltering tree,
Than winds that stir the branches round,
  And murmur of the bee.

And we will pray that, ere again
  The flowers of autumn bloom and die,
Our generals and their strong-armed men
  May lay their weapons by.

Then may ye warble, unafraid,
  Where hands, that wear the fetter now,
Free as your wings shall ply the spade,
  And guide the peaceful plough.

Then, as our conquering hosts return,
  What shouts of jubilee shall break
From placid vale and mountain stern,
  And shore of mighty lake!

And midland plain and ocean-strand
  Shall thunder: "Glory to the brave,

Peace to the torn and bleeding land,
  And freedom to the slave!"

March, 1864.

~~~~~******~~~~~

"HE HATH PUT ALL THINGS UNDER HIS FEET."

O North, with all thy vales of green!
  O South, with all thy palms!
From peopled towns and fields between
  Uplift the voice of psalms;
Raise, ancient East, the anthem high,
And let the youthful West reply.

Lo! in the clouds of heaven appears
  God's well-beloved Son;
He brings a train of brighter years:
  His kingdom is begun.
He comes, a guilty world to bless
With mercy, truth, and righteousness.

Oh, Father! haste the promised hour
  When, at His feet, shall lie
All rule, authority, and power,
  Beneath the ample sky;
When He shall reign from pole to pole,
The lord of every human soul;

When all shall heed the words He said
  Amid their daily cares,
And, by the loving life He led,
  Shall seek to pattern theirs;
And He, who conquered Death, shall win
The nobler conquest over Sin.

~~~~~******~~~~~

MY AUTUMN WALK.

On woodlands ruddy with autumn
  The amber sunshine lies;
I look on the beauty round me,
  And tears come into my eyes.

For the wind that sweeps the meadows
  Blows out of the far Southwest,
Where our gallant men are fighting,
  And the gallant dead are at rest.

The golden-rod is leaning,
  And the purple aster waves
In a breeze from the land of battles,
  A breath from the land of graves.

235

Full fast the leaves are dropping
  Before that wandering breath;
As fast, on the field of battle,
  Our brethren fall in death.

Beautiful over my pathway
  The forest spoils are shed;
They are spotting the grassy hillocks
  With purple and gold and red.

Beautiful is the death-sleep
  Of those who bravely fight
In their country's holy quarrel,
  And perish for the Right.

But who shall comfort the living,
  The light of whose homes is gone:
The bride that, early widowed,
  Lives broken-hearted on;

The matron whose sons are lying
  In graves on a distant shore;
The maiden, whose promised husband
  Comes back from the war no more?

I look on the peaceful dwellings
  Whose windows glimmer in sight,
With croft and garden and orchard,
  That bask in the mellow light;

And I know that, when our couriers
  With news of victory come,
They will bring a bitter message
  Of hopeless grief to some.

Again I turn to the woodlands,
  And shudder as I see
The mock-grape's blood-red banner[42]
  Hung out on the cedar-tree;

And I think of days of slaughter,
  And the night-sky red with flames,
On the Chattahoochee's meadows,
  And the wasted banks of the James.

Oh, for the fresh spring-season,
  When the groves are in their prime;
And far away in the future
  Is the frosty autumn-time!

Oh, for that better season,

---

[42] *Ampelopis*, mock-grape. I have here literally translated the botanical name of the Virginia creeper—an appellation too cumbro
for verse.

When the pride of the foe shall yield,
  And the hosts of God and Freedom
    March back from the well-won field;

And the matron shall clasp her first-born
  With tears of joy and pride;
And the scarred and war-worn lover
  Shall claim his promised bride!

The leaves are swept from the branches;
  But the living buds are there,
With folded flower and foliage,
  To sprout in a kinder air.

October, 1864.

~~~~~******~~~~~

DANTE.

Who, mid the grasses of the field
  That spring beneath our careless feet,
First found the shining stems that yield
  The grains of life-sustaining wheat:

Who first, upon the furrowed land,
  Strewed the bright grains to sprout, and grow,
And ripen for the reaper's hand—
  We know not, and we cannot know.

But well we know the hand that brought
  And scattered, far as sight can reach,
The seeds of free and living thought
  On the broad field of modern speech.

Mid the white hills that round us lie,
  We cherish that Great Sower's fame,
And, as we pile the sheaves on high,
  With awe we utter Dante's name.

Six centuries, since the poet's birth,
  Have come and flitted o'er our sphere:
The richest harvest reaped on earth
  Crowns the last century's closing year.

1865.

~~~~~******~~~~~

THE DEATH OF LINCOLN.

Oh, slow to smite and swift to spare,
  Gentle and merciful and just!
Who, in the fear of God, didst bear
  The sword of power, a nation's trust!

In sorrow by thy bier we stand,
  Amid the awe that hushes all,
And speak the anguish of a land
  That shook with horror at thy fall.

Thy task is done; the bond are free:
  We bear thee to an honored grave,
Whose proudest monument shall be
  The broken fetters of the slave.

Pure was thy life; its bloody close
  Hath placed thee with the sons of light,
Among the noble host of those
  Who perished in the cause of Right.

April, 1865.

～～～******～～～

THE DEATH OF SLAVERY.

O thou great Wrong, that, through the slow-paced years,
  Didst hold thy millions fettered, and didst wield
  The scourge that drove the laborer to the field,
And turn a stony gaze on human tears,
     Thy cruel reign is o'er;
     Thy bondmen crouch no more
In terror at the menace of thine eye;
  For He who marks the bounds of guilty power,
Long-suffering, hath heard the captive's cry,
  And touched his shackles at the appointed hour,
And lo! they fall, and he whose limbs they galled
Stands in his native manhood, disenthralled.

A shout of joy from the redeemed is sent;
  Ten thousand hamlets swell the hymn of thanks;
  Our rivers roll exulting, and their banks
Send up hosannas to the firmament!
     Fields where the bondman's toil
     No more shall trench the soil,
Seem now to bask in a serener day;
  The meadow-birds sing sweeter, and the airs
Of heaven with more caressing softness play,
  Welcoming man to liberty like theirs.
A glory clothes the land from sea to sea,
For the great land and all its coasts are free.

Within that land wert thou enthroned of late,
  And they by whom the nation's laws were made,
  And they who filled its judgment-seats obeyed
Thy mandate, rigid as the will of Fate.
     Fierce men at thy right hand,
     With gesture of command,
Gave forth the word that none might dare gainsay;
  And grave and reverend ones, who loved thee not,
Shrank from thy presence, and in blank dismay

Choked down, unuttered, the rebellious thought;
While meaner cowards, mingling with thy train,
Proved, from the book of God, thy right to reign.

Great as thou wert, and feared from shore to shore,
  The wrath of Heaven o'ertook thee in thy pride;
  Thou sitt'st a ghastly shadow; by thy side
Thy once strong arms hang nerveless evermore.
      And they who quailed but now
      Before thy lowering brow,
Devote thy memory to scorn and shame,
  And scoff at the pale, powerless thing thou art.
And they who ruled in thine imperial name,
  Subdued, and standing sullenly apart,
Scowl at the hands that overthrew thy reign,
And shattered at a blow the prisoner's chain.

Well was thy doom deserved; thou didst not spare
  Life's tenderest ties, but cruelly didst part
  Husband and wife, and from the mother's heart
Didst wrest her children, deaf to shriek and prayer;
      Thy inner lair became
      The haunt of guilty shame;
Thy lash dropped blood; the murderer, at thy side,
  Showed his red hands, nor feared the vengeance due.
Thou didst sow earth with crimes, and, far and wide,
  A harvest of uncounted miseries grew,
Until the measure of thy sins at last
Was full, and then the avenging bolt was cast!

Go now, accursed of God, and take thy place
  With hateful memories of the elder time,
  With many a wasting plague, and nameless crime,
And bloody war that thinned the human race;
      With the Black Death, whose way
      Through wailing cities lay,
Worship of Moloch, tyrannies that built
  The Pyramids, and cruel creeds that taught
To avenge a fancied guilt by deeper guilt—
  Death at the stake to those that held them not.
Lo! the foul phantoms, silent in the gloom
Of the flown ages, part to yield thee room.

I see the better years that hasten by
  Carry thee back into that shadowy past,
  Where, in the dusty spaces, void and vast,
The graves of those whom thou hast murdered lie.
      The slave-pen, through whose door
      Thy victims pass no more,
Is there, and there shall the grim block remain
  At which the slave was sold; while at thy feet
Scourges and engines of restraint and pain
  Moulder and rust by thine eternal seat.
There, mid the symbols that proclaim thy crimes,
Dwell thou, a warning to the coming times.

May, 1866.

~~~~~~******~~~~~~

"RECEIVE THY SIGHT."

When the blind suppliant in the way,
  By friendly hands to Jesus led,
Prayed to behold the light of day,
  "Receive thy sight," the Saviour said.

At once he saw the pleasant rays
  That lit the glorious firmament;
And, with firm step and words of praise,
  He followed where the Master went.

Look down in pity, Lord, we pray,
  On eyes oppressed by moral night,
And touch the darkened lids and say
  The gracious words, "Receive thy sight."

Then, in clear daylight, shall we see
  Where walked the sinless Son of God;
And, aided by new strength from Thee,
  Press onward in the path He trod.

~~~~~~******~~~~~~

A BRIGHTER DAY. [43]

FROM THE SPANISH.

    Harness the impatient Years,
O Time! and yoke them to the imperial car;
    For, through a mist of tears,
    The brighter day appears,
Whose early blushes tinge the hills afar.

    A brighter day for thee,
O realm! whose glorious fields are spread between
    The dark-blue Midland Sea
    And that immensity
Of Western waters which once hailed thee queen!

    The fiery coursers fling
Their necks aloft, and snuff the morning wind,
    Till the fleet moments bring
    The expected sign to spring
Along their path, and leave these glooms behind.

---

[43] This poem was written shortly after the author's return from a visit to Spain, and more than a twelvemonth before the overthrow of
the tyrannical government of Queen Isabella and the expulsion of the Bourbons. It is not "from the Spanish" in the ordinary sense of
the phrase, but is an attempt to put into a poetic form sentiments and hopes which the author frequently heard, during his visit to
Spain, from the lips of the natives. We are yet to see whether these expectations of an enlightened government and national liberty are
to become a reality under the new order of things.

Yoke them, and yield the reins
To Spain, and lead her to the lofty seat;
    But, ere she mount, the chains
    Whose cruel strength constrains
Her limbs must fall in fragments at her feet.

    A tyrant brood have wound
About her helpless limbs the steely braid,
    And toward a gulf profound
    They drag her, gagged and bound,
Down among dead men's bones, and frost and shade.

    O Spain! thou wert of yore
The wonder of the realms; in prouder years
    Thy haughty forehead wore,
    What it shall wear no more,
The diadem of both the hemispheres.

    To thee the ancient Deep
Revealed his pleasant, undiscovered lands;
    From mines where jewels sleep,
    Tilled plain and vine-clad steep,
Earth's richest spoil was offered to thy hands.

    Yet thou, when land and sea
Sent thee their tribute with each rolling wave,
    And kingdoms crouched to thee,
    Wert false to Liberty,
And therefore art thou now a shackled slave.

    Wilt thou not, yet again,
Put forth the sleeping strength that in thee lies,
    And snap the shameful chain,
    And force that tyrant train
To flee before the anger in thine eyes?

    Then shall the harnessed Years
Sweep onward with thee to that glorious height
    Which even now appears
    Bright through the mist of tears,
The dwelling-place of Liberty and Light.

October, 1867.

~~~~~******~~~~~

AMONG THE TREES.

Oh ye who love to overhang the springs,
And stand by running waters, ye whose boughs
Make beautiful the rocks o'er which they play,
Who pile with foliage the great hills, and rear
A paradise upon the lonely plain,
Trees of the forest, and the open field!
Have ye no sense of being? Does the air,

The pure air, which I breathe with gladness, pass
In gushes o'er your delicate lungs, your leaves,
All unenjoyed? When on your winter's sleep
The sun shines warm, have ye no dreams of spring?
And when the glorious spring-time comes at last,
Have ye no joy of all your bursting buds,
And fragrant blooms, and melody of birds
To which your young leaves shiver? Do ye strive
And wrestle with the wind, yet know it not?
Feel ye no glory in your strength when he,
The exhausted Blusterer, flies beyond the hills,
And leaves you stronger yet? Or have ye not
A sense of loss when he has stripped your leaves,
Yet tender, and has splintered your fair boughs?
Does the loud bolt that smites you from the cloud
And rends you, fall unfelt? Do there not run
Strange shudderings through your fibres when the axe
Is raised against you, and the shining blade
Deals blow on blow, until, with all their boughs,
Your summits waver and ye fall to earth?
Know ye no sadness when the hurricane
Has swept the wood and snapped its sturdy stems
Asunder, or has wrenched, from out the soil,
The mightiest with their circles of strong roots,
And piled the ruin all along his path?

  Nay, doubt we not that under the rough rind,
In the green veins of these fair growths of earth,
There dwells a nature that receives delight
From all the gentle processes of life,
And shrinks from loss of being. Dim and faint
May be the sense of pleasure and of pain,
As in our dreams; but, haply, real still.

  Our sorrows touch you not. We watch beside
The beds of those who languish or who die,
And minister in sadness, while our hearts
Offer perpetual prayer for life and ease
And health to the beloved sufferers.
But ye, while anxious fear and fainting hope
Are in our chambers, ye rejoice without.
The funeral goes forth; a silent train
Moves slowly from the desolate home; our hearts
Are breaking as we lay away the loved,
Whom we shall see no more, in their last rest,
Their little cells within the burial-place.
Ye have no part in this distress; for still
The February sunshine steeps your boughs
And tints the buds and swells the leaves within;
While the song-sparrow, warbling from her perch,
Tells you that spring is near. The wind of May
Is sweet with breath of orchards, in whose boughs
The bees and every insect of the air
Make a perpetual murmur of delight,
And by whose flowers the humming-bird hangs poised
In air, and draws their sweets and darts away.

The linden, in the fervors of July,
Hums with a louder concert. When the wind
Sweeps the broad forest in its summer prime,
As when some master-hand exulting sweeps
The keys of some great organ, ye give forth
The music of the woodland depths, a hymn
Of gladness and of thanks. The hermit-thrush
Pipes his sweet note to make your arches ring;
The faithful robin, from the wayside elm,
Carols all day to cheer his sitting mate;
And when the autumn comes, the kings of earth,
In all their majesty, are not arrayed
As ye are, clothing the broad mountain-side
And spotting the smooth vales with red and gold;
While, swaying to the sudden breeze, ye fling
Your nuts to earth, and the brisk squirrel comes
To gather them, and barks with childish glee,
And scampers with them to his hollow oak.

Thus, as the seasons pass, ye keep alive
The cheerfulness of Nature, till in time
The constant misery which wrings the heart
Relents, and we rejoice with you again,
And glory in your beauty; till once more
We look with pleasure on your varnished leaves,
That gayly glance in sunshine, and can hear,
Delighted, the soft answer which your boughs
Utter in whispers to the babbling brook.

Ye have no history. I cannot know
Who, when the hillside trees were hewn away,
Haply two centuries since, bade spare this oak,
Leaning to shade, with his irregular arms,
Low-bent and long, the fount that from his roots
Slips through a bed of cresses toward the bay—
I know not who, but thank him that he left
The tree to flourish where the acorn fell,
And join these later days to that far time
While yet the Indian hunter drew the bow
In the dim woods, and the white woodman first
Opened these fields to sunshine, turned the soil
And strewed the wheat. An unremembered Past
Broods, like a presence, mid the long gray boughs
Of this old tree, which has outlived so long
The flitting generations of mankind.

Ye have no history. I ask in vain
Who planted on the slope this lofty group
Of ancient pear-trees that with spring-time burst
Into such breadth of bloom. One bears a scar
Where the quick lightning scored its trunk, yet still
It feels the breath of Spring, and every May
Is white with blossoms. Who it was that laid
Their infant roots in earth, and tenderly
Cherished the delicate sprays, I ask in vain,
Yet bless the unknown hand to which I owe

243

This annual festival of bees, these songs
Of birds within their leafy screen, these shouts
Of joy from children gathering up the fruit
Shaken in August from the willing boughs.
  Ye that my hands have planted, or have spared,
Beside the way, or in the orchard-ground,
Or in the open meadow, ye whose boughs
With every summer spread a wider shade,
Whose herd in coming years shall lie at rest
Beneath your noontide shelter? who shall pluck
Your ripened fruit? who grave, as was the wont
Of simple pastoral ages, on the rind
Of my smooth beeches some beloved name?
Idly I ask; yet may the eyes that look
Upon you, in your later, nobler growth,
Look also on a nobler age than ours;
An age when, in the eternal strife between
Evil and Good, the Power of Good shall win
A grander mastery; when kings no more
Shall summon millions from the plough to learn
The trade of slaughter, and of populous realms
Make camps of war; when in our younger land
The hand of ruffian Violence, that now
Is insolently raised to smite, shall fall
Unnerved before the calm rebuke of Law,
And Fraud, his sly confederate, shrink, in shame,
Back to his covert, and forego his prey.

<div align="center">~~~~~~******~~~~~~</div>

MAY EVENING.

The breath of Spring-time at this twilight hour
    Comes through the gathering glooms,
And bears the stolen sweets of many a flower
    Into my silent rooms.

Where hast thou wandered, gentle gale, to find
    The perfumes thou dost bring?
By brooks, that through the wakening meadows wind,
    Or brink of rushy spring?

Or woodside, where, in little companies,
    The early wild-flowers rise,
Or sheltered lawn, where, mid encircling trees,
    May's warmest sunshine lies?

Now sleeps the humming-bird, that, in the sun,
    Wandered from bloom to bloom;
Now, too, the weary bee, his day's work done,
    Rests in his waxen room.

Now every hovering insect to his place
    Beneath the leaves hath flown;
And, through the long night hours, the flowery race
    Are left to thee alone.

O'er the pale blossoms of the sassafras
    And o'er the spice-bush spray,
Among the opening buds, thy breathings pass,
    And come embalmed away.

Yet there is sadness in thy soft caress,
    Wind of the blooming year!
The gentle presence, that was wont to bless
    Thy coming, is not here.

Go, then; and yet I bid thee not repair,
    Thy gathered sweets to shed,
Where pine and willow, in the evening air,
    Sigh o'er the buried dead.

Pass on to homes where cheerful voices sound,
    And cheerful looks are cast,
And where thou wakest, in thine airy round,
    No sorrow of the past.

Refresh the languid student pausing o'er
    The learned page apart,
And he shall turn to con his task once more
    With an encouraged heart.

Bear thou a promise, from the fragrant sward,
    To him who tills the land,
Of springing harvests that shall yet reward
    The labors of his hand.

And whisper, everywhere, that Earth renews
    Her beautiful array,
Amid the darkness and the gathering dews,
    For the return of day.

<div align="center">~~~~******~~~~</div>

OCTOBER, 1866.

'Twas when the earth in summer glory lay,
  We bore thee to thy grave; a sudden cloud
Had shed its shower and passed, and every spray
  And tender herb with pearly moisture bowed.

How laughed the fields, and how, before our door,
  Danced the bright waters!—from his perch on high
The hang-bird sang his ditty o'er and o'er,
  And the song-sparrow from the shrubberies nigh.

Yet was the home where thou wert lying dead
  Mournfully still, save when, at times, was heard,
From room to room, some softly-moving tread,
  Or murmur of some softly-uttered word.

Feared they to break thy slumber? As we threw

A look on that bright bay and glorious shore,
  Our hearts were wrung with anguish, for we knew
  Those sleeping eyes would look on them no more.

Autumn is here; we cull his lingering flowers
  And bring them to the spot where thou art laid;
The late-born offspring of his balmier hours,
  Spared by the frost, upon thy grave to fade.

The sweet calm sunshine of October, now
  Warms the low spot; upon its grassy mould
The purple oak-leaf falls; the birchen bough
  Drops its bright spoil like arrow-heads of gold.

And gorgeous as the morn, a tall array
  Of woodland shelters the smooth fields around;
And guarded by its headlands, far away
  Sail-spotted, blue and lake-like, sleeps the sound.

I gaze in sadness; it delights me not
  To look on beauty which thou canst not see;
And, wert thou by my side, the dreariest spot
  Were, oh, how far more beautiful to me!

In what fair region dost thou now abide?
  Hath God, in the transparent deeps of space,
Through which the planets in their journey glide,
  Prepared, for souls like thine, a dwelling-place?

Fields of unwithering bloom, to mortal eye
  Invisible, though mortal eye were near,
Musical groves, and bright streams murmuring by,
  Heard only by the spiritual ear?

Nay, let us deem that thou dost not withdraw
  From the dear places where thy lot was cast,
And where thy heart, in love's most holy law,
  Was schooled by all the memories of the past.

Here on this earth, where once, among mankind,
  Walked God's beloved Son, thine eyes may see
Beauty to which our dimmer sense is blind
  And glory that may make it heaven to thee.

May we not think that near us thou dost stand
  With loving ministrations, for we know
Thy heart was never happy when thy hand
  Was forced its tasks of mercy to forego!

Mayst thou not prompt, with every coming day,
  The generous aim and act, and gently win
Our restless, wandering thoughts to turn away
  From every treacherous path that ends in sin!

~~~~~******~~~~~

THE ORDER OF NATURE.

FROM BOETHIUS DE CONSOLATIONE.

Thou who wouldst read, with an undarkened eye,
  The laws by which the Thunderer bears sway,
Look at the stars that keep, in yonder sky,
  Unbroken peace from Nature's earliest day.

The great sun, as he guides his fiery car,
  Strikes not the cold moon in his rapid sweep;
The Bear, that sees star setting after star
  In the blue brine, descends not to the deep.

The star of eve still leads the hour of dews;
  Duly the day-star ushers in the light;
With kindly alternations Love renews
  The eternal courses bringing day and night.

Love drives away the brawler War, and keeps
  The realm and host of stars beyond his reach;
In one long calm the general concord steeps
  The elements, and tempers each to each.

The moist gives place benignly to the dry;
  Heat ratifies a faithful league with cold;
The nimble flame springs upward to the sky;
  Down sinks by its own weight the sluggish mould.

Still sweet with blossoms is the year's fresh prime;
  Her harvests still the ripening Summer yields;
Fruit-laden Autumn follows in his time,
  And rainy Winter waters still the fields.

The elemental harmony brings forth
  And rears all life, and, when life's term is o'er,
It sweeps the breathing myriads from the earth,
  And whelms and hides them to be seen no more:

While the Great Founder, he who gave these laws,
  Holds the firm reins and sits amid his skies
Monarch and Master, Origin and Cause,
  And Arbiter supremely just and wise.

He guides the force he gave; his hand restrains
  And curbs it to the circle it must trace:
Else the fair fabric which his power sustains
  Would fall to fragments in the void of space.

Love binds the parts together, gladly still
  They court the kind restraint nor would be free;
Unless Love held them subject to the Will
  That gave them being, they would cease to be.

******

TREE-BURIAL.

Near our southwestern border, when a child
Dies in the cabin of an Indian wife,
She makes its funeral-couch of delicate furs,
Blankets and bark, and binds it to the bough
Of some broad branching tree with leathern thongs
And sinews of the deer. A mother once
Wrought at this tender task, and murmured thus:
  "Child of my love, I do not lay thee down
Among the chilly clods where never comes
The pleasant sunshine. There the greedy wolf
Might break into thy grave and tear thee thence,
And I should sorrow all my life. I make
Thy burial-place here, where the light of day
Shines round thee, and the airs that play among
The boughs shall rock thee. Here the morning sun,
Which woke thee once from sleep to smile on me,
Shall beam upon thy bed, and sweetly here
Shall lie the red light of the evening clouds
Which called thee once to slumber. Here the stars
Shall look upon thee—the bright stars of heaven
Which thou didst wonder at. Here too the birds,
Whose music thou didst love, shall sing to thee,
And near thee build their nests and rear their young
With none to scare them. Here the woodland flowers,
Whose opening in the spring-time thou didst greet
With shouts of joy, and which so well became
Thy pretty hands when thou didst gather them,
Shall spot the ground below thy little bed.
  "Yet haply thou hast fairer flowers than these,
Which, in the land of souls, thy spirit plucks
In fields that wither not, amid the throng
Of joyous children, like thyself, who went
Before thee to that brighter world and sport
Eternally beneath its cloudless skies.
Sport with them, dear, dear child, until I come
To dwell with thee, and thou, beholding me,
From far, shalt run and leap into my arms,
And I shall clasp thee as I clasped thee here
While living, oh most beautiful and sweet
Of children, now more passing beautiful,
If that can be, with eyes like summer stars—
A light that death can never quench again.
  "And now, oh wind, that here among the leaves
Dost softly rustle, breathe thou ever thus
Gently, and put not forth thy strength to tear
The branches and let fall their precious load,
A prey to foxes. Thou, too, ancient sun,
Beneath whose eye the seasons come and go,
And generations rise and pass away,
While thou dost never change—oh, call not up,
With thy strong heats, the dark, grim thunder-cloud,
To smite this tree with bolts of fire, and rend
Its trunk and strew the earth with splintered boughs.
Ye rains, fall softly on the couch that holds

My darling. There the panther's spotted hide
Shall turn aside the shower; and be it long,
Long after thou and I have met again,
Ere summer wind or winter rain shall waste
This couch and all that now remains of thee,
To me thy mother. Meantime, while I live,
With each returning sunrise I shall seem
To see thy waking smile, and I shall weep;
And when the sun is setting I shall think
How, as I watched thee, o'er thy sleepy eyes
Drooped the smooth lids, and laid on the round cheek
Their lashes, and my tears will flow again;
And often, at those moments, I shall seem
To hear again the sweetly prattled name
Which thou didst call me by, and it will haunt
My home till I depart to be with thee."

<center>~~~~~~******~~~~~~</center>

A LEGEND OF THE DELAWARES.

The air is dark with cloud on cloud,
  And, through the leaden-colored mass,
With thunder-crashes quick and loud,
  A thousand shafts of lightning pass.

And to and fro they glance and go,
  Or, darting downward, smite the ground.
What phantom arms are those that throw
  The shower of fiery arrows round?

A louder crash! a mighty oak
  Is smitten from that stormy sky.
Its stem is shattered by the stroke;
  Around its root the branches lie.

Fresh breathes the wind; the storm is o'er;
  The piles of mist are swept away;
And from the open sky, once more,
  Streams gloriously the golden day.

A dusky hunter of the wild
  Is passing near, and stops to see
The wreck of splintered branches piled
  About the roots of that huge tree.

Lo, quaintly shaped and fairly strung,
  Wrought by what hand he cannot know,
On that drenched pile of boughs, among
  The splinters, lies a polished bow.

He lifts it up; the drops that hang
  On the smooth surface glide away:
He tries the string, no sharper twang
  Was ever heard on battle-day.

249

Homeward Onetho bears the prize:
  Who meets him as he turns to go?
An aged chief, with quick, keen eyes,
  And bending frame, and locks of snow.

"See, what I bring, my father, see
  This goodly bow which I have found
Beneath a thunder-riven tree,
  Dropped with the lightning to the ground."

"Beware, my son; it is not well" —
  The white-haired chieftain makes reply—
"That we who in the forest dwell
  Should wield the weapons of the sky.

"Lay back that weapon in its place;
  Let those who bore it bear it still,
Lest thou displease the ghostly race
  That float in mist from hill to hill."

"My father, I will only try
  How well it sends a shaft, and then,
Be sure, this goodly bow shall lie
  Among the splintered boughs again."

So to the hunting-ground he hies,
  To chase till eve the forest-game,
And not a single arrow flies,
  From that good bow, with erring aim.

And then he deems that they, who swim
  In trains of cloud the middle air,
Perchance had kindly thoughts of him
  And dropped the bow for him to bear.

He bears it from that day, and soon
  Becomes the mark of every eye,
And wins renown with every moon
  That fills its circle in the sky.

None strike so surely in the chase;
  None bring such trophies from the fight;
And, at the council-fire, his place
  Is with the wise and men of might.

And far across the land is spread,
  Among the hunter tribes, his fame;
Men name the bowyer-chief with dread
  Whose arrows never miss their aim.

See next his broad-roofed cabin rise
  On a smooth river's pleasant side,
And she who has the brightest eyes
  Of all the tribe becomes his bride.

A year has passed; the forest sleeps

In early autumn's sultry glow;
  Onetho, on the mountain-steeps,
Is hunting with that trusty bow.

But they, who by the river dwell,
  See the dim vapors thickening o'er
Long mountain-range and severing dell,
  And hear the thunder's sullen roar.

Still darker grows the spreading cloud
  From which the booming thunders sound,
And stoops and hangs a shadowy shroud
  Above Onetho's hunting-ground.

Then they who, from the river-vale,
  Are gazing on the distant storm,
See in the mists that ride the gale
  Dim shadows of the human form—

Tall warriors, plumed, with streaming hair
  And lifted arms that bear the bow,
And send athwart the murky air
  The arrowy lightnings to and fro.

Loud is the tumult of an hour—
  Crash of torn boughs and howl of blast,
And thunder-peal and pelting shower,
  And then the storm is overpast.

Where is Onetho? what delays
  His coming? why should he remain
Among the plashy woodland ways,
  Swoln brooks and boughs that drip with rain?

He comes not, and the younger men
  Go forth to search the forest round.
They track him to a mountain-glen,
  And find him lifeless on the ground.

The goodly bow that was his pride
  Is gone, but there the arrows lie;
And now they know the death he died,
  Slain by the lightnings of the sky.

They bear him thence in awe and fear
  Back to the vale with stealthy tread;
There silently, from far and near,
  The warriors gather round the dead.

But in their homes the women bide;
  Unseen they sit and weep apart,
And, in her bower, Onetho's bride
  Is sobbing with a broken heart.

They lay in earth their bowyer-chief,
  And at his side their hands bestow

His dreaded battle-axe and sheaf
  Of arrows, but without a bow.

"Too soon he died; it is not well" —
  The old men murmured, standing nigh—
"That we, who in the forest dwell,
  Should wield the weapons of the sky."

<center>~~~~~******~~~~~</center>

A LIFETIME.

I sit in the early twilight,
  And, through the gathering shade,
I look on the fields around me
  Where yet a child I played.

And I peer into the shadows,
  Till they seem to pass away,
And the fields and their tiny brooklet
  Lie clear in the light of day.

A delicate child and slender,
  With lock of light-brown hair,
From knoll to knoll is leaping
  In the breezy summer air.

He stoops to gather blossoms
  Where the running waters shine;
And I look on him with wonder,
  His eyes are so like mine.

I look till the fields and brooklet
  Swim like a vision by,
And a room in a lowly dwelling
  Lies clear before my eye.

There stand, in the clean-swept fireplace,
  Fresh boughs from the wood in bloom,
And the birch-tree's fragrant branches
  Perfume the humble room.

And there the child is standing
  By a stately lady's knee,
And reading of ancient peoples
  And realms beyond the sea:

Of the cruel King of Egypt
  Who made God's people slaves,
And perished, with all his army,
  Drowned in the Red Sea waves;

Of Deborah who mustered
  Her brethren long oppressed,
And routed the heathen army,
  And gave her people rest;

And the sadder, gentler story
  How Christ, the crucified,
With a prayer for those who slew him,
  Forgave them as he died.

I look again, and there rises
  A forest wide and wild,
And in it the boy is wandering,
  No longer a little child.

He murmurs his own rude verses
  As he roams the woods alone;
And again I gaze with wonder,
  His eyes are so like my own.

I see him next in his chamber,
  Where he sits him down to write
The rhymes he framed in his ramble,
  And he cons them with delight.

A kindly figure enters,
  A man of middle age,
And points to a line just written,
  And 'tis blotted from the page.

And next, in a hall of justice,
  Scarce grown to manly years,
Mid the hoary-headed wranglers
  The slender youth appears.

With a beating heart he rises,
  And with a burning cheek,
And the judges kindly listen
  To hear the young man speak.

Another change, and I see him
  Approach his dwelling-place,
Where a fair-haired woman meets him,
  With a smile on her young face—

A smile that spreads a sunshine
  On lip and cheek and brow;
So sweet a smile there is not
  In all the wide earth now.

She leads by the hand their first-born,
  A fair-haired little one,
And their eyes as they meet him sparkle
  Like brooks in the morning sun.

Another change, and I see him
  Where the city's ceaseless coil
Sends up a mighty murmur
  From a thousand modes of toil.

And there, mid the clash of presses,
  He plies the rapid pen
In the battles of opinion,
  That divide the sons of men.

I look, and the clashing presses
  And the town are seen no more,
But there is the poet wandering
  A strange and foreign shore.

He has crossed the mighty ocean
  To realms that lie afar,
In the region of ancient story,
  Beneath the morning star.

And now he stands in wonder
  On an icy Alpine height;
Now pitches his tent in the desert
  Where the jackal yells at night;

Now, far on the North Sea islands,
  Sees day on the midnight sky,
Now gathers the fair strange fruitage
  Where the isles of the Southland lie.

I see him again at his dwelling,
  Where, over the little lake,
The rose-trees droop in their beauty
  To meet the image they make.

Though years have whitened his temples,
  His eyes have the first look still,
Save a shade of settled sadness,
  A forecast of coming ill.

For in that pleasant dwelling,
  On the rack of ceaseless pain,
Lies she who smiled so sweetly,
  And prays for ease in vain.

And I know that his heart is breaking,
  When, over those dear eyes,
The darkness slowly gathers,
  And the loved and loving dies.

A grave is scooped on the hillside
  Where often, at eve or morn,
He lays the blooms of the garden—
  He, and his youngest born.

And well I know that a brightness
  From his life has passed away,
And a smile from the green earth's beauty,
  And a glory from the day.

But I behold, above him,

In the far blue deeps of air,
Dim battlements shining faintly,
  And a throng of faces there;

See over crystal barrier
  The airy figures bend,
Like those who are watching and waiting
  The coming of a friend.

And one there is among them,
  With a star upon her brow,
In her life a lovely woman,
  A sinless seraph now.

I know the sweet calm features;
  The peerless smile I know,
And I stretch my arms with transport
  From where I stand below.

And the quick tears drown my eyelids,
  But the airy figures fade,
And the shining battlements darken
  And blend with the evening shade.

I am gazing into the twilight
  Where the dim-seen meadows lie,
And the wind of night is swaying
  The trees with a heavy sigh.

~~~~~******~~~~~

THE TWO TRAVELLERS.

'Twas evening, and before my eyes
  There lay a landscape gray and dim—
Fields faintly seen and twilight skies,
  And clouds that hid the horizon's brim.

I saw—or was it that I dreamed?
  A waking dream?—I cannot say,
For every shape as real seemed
  As those which meet my eyes to-day.

Through leafless shrubs the cold wind hissed;
  The air was thick with falling snow,
And onward, through the frozen mist,
  I saw a weary traveller go.

Driven o'er the landscape, bare and bleak,
  Before the whirling gusts of air,
The snow-flakes smote his withered cheek,
  And gathered on his silver hair.

Yet on he fared through blinding snows,
  And murmuring to himself he said:
"The night is near; the darkness grows,

And higher rise the drifts I tread.

"Deep, deep, each autumn flower they hide;
  Each tuft of green they whelm from sight;
And they who journeyed by my side,
  Are lost in the surrounding night.

"I loved them; oh, no words can tell
  The love that to my friends I bore;
They left me with the sad farewell
  Of those who part to meet no more.

"And I, who face this bitter wind
  And o'er these snowy hillocks creep,
Must end my journey soon, and find
  A frosty couch, a frozen sleep."

As thus he spoke, a thrill of pain
  Shot to my heart—I closed my eyes;
But when I opened them again,
  I started with a glad surprise.

'Twas evening still, and in the west
  A flush of glowing crimson lay;
I saw the morrow there, and blest
  That promise of a glorious day.

The waters, in their glassy sleep,
  Shone with the hues that tinged the sky,
And rugged cliff and barren steep
  Gleamed with the brightness from on high.

And one was there whose journey lay
  Into the slowly-gathering night;
With steady step he held his way,
  O'er shadowy vale and gleaming height.

I marked his firm though weary tread,
  The lifted eye and brow serene;
And saw no shade of doubt or dread
  Pass o'er that traveller's placid mien.

And others came, their journey o'er,
  And bade good-night, with words of cheer:
"To-morrow we shall meet once more;
  'Tis but the night that parts us here."

"And I," he said, "shall sleep ere long;
  These fading gleams will soon be gone;
Shall sleep to rise refreshed and strong
  In the bright day that yet will dawn."

I heard; I watched him as he went,
  A lessening form, until the light
Of evening from the firmament
  Had passed, and he was lost to sight.

CHRISTMAS IN 1875.

SUPPOSED TO BE WRITTEN BY A SPANIARD.

No trumpet-blast profaned
The hour in which the Prince of Peace was born;
　No bloody streamlet stained
Earth's silver rivers on that sacred morn;
　But, o'er the peaceful plain,
The war-horse drew the peasant's loaded wain.

　The soldier had laid by
The sword and stripped the corselet from his breast,
　And hung his helm on high—
The sparrow's winter home and summer nest;
　And, with the same strong hand
That flung the barbed spear, he tilled the land.

　Oh, time for which we yearn;
Oh, sabbath of the nations long foretold!
　Season of peace, return,
Like a late summer when the year grows old,
　When the sweet sunny days
Steeped mead and mountain-side in golden haze.

　For now two rival kings
Flaunt, o'er our bleeding land, their hostile flags,
　And every sunrise brings
The hovering vulture from his mountain-crags
　To where the battle-plain
Is strewn with dead, the youth and flower of Spain.

　Christ is not come, while yet
O'er half the earth the threat of battle lowers,
　And our own fields are wet,
Beneath the battle-cloud, with crimson showers—
　The life-blood of the slain,
Poured out where thousands die that one may reign.

　Soon, over half the earth,
In every temple crowds shall kneel again
　To celebrate His birth
Who brought the message of good-will to men,
　And bursts of joyous song
Shall shake the roof above the prostrate throng.

　Christ is not come, while there
The men of blood whose crimes affront the skies
　Kneel down in act of prayer,
Amid the joyous strains, and when they rise
　Go forth, with sword and flame,
To waste the land in His most holy name.

Oh, when the day shall break
O'er realms unlearned in warfare's cruel arts,
  And all their millions wake
To peaceful tasks performed with loving hearts,
  On such a blessed morn,
Well may the nations say that Christ is born.

******

THE FLOOD OF YEARS.

A mighty Hand, from an exhaustless Urn,
Pours forth the never-ending Flood of Years,
Among the nations. How the rushing waves
Bear all before them! On their foremost edge,
And there alone, is Life. The Present there
Tosses and foams, and fills the air with roar
Of mingled noises. There are they who toil,
And they who strive, and they who feast, and they
Who hurry to and fro. The sturdy swain—
Woodman and delver with the spade—is there,
And busy artisan beside his bench,
And pallid student with his written roll.
A moment on the mounting billow seen,
The flood sweeps over them and they are gone.
There groups of revellers whose brows are twined
With roses, ride the topmost swell awhile,
And as they raise their flowing cups and touch
The clinking brim to brim, are whirled beneath
The waves and disappear. I hear the jar
Of beaten drums, and thunders that break forth
From cannon, where the advancing billow sends
Up to the sight long files of armed men,
That hurry to the charge through flame and smoke.
The torrent bears them under, whelmed and hid
Slayer and slain, in heaps of bloody foam.
Down go the steed and rider, the plumed chief
Sinks with his followers; the head that wears
The imperial diadem goes down beside
The felon's with cropped ear and branded cheek.
A funeral-train—the torrent sweeps away
Bearers and bier and mourners. By the bed
Of one who dies men gather sorrowing,
And women weep aloud; the flood rolls on;
The wail is stifled and the sobbing group
Borne under. Hark to that shrill, sudden shout,
The cry of an applauding multitude,
Swayed by some loud-voiced orator who wields
The living mass as if he were its soul!
The waters choke the shout and all is still.
Lo! next a kneeling crowd, and one who spreads
The hands in prayer—the engulfing wave o'ertakes
And swallows them and him. A sculptor wields
The chisel, and the stricken marble grows
To beauty; at his easel, eager-eyed,
A painter stands, and sunshine at his touch

Gathers upon his canvas, and life glows;
A poet, as he paces to and fro,
Murmurs his sounding lines. Awhile they ride
The advancing billow, till its tossing crest
Strikes them and flings them under, while their tasks
Are yet unfinished. See a mother smile
On her young babe that smiles to her again;
The torrent wrests it from her arms; she shrieks
And weeps, and midst her tears is carried down.
A beam like that of moonlight turns the spray
To glistening pearls; two lovers, hand in hand,
Rise on the billowy swell and fondly look
Into each other's eyes. The rushing flood
Flings them apart: the youth goes down; the maid
With hands outstretched in vain, and streaming eyes,
Waits for the next high wave to follow him.
An aged man succeeds; his bending form
Sinks slowly. Mingling with the sullen stream
Gleam the white locks, and then are seen no more.
   Lo! wider grows the stream—a sea-like flood
Saps earth's walled cities; massive palaces
Crumble before it; fortresses and towers
Dissolve in the swift waters; populous realms
Swept by the torrent see their ancient tribes
Engulfed and lost; their very languages
Stifled, and never to be uttered more.
   I pause and turn my eyes, and looking back
Where that tumultuous flood has been, I see
The silent ocean of the Past, a waste
Of waters weltering over graves, its shores
Strewn with the wreck of fleets where mast and hull
Drop away piecemeal; battlemented walls
Frown idly, green with moss, and temples stand
Unroofed, forsaken by the worshipper.
There lie memorial stones, whence time has gnawed
The graven legends, thrones of kings o'erturned,
The broken altars of forgotten gods,
Foundations of old cities and long streets
Where never fall of human foot is heard,
On all the desolate pavement. I behold
Dim glimmerings of lost jewels, far within
The sleeping waters, diamond, sardonyx,
Ruby and topaz, pearl and chrysolite,
Once glittering at the banquet on fair brows
That long ago were dust, and all around
Strewn on the surface of that silent sea
Are withering bridal wreaths, and glossy locks
Shorn from dear brows, by loving hands, and scrolls
O'er written, haply with fond words of love
And vows of friendship, and fair pages flung
Fresh from the printer's engine. There they lie
A moment, and then sink away from sight.
   I look, and the quick tears are in my eyes,
For I behold in every one of these
A blighted hope, a separate history
Of human sorrows, telling of dear ties

Suddenly broken, dreams of happiness
Dissolved in air, and happy days too brief
That sorrowfully ended, and I think
How painfully must the poor heart have beat
In bosoms without number, as the blow
Was struck that slew their hope and broke their peace.
Sadly I turn and look before, where yet
The Flood must pass, and I behold a mist
Where swarm dissolving forms, the brood of Hope,
Divinely fair, that rest on banks of flowers,
Or wander among rainbows, fading soon
And reappearing, haply giving place
To forms of grisly aspect such as Fear
Shapes from the idle air—where serpents lift
The head to strike, and skeletons stretch forth
The bony arm in menace. Further on
A belt of darkness seems to bar the way
Long, low, and distant, where the Life to come
Touches the Life that is. The Flood of Years
Rolls toward it near and nearer. It must pass
That dismal barrier. What is there beyond?
Hear what the wise and good have said. Beyond
That belt of darkness, still the Years roll on
More gently, but with not less mighty sweep.
They gather up again and softly bear
All the sweet lives that late were overwhelmed
And lost to sight, all that in them was good,
Noble, and truly great, and worthy of love—
The lives of infants and ingenuous youths,
Sages and saintly women who have made
Their households happy; all are raised and borne
By that great current in its onward sweep,
Wandering and rippling with caressing waves
Around green islands with the breath
Of flowers that never wither. So they pass
From stage to stage along the shining course
Of that bright river, broadening like a sea.
As its smooth eddies curl along their way
They bring old friends together; hands are clasped
In joy unspeakable; the mother's arms
Again are folded round the child she loved
And lost. Old sorrows are forgotten now,
Or but remembered to make sweet the hour
That overpays them; wounded hearts that bled
Or broke are healed forever. In the room
Of this grief-shadowed present, there shall be
A Present in whose reign no grief shall gnaw
The heart, and never shall a tender tie
Be broken; in whose reign the eternal Change
That waits on growth and action shall proceed
With everlasting Concord hand in hand.

~~~~~~******~~~~~~

OUR FELLOW-WORSHIPPERS.

Think not that thou and I
Are here the only worshippers to day,
  Beneath this glorious sky,
Mid the soft airs that o'er the meadows play;
  These airs, whose breathing stirs
The fresh grass, are our fellow-worshippers.

  See, as they pass, they swing
The censers of a thousand flowers that bend
  O'er the young herbs of spring,
And the sweet odors like a prayer ascend,
  While, passing thence, the breeze
Wakes the grave anthem of the forest-trees.

  It is as when, of yore,
The Hebrew poet called the mountain-steeps,
  The forests, and the shore
Of ocean, and the mighty mid-sea deeps,
  And stormy wind, to raise
A universal symphony of praise.

  For, lo! the hills around,
Gay in their early green, give silent thanks;
  And, with a joyous sound,
The streamlet's huddling waters kiss their banks,
  And, from its sunny nooks,
To heaven, with grateful smiles, the valley looks.

  The blossomed apple-tree,
Among its flowery tufts, on every spray,
  Offers the wandering bee
A fragrant chapel for his matin-lay;
  And a soft bass is heard
From the quick pinions of the humming-bird.

  Haply—for who can tell? —
Aerial beings, from the world unseen,
  Haunting the sunny dell,
Or slowly floating o'er the flowery green,
  May join our worship here,
With harmonies too fine for mortal ear.

****

SHORT STORY
~⁓**⁓~

THE SKELETON'S CAVE.

From *Tales of the Glauber Spa* (1832).

CHAPTER I.

Qual e quella ruina che, nel fianco
Di qua da Trento, l'Adige percosse.
O per tremuoto, o per sostegno manco,
Che, da cima del monte onde si mosse,
Al piano i: si la rocca discoseesa,
Ch' alcuna via darebbe a chi su fosse—
Cotal di quel burrato era la scesa.
~Dante, *Inferno*.

We hold our existence at the mercy of the elements; the life of man is a state of continual vigilance against their warfare. The heats of noon would wither him like the severed herb; the chills and dews of night would fill his bones with pain; the winter frost would extinguish life in an hour; the hail would smite him to death, did he not seek shelter and protection against them. His clothing is the perpetual armour he wears for his defence, and his dwelling the fortress to which he retreats for safety. Yet, even there the elements attack him; the winds overthrow his habitation; the waters sweep it away. The fire, that warmed and brightened it within, seizes upon its walls and consumes it, with his wretched family. The earth, where she seems to spread a paradise for his abode, sends up death in exhalations from her bosom; and the heavens dart down lightnings to destroy him. The drought consumes the harvests on which he relied for sustenance; or the rains cause the green corn to "rot ere its youth attains a beard." A. sudden blast engulfs him in the waters of the lake or bay from which he seeks his food; a false step, or a broken twig, precipitates him from the tree which he had climbed for its fruit; oaks falling in the storm, rocks toppling down from the precipices are so many dangers which beset his life. Even his erect attitude is a continual affront to the great law of gravitation, which is sometimes fatally avenged when he loses the balance preserved by constant care, and falls on a hard surface. The very arts on which he relies for protection from the unkindness of the elements betray him to the fate he would avoid, in some moment of negligence, or by some misdirection of skill, and he perishes miserably by his own inventions. Amid these various causes of accidental death, which thus surround us at every moment, it is only wonderful that their proper effect is not oftener produced—so admirably has the Framer of the universe adapted the faculties by which man provides for his safety, to the perils of the condition in which he is placed. Yet there are situations in which all his skill and strength are vain to protect him from a violent death, by some unexpected chance which executes upon him a sentence as severe and inflexible as the most pitiless tyranny of human despotism. But I began with the intention of relating a story, and I will not by my reflections anticipate the catastrophe of my narrative.

One pleasant summer morning a party of three persons set out from a French settlement in the western region of the United States, to visit a remarkable cavern in its vicinity. They had already proceeded for the distance of about three miles, through the tall original forest, along a path so rarely trodden that i required all their attention to keep its track. They now perceived through the trees the sunshine at a distance, and as they drew nearer they saw that it came down into a kind of natural opening, at the foot of a steep precipice. At every step the vast wall seemed to rise higher and higher; its seams and fissures, and inequalities became more and more distinct; and far up, nearly midway from the bottom, appeared a dar opening, under an impending crag. The precipice seemed between two and three hundred feet in height, an quite perpendicular. At its base, the earth for several rods around was heaped with loose fragments of rock which had evidently been detached from the principal mass, and shivered to pieces in the fall. A few tree among which were the black walnut and the slippery elm, and here and there an oak, grew scattered amon the rocks, and attested by their dwarfish stature the ungrateful soil in which they had taken root. But th wild grape vines which trailed along the ground, and sent out their branches to overrun the trees around them, showed by their immense size how much they delighted in the warmth of the rocks and the sunshine. The celastrus also here and there had wound its strong rings round and round the trunks and the boughs, till they died in its embrace, and then clothed the leafless branches in a thick drapery of its own foliage. Into this open space the party at length emerged from the forest, and for a moment stopped.

"Yonder is the Skeleton's Cave," said one of them, who stood a little in front of the rest. As he spoke he raised his arm, and pointed to the dark opening in the precipice already mentioned.

The speaker was an aged man, of spare figure, and a mild, subdued expression of countenance. Whoever looked at his thin gray hairs, his stooping form, and the emaciated hand which he extended; might have taken him for one who had passed the Scripture limit of threescore years and ten; but a glance at his clear and bright hazel eye would have induced the observer to set him down at some five years younger. A broad-brimmed palmetto hat shaded his venerable features from the sun, and his black gown and rosary denoted him to be an ecclesiastic of the Romish faith.

The two persons whom he addressed were much younger. One of them was in the prime of manhood and personal strength, rather tall, and of a vigorous make. He wore a hunting-cap, from the lower edge of which curled a profusion of strong dark hair, rather too long for the usual mode in the Atlantic States, shading a fresh-coloured countenance, lighted by a pair of full black eyes, the expression of which was compounded of boldness and good-humour. His dress was a blue frock-coat trimmed with yellow fringe, and bound by a sash at the waist, deer-skin pantaloons, and deer-skin mocasins. He carried a short rifle on his left shoulder; and wore on his left side a leathern bag of rather ample dimensions, and on his right a powder flask. It was evident that he was either a hunter by occupation, or at least one who made hunting his principal amusement; and there was something in his air and the neatness of his garb and equipments that bespoke the latter.

On the arm of this person leaned the third individual of the party, a young woman apparently about nineteen or twenty years of age, slender and graceful as a youthful student of the classic poets might imagine a wood-nymph. She was plainly attired in a straw hat and a dress of russet-colour, fitted for a ramble through that wild forest. The faces of her two companions were decidedly French in their physiognomy; hers was as decidedly Anglo-American. Her brown hair was parted away from a forehead of exceeding fairness, more compressed on the sides than is usual with the natives of England; and showing in the profile that approach to the Grecian outline which is remarked among their descendants in America. To complete the picture, imagine a quiet blue eye, features delicately moulded, and just colour enough on her cheek to make it interesting to watch its changes, as it deepened or grew paler with the varying and flitting emotions which slight cause will call up in a youthful maiden's bosom.

Notwithstanding this difference of national physiognomy, there was nothing peculiar in her accent, as she answered the old man who had just spoken.

"I see the mouth of the cave, but how are we to reach it, Father Ambrose? I perceive no way of getting to it without wings, either from the bottom or the top of the precipice."

"Look a few rods to the right, Emily. Do you see that pile of broken rocks reaching up to the middle of the precipice, looking as if a huge column of that mighty wall had been shivered into a pyramid of fragments? Our path lies that way."

"I see it, father," returned the fair questioner; "but when we arrive at the top, it appears to me we shall be no nearer the cave than we now are."

"From the top of that pile you may perceive a horizontal seam in the precipice extending to the mouth of the cave. Along that line, though you cannot discern it from the place where we stand, is a safe and broad footing, leading to our place of destination. Do you see, Le Maire," continued Father Ambrose, addressing himself to his other companion, "do you see that eagle sitting so composedly on a bough of that leafless tree, which seems a mere shrub on the brow of the precipice directly over the cavern? Nay, never lift your rifle, my good friend; the bird is beyond your reach, and you will only waste your powder. The superfluous rains which fall on the highlands beyond are collected in the hollow over which hangs the tree I showed you, and pour down the face of the rock directly over the entrance of the cave. Generally, you will see the bed of that hollow perfectly dry, as it is at present, but during a violent shower, or after several days' rain, there descends from that spot a sheet of water, white as snow, deafening with its noise the quiet solitudes around us, and rivalling in beauty some of the cascades that tumble from the cliffs of the Alps. But let us proceed."

The old man led the party to the pile of rocks which he had pointed out to their notice, and began to ascend from one huge block to another with an agility scarcely impaired by age. They could now perceive that human steps had trodden that rough path before them; in some places the ancient moss was effaced from the stones, and in others their surfaces had been worn smooth. Emily was about to follow her venerable conductor, when Le Maire offered to assist her.

"Nay, uncle," said she, "I know you are the politest of men, but I think your rifle will give you trouble enough. I have often heard you call it your wife; so I beg you will wait on Madame Le Maire, and leave me to make the best of my way by myself. I am not now to take my first lesson in climbing rocks, as you well know."

"Well, if this rifle be my spouse," rejoined the hunter, "I will say that it is not every wife who has so devoted a husband, nor every husband who is fortunate enough to possess so true a wife. She has another good quality—she never speaks but when she is bid, and then always to the point. I only wish for your sake, since I am not permitted to assist you, that Henry Danville were here. I think we should see the wildness of the paces that carry you so lightly over these rocks, a little chastised, while the young gentleman tenderly and respectfully handed you up this rude staircase, too rude for such delicate feet. Ah, I beg pardon, I forgot that you had quarrelled. Well, it is only a lover's quarrel, and the reconciliation will be the happier for being delayed so long. Henry is a worthy lad and an excellent marksman."

A heroine in a modern novel would have turned back this raillery with a smart or proud reply, but Emily was of too sincere and ingenuous a nature to answer a jest on a subject in which her heart was so deeply interested. Her cheek burned with a blush of the deepest crimson, as she turned away without speaking, and fled up the rocks. But though she spoke not, a tumult of images and feelings passed rapidly through her mind. One vivid picture of the past after another came before her recollection, and one well-known form and face were present in them all. She saw Henry Danville as when she first beheld, and was struck with his frank, intelligent aspect and graceful manners,—respectful, attentive, eager to attract her notice, and fearing to displease,—then again as the accepted and delighted lover,—and finally, as he was now, offended, cold, and estranged. A rustic ball rose before her imagination—a young stranger from the Atlantic States appears among the revellers—the phrases of the gay and animated conversation she held with him again vibrate on her ear—and again she sees Henry standing aloof, and looking gloomy and unhappy. She remembered how she had undertaken to discipline him for this unreasonable jealousy, by appearing charmed with her new acquaintance, and accepting his civilities with affected pleasure; how he had taken fire at this—had withdrawn himself from her society, and transferred his attentions to others. It was but the simple history of what is common enough among youthful lovers; but it was not of the less moment to her whose heart now throbbed with mingled pride and anguish, as these incidents came thronging back upon her memory. She regretted her own folly, but her thoughts severely blamed Henry for making so trifling a matter a ground of serious offence, and she sought consolation in reflecting how unhappy she must have been had she been united for life to one of so jealous a temper. "I am confident," said she to herself, "that his present indifference is all a pretence; he will soon sue for a reconciliation, and shall then show him that I can be as indifferent as himself."

Occupied with these reflections, Emily, before she was aware, found herself at the summit of the pile of broken rocks, and midway up the precipice.

264

CHAPTER II.

> ——I'll look no more,
> Lest my brain turn.——
> ~*King Lear.*

The ecclesiastic was the first of the party who arrived at the summit. He had seated himself on one of the blocks of stone which composed the pile, with his back against the wall of the precipice, and had taken the hat from his brow that he might enjoy the breeze which played lightly about the cliffs; and the coolness of which was doubly grateful after the toil of the ascent. In doing this he uncovered a high and ample forehead, such as artists love to couple with the features of old age, when they would represent a countenance at once noble and venerable. This is the only feature of the human face which Time spares: he dims the lustre of the eye; he shrivels the cheek; he destroys the firm or sweet expression of the mouth; he thins and whitens the hairs; but the forehead, that temple of thought, is beyond his reach, or rather, it shows more grand and lofty for the ravages which surround it.

The spot on which they now stood commanded a view of a wide extent of uncultivated and uninhabited country. An eminence interposed to hide from sight the village they had left; and on every side were the summits of the boundless forest, here and there diversified with a hollow of softer and richer verdure, where the hurricane, a short time before, had descended to lay prostrate the gigantic trees, and a young growth had shot up in their stead. Solitary savannas opened in the depth of the woods, and far off a lonely stream was flowing away in silence, sometimes among venerable trees, and sometimes through natural meadows, crimson with blossoms. All around them was the might, the majesty of vegetable life, untamed by the hand of man, and pampered by the genial elements into boundless luxuriance. The ecclesiastic pointed out to his companions the peculiarities of the scenery; he expatiated on the flowery beauty of those unshorn lawns; and on the lofty growth, and the magnificence and variety of foliage which distinguish the American forests, so much the admiration of those who have seen only the groves of Europe.

The conversation was interrupted by a harsh stridulous cry, and looking up, the party beheld the eagle who had left his perch on the top of the precipice, and having passed over their heads, was winging his way towards the stream in the distance.

"Ah," exclaimed Le Maire, "that is a hungry note, and the bird is a shrewd one, for he is steering to a place where there is plenty of game to my certain knowledge. It is the golden eagle; the war eagle, as the Indians call him, and no chicken either, as you may understand from the dark colour of his plumage. I warrant he has gorged many a rabbit and prairie hen on these old cliffs. At all events, he has made me think of my dinner: unless we make haste, good Father Am. brose, I am positive that we shall be late to our venison and claret."

"We must endeavour to prevent so great a misfortune," said Father Ambrose, rising from the rock where he sat, and proceeding on the path towards the cavern. It was a kind of narrow terrace, varying in width from four to ten feet, running westwardly along the face of the steep solid rock, and apparently formed by the breaking away of the upper part of one of the perpendicular strata of which the precipice was composed. That event must have happened at a very remote period, for in some places the earth had accumulated on the path to a considerable depth, and here and there grew a hardy and dwarfish shrub, or a tuft of wildflowers hanging over the edge. As they proceeded, the great height at which they stood, and the steepness of the rocky wall above and below them, made Emily often tremble and grow pale as she looked down. A few rods brought the party to a turn in the rock, where the path was narrower than elsewhere, and precisely in the angle a portion of the terrace on which they walked had fallen, leaving a chasm of about two feet in width, through which their distance from the base was fearfully apparent. Le Maire had already passed it, but Emily, when she arrived at the spot, shrunk back and leaned against the rock.

"I fear I shall not be able to cross the chasm," said she, in a tone of alarm. "My poor head grows giddy from a single look at it."

"Le Maire will assist you, my child," said the old man, who walked behind her.

"With the greatest pleasure in life," answered Le Maire; "though I confess I little expected that the daughter of a clear-headed Yankee would complain of being giddy in any situation. But this comes of having a French mother I suppose. Let me provide a convenient station for Madame le Maire, as you call her, and I will help you over." He then placed his rifle against the rock, where the path immediately beyond him grew wider, and advancing to the edge of the chasm, held forth both hands to Emily, taking hold of her arms near the elbow. In doing this he perceived that she trembled.

"You are as safe here as when you were in the woods below," said Le Maire, "if you would but think so. Step forward now, firmly, and look neither to the right nor left."

She took the step, but at that moment the strange inclination which we sometimes feel when standing on a dizzy height, to cast ourselves to the ground, came powerfully over her, and she leaned involuntarily and heavily towards the verge of the precipice. Le Maire was instantly aware of the movement, and bracing himself firmly, strove with all his might to counteract it. Had his grasp been less steady, or his self-possession less perfect, they would both inevitably have been precipitated from where they stood; but Le Maire was familiar with all the perilous situations of the wilderness, and the presence of mind he had learned in such a school did not now desert him. His countenance bore witness to the intense exertion he was making; it was flushed, and its muscles were working powerfully; his lips were closely compressed; the veins on his brow swelled, and his arms quivered with the strong tension given to their sinews. For an instant the fate of the two seemed in suspense, but the strength of the hunter prevailed, and he placed the damsel beside him on the rock, fainting and pallid as a corpse.

"God be praised," said the priest, drawing heavily the breath which he had involuntarily held during that fearful moment, while he had watched the scene, unable to render the least assistance.

CHAPTER III

— A hollow cave
Far underneath a craggy cliff ypight,
Dark, doleful, dreary, like a greedy grave.
                    ~*Spenser.*

——Beneath whose sable roof,
——ghostly shapes
Might meet at noontide,
—Fear and trembling Hope—
Silence and Foresight,—Death the Skeleton, .
And Time the Shadow.—
                    ~*Wordsworth.*

Some moments of repose were necessary before Emily was sufficiently recovered from her agitation to be able to proceed. The tears filled her eyes as she briefly but warmly thanked Le Maire for his generous exertions to save her, and begged his pardon for the foolish and awkward timidity, as she termed it, which had put his life as well as her own in such extreme peril.

"I confess," answered he, good-naturedly, "that had you been of as solid a composition as some ladies with whom I have the honour of an acquaintance, Madame Le Maire here would most certainly have been a widow. I understood my own strength, however,'' added he, for on this point he was 'somewhat vain, "and if I had not, I should still have been willing to risk something rather than to lose you. But I will take care, Emily, that you do not lead me into another scrape of the kind. When we return I shall, by your leave, take you in my arms and carry you over the chasm, and you may shut your eyes while I do it, if you please."

They now again set out, and in a few moments arrived at the mouth of the cavern they had come to visit. A projecting mass of rock impended over it, so low as not to allow in front an entrance to a person standing upright, but on each side it receded upwards in such a manner as to leave two high narrow openings, giving it the appearance of being suspended from the cavern roof. Beneath it the floor, which was a continuation of the terrace leading to the spot, was covered, in places, to a considerable depth, with soil formed by the disintegration of the neighbouring rocks, and traversed by several fissures nearly filled with earth. As they entered by one of the narrow side openings, Emily looked up to the crag with a slight shudder. "If it should fall!" thought she to herself; but a feeling of shame at the idle fear she had lately manifested restrained her from giving utterance to the thought. The good ecclesiastic perceived what was passing in her mind, and said, with a smile—.

"There is no danger, my child; that rock has been suspended over the entrance for centuries, for thousands of years perhaps, and is not likely to fall today. Ages must have elapsed before the crags could have crumbled to form the soil now under our feet. It is true that there is no place sacred from the intrusion of accident; everywhere may unforeseen events surprise and crush us, as the foot of man surprises and crushes the insect in his path; but to suppose peculiar danger in a place which has known no change for hundreds of years is to distrust Providence. Come, Le Maire," said Father Ambrose, "will you oblige us by striking a light ! Our eyes have been too much in the sunshine to distinguish objects in this dark place."

Le Maire produced from his hunting bag a roll of tinder, and lighting it with a spark from his rifle, kindled in a few moments a large pitch-pine torch. The circumstance which first struck the attention of the party was the profound and solemn stillness of the place. The most quiet day has under the open sky its multitude of sounds—the lapse of waters, the subtle motions of the apparently slumbering air among forests, grasses, and rocks, the flight and note of insects, the voices of animals, the rising of exhalations, the mighty process of change, of perpetual growth and decay, going on all over the earth, produce a chorus of noises which the hearing cannot analyze—which, though it may seem to you silence, is not so; and when from such a scene you pass directly into one of the rocky chambers of the earth, you perceive your error by the contrast. As the three went forward they passed through a heap of dry leaves lightly piled, which the winds of the last autumn had blown into the cave from the summit of the surrounding forest, and the rustling made by their steps sounded strangely loud amid that death-like silence. A spacious cavern presented itself to their sight, the roof of which near the entrance was low, but several paces beyond it rose to a great height, where the smoke of the torch ascending, mingled with the darkness, but the flame did not reveal the face of the vault.

They soon came to where, as Father Ambrose informed them, the cave divided into two branches. "That on the left," said he, "soon becomes a low and narrow passage among the rocks; this on the right leads to a large chamber, in which lie the bones from which the cavern takes its name."

He now took the torch from the hand of Le Maire, and turning to the right guided his companions to a lofty and wide apartment of the cave, in one corner of which he showed them a human skeleton lying extended on the rocky floor. Some decayed fragments, apparently of the skins of animals, lay under it in places, and one small remnant passed over the thighs, but the bones, though they had acquired from the atmosphere of the cave a greenish yellow hue, were seemingly unmouldered. They still retained their original relative position, and appeared as never disturbed since the sleep of death came over the frame to which they once belonged. Emily gazed on the spectacle with that natural horror which the remains of the dead inspire. Even Le Maire, with all his vivacity and garrulity, was silent for a moment.

"Is any thing known of the manner in which this poor wretch came to his end?" he at length inquired.

"Nothing. The name of Skeleton's Cave was given to this place by the aborigines; but I believe they have no tradition concerning these remains. If you look at the right leg you will perceive that the bone is fractured: it is most likely the man was wounded on these very cliffs either by accident or by some enemy, and that he crawled to this retreat, where he perished from want of attendance and from famine."

"What a death!" murmured Emily.

The ecclesiastic then directed their attention to another part of the same chamber, where he said it was formerly not uncommon for persons benighted in these parts, particularly hunters, to pass the night. "You perceive," added he, "that this spot is higher than the rest of the cavern, and drier also; indeed no part of the cavern is much subject to moisture. A bed of leaves on this rock with a good blanket, is no bad accommodation for a night's rest, as I can assure you, having once made the experiment myself many years since, when I came hither from Europe. Ah, what have we here 1 coals, brands, splinters of pitch-pine! The cave must have been occupied very lately for the purpose I mentioned, and by people too who, I dare say, from the preparations they seem to have made, passed the night very comfortably."

"I dare say they did so, though they had an ugly bedfellow yonder," answered Le Maire; "but I hope you do not think of following their example. As you have shown us, I presume, the principal curiosities of the cave, I take the liberty of suggesting the propriety of getting as fast as we can out of this melancholy place, which has already put me out of spirits. That poor wretch who died of famine!—I shall never get him out of my head till I am fairly set down to dinner. Not that I care more for my dinner than any other man when there is any thing of importance in the way, as, for example, a buffalo, or a fat buck, or a bear to be killed; but you will allow, Father Ambrose, that a saddle of venison, or a hump of buffalo and a sober bottle of claret are a prettier spectacle, particularly at this time of day, than that mouldy skeleton yonder. I had intended to shoot something in my way back just to keep my hand and eye in practice, but it is quite too late to think of that. Besides, here is Emily, poor thing, whom we have contrived to get up to this place, and whom we must manage to get down again as well as we can."

The good priest, though by no means participating in Le Maire's haste to be gone, mildly yielded to his instances, particularly as they were seconded by Emily, and they accordingly prepared to return. On reaching the mouth of the cave, they were struck with the change in the aspect of the heavens. Dark heavy clouds, the round summits of which were seen one beyond the other, were rapidly rising in the west; and through the grayish blue haze which suffused the sky before them, the sun appeared already shorn of his beams. A sound was heard afar of mighty winds contending with the forest, and the thunder rolled at a distance.

"We must stay at least until the storm is over," said Father Ambrose; "it would be upon us before we could descend these cliffs. Let us watch it from where we stand above the tops of these old woods: I can promise you it will be a magnificent spectacle."

Emily, though she would gladly have left the cave, could say nothing against the propriety of this advice; and even Le Maire, notwithstanding that he declared he had rather see a well-loaded table at that moment than all the storms that ever blew, preferred remaining to the manifest inconvenience of attempting a descent. In a few moments the dark array of clouds swept over the face of the sun, and a tumult in the woods announced the coming of the blast. The summits of the forest waved and stooped before it, like a field of young flax in the summer breeze,—another and fiercer gust descended,—another and stronger convulsion of the forest ensued. The trees rocked backward and forward, leaned and rose, and tossed and swung their branches in every direction, and the whirling air above them was filled with their leafy spoils. The roar was tremendous,—the noise of the ocean in a tempest is not louder,—it seemed as if tha innumerable multitude of giants of the wood, raised a universal voice of wailing under the fury that smote and tormented them. At length the rain began to fall, first in large and rare drops, and then the thunder burs over head, and the waters of the firmament poured down in torrents, and the blast that howled in the wood fled before them as if from an element that it feared. The trees again stood erect, and nothing was heard bu the rain beating heavily on the immense canopy of leaves around, and the occasional crashings of th thunder, accompanied by flashes of lightning, that threw a vivid light upon the walls of the cavern. Th priest and his companions stood contemplating this scene in silence, when a rushing of water close at han was heard. Father Ambrose showed the others where a stream, formed from the rains collected on th highlands above, descended on the crag that overhung the mouth of the cavern, and shooting clear of th rocks on which they stood, fell in spray to the broken fragments at the base of the precipice.

A gust of wind drove the rain into the opening where they stood, and obliged them to retire farth within. The priest suggested that they should take this opportunity to examine that part of the cave which going to the skeleton's chamber they had passed on their left, observing, however, that he believed it was no otherwise remarkable than for its narrowness and its length. Le Maire and Emily assented, and the former taking up the torch which he had stuck in the ground, they went back into the interior. They had just reached the spot where the two passages diverged from each other, when a hideous and intense glare of light filled the cavern, showing for an instant the walls, the roof, the floor, and every crag and recess, with the distinctness of the broadest sunshine. A frightful crash accompanied it, consisting of several sharp and deafening explosions, as if the very heart of the mountain was rent asunder by the lightning, and immediately after a body of immense weight seemed to fall at their very feet with a heavy sound, and a shock that caused the place where they stood to tremble as if shaken by an earthquake. A strong blast of air rushed by them, and a suffocating odour filled the cavern.

Father Ambrose had fallen upon his knees in mental prayer, at the explosion; but the blast from the mouth of the cavern threw him to the earth, t He raised himself, however, immediately, and found himself in utter silence and darkness, save that a livid image of that insufferable glare floated yet before his eyeballs. He called first upon Emily, who did not answer, then upon Le Maire, who replied from the ground a few paces nearer the entrance of the cave. He also had been thrown prostrate, and the torch he carried was extinguished. It was but the work of an instant to kindle it again, and they then discovered Emily extended near them in a swoon.

"Let us bear her to the mouth of the cavern," said Le Maire; "the fresh air from without will revive her." He took her in his arms, but on arriving at the spot he placed her suddenly on the ground, and raising both hands, exclaimed, with an accent of despair, " The rock is fallen!—the entrance is closed!"

It was but too evident,—Father Ambrose needed but a single look to convince him of its truth,— the huge rock which impended over the entrance had been loosened by the thunderbolt, and had fallen upon the floor of the cave, closing all return to the outer world.

CHAPTER IV.

Had one been there, with spirit strong and high,
Who could observe as he prepared to die;
He might have seen of hearts the varying kind,
And traced the movements of each different mind;
He might have seen that not the gentle maid
Was more than stern and haughty man afraid.
~ *Crabbe.*

Before inquiring further into the extent of the disaster, an office of humanity was to be performed. Emily was yet lying on the floor of the cave in a swoon, and the old man, stooping down and placing her head in his lap, began to use the ordinary means of recovery, and called on Le Maire to assist him. The hunter, after being spoken to several times, started from his gloomy revery, and kneeling down by the side of the priest, aided him in chafing her temples and hands, and fanned her cheek with his cap until consciousness was restored, when the priest communicated the terrible intelligence of what had happened.

Presence of mind and fortitude do not always dwell together. Those who are most easily overcome by the appearance of danger often support the calamity after it has fallen with the most composure. Le Maire had presence of mind, but he had not learned to submit with patience to irremediable misfortune; Emily could not command her nerves in sudden peril, but she could suffer with a firmness which left her mind at liberty to employ its resources. The very disaster which had happened seemed to inspire both her mind and her frame with new strength. The vague apprehensions which had haunted her were now reduced to certainty; she saw the extent of the calamity, and felt the duties it imposed. She rose from the ground without aid and with a composed countenance, and began to confer with Father Ambrose on the probabilities and means of escape from their present situation.

In the mean time, Le Maire, who had left them as soon as Emily came to herself, was eagerly employed in examining the entrance where the rock had fallen. On one side it lay close against the wall of the cavern; on the other was an opening of about a hand's breadth, which appeared, so far as he could distinguish, to communicate with the outer atmosphere. He looked above, but there the low roof, which met the wavering flame of his torch, showed a collection of large blocks firmly wedged together; he cast his eyes downwards, but there the lower edge of the vast mass which had fallen lay imbedded in the soil; he placed his shoulder against it and exerted his utmost strength to discover if it were moveable, but it yielded no more than the rock on which it rested.

"It is all over with us," said he, at length, dashing to the ground the torch, which the priest, approaching, prudently took up before it was extinguished; "it is all over with us; and we must perish in this horrid place like wild beasts in a trap. There is no opening, no possible way for escape, and not a soul on the wide earth knows where we are, or what is our situation." Then turning fiercely to the priest, and losing his habitual respect for his person and office in the bitterness of his despair, he said, "This is all your doing,— it was you who decoyed us hither to lay our bones beside those of that savage yonder"

"My son—" said the old man.

"Call me not son,—this is no time for cant. You take my life, and when I reproach you, you give me fine words. You call yourself a man of God,—can you pray us out of this horrible dungeon into which you have enticed us to bury us alive?"

"Say not that I take your life," said Father Ambrose mildly, without otherwise noticing his reproaches; "there is no reason as yet to suppose our case hopeless. Though we informed no person of the place to which we were going, it does not follow that we shall not be missed, or that no inquiry will be made for us. With to-morrow morning the whole settlement will doubtless be out to search for us, and as it is probable that some of them will pass this way, we may make ourselves heard by them from the mouth of the cavern. Besides, as Emily has just suggested, it is not impossible that the cave may have some other outlet, and that the part we were about to examine may afford a passage to the daylight."

Le Maire caught eagerly at the hope thus presented. "I beg your pardon, father," said he, "I was hasty— I was furious—but it is terrible, you will allow, to be shut up in this sepulchre, with the stone rolled to its mouth, and left to die. It is no light trial of patience merely to pass the night here, particularly," said he, with a smile, "when you know that dinner is waiting for you at home. Well, if the cave is to be explored, let us set about it immediately; if there is any way of getting out, let us discover it as soon as possible."

They again went to the passage which diverged from the path leading to the skeleton's chamber. It was a low, irregular passage, sometimes so narrow that they were obliged to walk one behind the other, and sometimes wide enough to permit them to walk abreast.

After proceeding a few rods it became so low that they were obliged to stoop.

"Remain here," said Le Maire, "and give me the torch. If there be any way of reaching daylight by this part of the cavern, I will give an account of it in due time."

Father Ambrose and Emily then seated themselves on a low bench of stone in the side of the cavern, while he went forward. The gleam of his torch appearing and disappearing showed the windings of the passage he was treading, and sometimes the sound of measured steps on the rock announced that he was walking upright, and sometimes a confused and struggling noise denoted that he was making his way on his elbows and knees. At length the sound was heard no longer, and the gleam of the torch ceased altogether to be descried in the passage.

"Father Ambrose!" said Emily, after a long interval. These words, though in the lowest key of her voice were uttered in such a tone of awe, and sounded, moreover, with such an unnatural distinctness in the midst of that perfect stillness, that the good father started.

"What would you, my daughter?"

"This darkness and this silence are frightful, and I spoke that you might reassure me by the sound of your voice. My uncle is long in returning."

"The passage is a long and intricate one."

"But is there no danger? I have heard of death-damps in pits and deep caverns, by the mere breathing of which a man dies silently and without a struggle. If my poor uncle should never return!"

"Let us not afflict ourselves with supposable evils, while a real calamity is impending over us. The cavern has been explored to a considerable distance without any such consequence as you mention to those who undertook it."

"God grant that he may discover a passage out of the cave! But I am afraid of the effect of a disappointment, he is so impatient—so impetuous."

"God grant us all grace to submit to his good pleasure," rejoined the priest; "but I think I hear him on the return. Listen, my child, you can distinguish sounds inaudible to my dull ears.'"

Emily listened, but in vain. At length, after another long interval, a sound of steps was heard, seemingly at a vast distance. In a little while a faint light showed itself in the passage, and after some minutes Le Maire appeared, panting with exertion, his face covered with perspiration, and his clothes soiled with the dust and slime of the rocks. He was about to throw himself on the rocky seat beside them without speaking.

"I fear your search has been unsuccessful," said Father Ambrose.

"There is no outlet in that quarter," rejoined Le Maire sullenly. "I have explored every winding and every cranny of the passage, and have been brought up at last, in every instance, against the solid rock."

"There is no alternative, then," said the ecclesiastic, "but to make ourselves as tranquil and comfortable as we can for the night. I shall have the honour of installing you in my old bed-chamber, where, if you sleep as soundly as I did once, you will acknowledge to-morrow morning that you might have passed a worse night. It is true, Emily, that one corner of it is occupied by an ill-looking inmate, but I can promise you from my own experience that he will do you no harm. So let us adjourn to the skeleton's chamber, and leave to Providence the events of the morrow."

To the skeleton's chamber they went accordingly, taking the precaution to remove thither a quantity of the dry leaves which lay heaped not far from the mouth of the cave, to form couches for their night's repose. A log of wood of considerable size was found in this part of the cavern, apparently left there by those who had lately occupied it for the night; and on collecting the brands and bits of wood which lay scattered about they found themselves in possession of a respectable stock of fuel. A fire was kindled, and the warmth, the light, the crackling brands, and the ever-moving flames, with the dancing shadows they threw on the walls, and the waving trains of smoke that mounted like winged serpents to the roof and glided away to the larger and loftier apartment of the cave, gave to that recess lately so still, dark, and damp, a kind of wild cheerfulness and animation, which, under other circumstances, could not have failed to raise the spirits of the party. They placed themselves around that rude hearth, Emily taking care to turn her back to the corner where lay the skeleton. Father Ambrose had been educated in Europe; he had seen much of men and manners, and he now exerted himself to entertain his companions by the narrative of what had fallen under his observation in that ancient abode of civilized man. He was successful, and the little circle forgot for a while in the charm of his conversation their misfortune and their danger. Even Le Maire was enticed into relating one or two of his hunting exploits, and Emily suffered a few of the arch sallies that distinguished her in more cheerful moments to escape her. At length Le Maire's hunting watch

271

pointed to the hour of ten, and the good priest counselled them to seek repose. He gave them his blessing, recommending them to the great Preserver of men, and then laying themselves down on their beds of leaves around the fire, they endeavoured to compose themselves to rest.

But now that each was left to the companionship of his own thoughts, the idea of their situation intruded upon their minds with a sense of pain and anxiety which repulsed the blessing of sleep. The reflections of each on the events of the day and the prospects of the morrow were different; those of Emily were the most cheerful, as her hopes of deliverance were the most sanguine. Her imagination had formed a picture of the incidents of her rescue from the fate that threatened her, a little romance in anticipation, which she would not for the world have revealed to living ear, but which she dwelt upon fondly and perpetually in the secrecy of her own meditations. She thought what must be the effect of her mysterious absence from the village upon Henry Danville, whose very jealousy, causeless as it was, demonstrated the sincerity and depth of his affection. She represented him to herself as the leader in the search that would be set on foot for the lost ones, as the most adventurous of the band, the most persevering, the most inventive, and the most successful.

"He will pass by this precipice to-morrow," thought she; "like others, he has heard of this cave; he will see that the fall of the rock has closed the entrance, his quick apprehension will divine the place of our imprisonment, he will call upon those who are engaged in the search, he will climb the precipice, he will deliver us, and I shall forgive him. But should it be my fate to perish: should none ever know the manner and place of my death; there will be one at least who will remember and regret me. He will bitterly repent the wrong he has done me, and the tears will start into his eyes at the mention of my name." A tear gushed out from between the closed lids of the fair girl as this thought passed through her mind, but it was such a tear as maidens love to shed, and it did not delay the slumber that already began to steal over her.

Sleep was later in visiting the eyes of Le Maire. The impatience which a bold and adventurous man, accustomed to rely on his own activity and address for escape in perilous emergencies, feels under the pressure of a calamity which no exertion of his own can remedy, had chafed and almost maddened his spirit. His heart sank within him at the thought of the lingering death he must die if not liberated from his living tomb. Long and uneasily he tossed on his bed of leaves, but he too had his hopes of deliverance by the people of the village, who would unquestionably assemble in the morning to search for their lost neighbours, and who might discover their situation. These thoughts at length prevailed over those of a gloomier kind; and the fatigues of the day overcoming his eyes with drowsiness, he fell into a slumber, profound, as it seemed from his hard drawn breath, but uneasy and filled with unpleasant dreams, as was evident from frequent starts and muttered exclamations.' When it was certain that both were asleep, Father Ambrose raised himself from his place and regarded them sorrowfully and attentively. He had not slept, though from his motionless posture and closed eyes, an observer might have thought him buried in a deep slumber. His own apprehensions, notwithstanding that he had endeavoured to prevent his companions from yielding themselves up to despair, were more painful than he had permitted himself to utter. That there was a possibility of their deliverance was true, but it was hardly to be expected that those who sought for them would think of looking for them in the cavern, nor was it likely that any cry they could utter would be heard below. The old man's thoughts gradually formed themselves into a kind of soliloquy, uttered, as is often the case with men much given to solitary meditation and prayer, in a low but articulate voice. "For myself," said he, "my life is near its close, and the day of decrepitude may be even yet nearer than the day of death. repine not, if it be the will of God that my existence on earth, already mercifully protracted to the ordinary limits of usefulness, should end here. But my heart bleeds to think that this maiden, in the blossom of her beauty and in the spring-time of her hopes, and that he who slumbers near me, in the pride and strength of manhood, should be thus violently divorced from a life which nature perhaps intended for as long a date as mine. I little thought, when the mother of that fair young creature in dying committed her to my charge that I should be her guide to a place where she should meet with a frightful and unnatural death. Accustomed as I am to protracted fastings, it is not impossible that I may outlive them both, and after having closed their eyes, who should have closed mine, I may be delivered and go forth in my uselessness from the sepulchre of those who should have been the delight and support of their friends. Let it not displease thee, O, my Maker! if, like the patriarch of old, I venture to expostulate with thee." And the old man placed himself in an attitude of supplication, clasping his hands and raising them towards heaven

272

Long did he remain in that posture motionless, and at length lowering his hands, he cast a look upon the sleepers near him, and laying himself down upon his bed of leaves, was soon asleep also.

CHAPTER V.

> A dull imprisoned ray,
> A sunbeam that hath lost its way,
> And through the crevice and the cleft
> Of the thick wall is fallen and left.
> ~ *Prisoners of Chillon.*

Of course the slumbers of none of the party were long protracted. They were early dispersed by the idea of their imprisonment in that mountain dungeon, which now and then showed itself painfully in the imagery of their dreams. When Emily awoke she found herself alone in the skeleton's chamber. Her eyes, accustomed to the darkness, could now distinguish most of the objects around her by the help of a gleam of light, which appeared to come in from the larger apartment. The fire, kindled the night previous, was now a mass of ashes and blackened brands; and the couches of her two companions yet showed the pressure of their forms. She rose, and not without casting a look at the grim inmate of the place, whose discoloured bones were just distinguishable in that dim twilight, passed into the outer chamber. Here she found the priest and Le Maire standing near the mouth of the cavern, where a strong light, at least so it seemed to her eyes, streamed in through the opening between the well and the fallen rock, showing that the short night of summer was already past.

"We are watching the increasing light of the morning," said the priest.

"And waiting for the friends whom it will bring to deliver us," added Le Maire*

"You will admit me to share in the occupation, I hope," answered Emily. "I am fit for nothing else, as you know, but to watch and wait, and I will endeavour to do that patiently."

It was not long before a brighter and a steady light, through the aperture, informed the prisoners that the sun had risen over the forest tops; and that the perfect day now shone upon the earth. To those, who could look upon the woods and savannas, the hills and the waters around, that morning was one of the most beautiful of the beautiful season to which it belonged. The aspect of nature, like one of those human countenances we sometimes meet with, so radiant with cheerfulness that it seems as if they had never known the expression of sorrow, showed, in the gladness it now put on, no traces of the tempest of the preceding day. The intensity of the sun's light was tempered by the white clouds that now and then floated over it, trailing through a soft blue sky; and the light and fresh breezes seemed to hover in the air, to rise and descend, with a motion like the irregular and capricious course of the butterfly; now stooping to wrinkle the surface of the stream, now rising to murmur in the leaves of the forest, and again descending to shake the dew from the cups of the opening flowers in the natural meadows. The replenished brooks had a livelier warble, and the notes of innumerable birds rang more cheerfully through the clear atmosphere. The prisoners of the cavern, however, could only distinguish the beauty of the morning by slight tokens,—now and then a sweep of the winds over the forest tops—sometimes the note of the woodthrush, or of the cardinal bird as he flew by the face of the rocks; and occasionally a breath of the perfumed atmosphere flowing through the aperture. These intimations of liberty and enjoyment from the world without only heightened their impatience at the imprisonment to which they were doomed.

"Listen!" said Emily; "I think I hear a human voice."

"There is certainly a distant call in the woods," said Le Maire, after a moment's silence. "Let us all shout together for assistance."

They shouted accordingly, Le Maire exerting his clear and powerful voice to the utmost, and the others aiding him as well as they were able, with their feebler and less practised organs. A shrill discordant cry replied, apparently from the cliffs close to the cave.

"A parrokeet," exclaimed Le Maire. "The noisy pest! I wish the painted rascal were within reach of my rifle. You see, Father Ambrose, we are forgotten by mankind; and the very birds of the wilderness mock our cries for assistance."

"You have a quick fancy, my son," answered the priest; "but it is yet quite too soon to give over. It is now the very hour when we may expect our neighbours to be looking for us in these parts."

They continued therefore to remain by the opening; and from time to time to raise that shout for assistance. Hour after hour passed, and no answer was returned to their cries, which indeed could have been but feebly heard, if heard at all, at the foot of the precipice; hour after hour passed, and no foot climbed the rocky stair that led to their prison. The pangs of hunger in the mean time began to assail them, and, more intolerable than these, a feverish and tormenting thirst.

"You have practised fasting," said Le Maire to Father Ambrose; "and so have I when I could get nothing to eat. In my hunting excursions I have sometimes gone without tasting food from morning till the night of the next day. I found relief from an expedient which I learned of the old hunters, but which I presume you churchmen are not acquainted with. Here it is."

Saying this, he passed the sash he wore once more round his body, drawing it tightly, and securing it by a firm knot. Father Ambrose declined adopting, for the present, a similar expedient, alleging that as yet he had suffered little inconvenience from want of food, except a considerable degree of thirst; but Emily, already weak from fasting, allowed her slender waist to be wrapped tightly in the folds of a silk shawl which she had brought with her. The importunities of hunger were thus rendered less painful, and a new tension was given to the enervated frame; but the burning thirst was not at all allayed. The cave was then explored for water; every corner was examined, and holes were dug in the soil which in some places covered the rocky floor, but in vain. Le Maire again ventured into the long narrow passage which he had followed to its termination the day previous, in the hope of now discovering some concealed spring, or some place where the much desired element fell in drops from the roof, but he returned fatigued and unsuccessful. As he came forth into the larger apartment a light fluttering sound, as of the waving of a thin garment, attracted the attention of the party. On listening attentively it appeared to be within the cavern; but what most excited their surprise was, that it passed suddenly and mysteriously from place to place, while the agent continued invisible, in spite of all their endeavours to discover it. Sometimes it was heard on the one side, sometimes on the other, now from the roof, and now from the floor, near, and at a distance. At length it passed directly over their heads.

"It is precisely the sound of a light robe agitated by the wind, or by a swift motion of the person wearing it," said Emily.

"It is no sound of this earth, I will depose in a court of justice," said Le Maire, who was naturally of a superstitious turn; "or we should see the thing that makes it."

"All we can say at present," answered the priest, "is, that we cannot discover the cause; but it does not therefore follow that it is any thing supernatural. What is perceived by one of our senses only does not necessarily belong to the other world. I have no doubt however, that we shall discover the cause before we leave the cavern."

"Nor I either," rejoined Le Maire, with a look and tone which showed the awe that had mastered him; "I am satisfied of the cause already. It is a warning of approaching death. We must perish in this cavern."

Emily, much as she was accustomed to rely on the opinions of the priest, felt in spite of herself the infection of that feeling of superstitious terror which had seized upon her uncle, and her heart had begun to beat thick, when a weak chirp was heard.

"The mystery is resolved," exclaimed Father Ambrose, "and your ghost, my good friend, is only a harmless fellow-prisoner, a poor bird, which the storm doubtless drove into the cave, and which has been confined here ever since." As he spoke, Emily, who had looked to the quarter whence the sound proceeded, pointed out the bird sitting on a projection of rock at no great distance.

"A godsend!" cried Le Maire; "the bird is ours, though his little carcass will hardly furnish a mouthful for each of us." Saying this, he took up his rifle, which stood leaning against the wall of the cavern, and raised the piece to his eye. Another instant and the bird would have fallen, but Emily laid her hand on his arm.

"Cannot we take him alive," asked she; "and make him the agent of our deliverance?"

"How will you do that?" said Le Maire, without lowering his rifle.

"Send him out at the opening yonder with a letter tied to his wing to inform our friends of our situation. It will at least increase the chances of our escape."

"It is well thought of," answered Le Maire; "and now, Emily, you shall see how an experienced hunter takes a bird without harming a single feather of his wings."

Saying this, he went to the mouth of the cave, and began to turn up, with a splinter of wood, the fresh earth. After considerable examination he drew forth a beetle, and producing from his hunting-bag a quantity of packthread, he tied the insect to one end of it, and having placed it on the point of a crag, retired to a little distance with the other end of the packthread in his hand. By frequently changing his place, he caused the bird to approach the spot where he had laid the insect. It was a tedious process; but when at length the bird perceived his prey, he flew to it and snapped it up in an instant, with the eagerness of famine. By a similar piece of management he contrived to get the thread wound several times about one of the legs of the little creature; and when this was effected, he suddenly drew it in, bringing him fluttering and struggling to his hand. It proved to be of the species commonly called the cedar bird.

"Ah, Father Ambrose," cried Le Maire, whose vivacity returned with whatever revived his hopes, " we have caught you a brother ecclesiastic, a recollet, as we call him from the gray hood he wears. No wonder we did not see him before, for his plumage is exactly of the colour of the rocks. But he is the very bird for a letter; look at the sealing-wax he carries on his wings." As he spoke he displayed the glossy brown pinions, the larger feathers of which were ornamented at their tops with little appendages of a vermilion colour, like drops of delicate red sealing-wax.

"And now let us think," continued he, "of writing the letter which this dapper little monk is to carry for us." A piece of charcoal was brought from the skeleton's chamber, and Le Maire having produced some paper from his hunting-bag, the priest wrote upon it a few lines, giving a brief account of their situation. The letter, being folded, and properly addressed, was next perforated with holes, through which a string was inserted, and tied under the wing of the bird. Emily then carried him to the opening, through which he darted forth in apparent joy at regaining his liberty. "Would that we could pass out," said she, with a sigh, "as easily as the little creature which we have just set free. But the *recollet* is a lover of gardens, and he will soon be found seeking his food in those of the village."

The hopes to which this little expedient gave birth in the bosoms of all contributed somewhat to cheer the gloom of their confinement. But night came at length, to close that long and weary day; a night till more long and weary. The light which came in at the aperture began to wane, and Emily watched it as it faded, with a sickness of the heart which grew almost to agony, when finally it ceased to shine altogether. She had continued during the day to cherish the dream of deliverance by the sagacity and exertions of her lover; and had scarcely allowed herself to contemplate the possibility of remaining in the cavern another night. It was therefore in unspeakable bitterness of spirit that she accompanied the priest and Le Maire to the skeleton's chamber, where they collected the brands which remained of the fire of the preceding flight, and kindled them into a dull and meager flame. That evening was a silent one—the day had been passed in various speculations on the probability of their release, in searching the cave for water, and in shouting at the entrance for assistance. But the hour of darkness,— the hour which carried their neighbours of the village to their quiet and easy beds, in their homes, overflowing with abundance, filled with the sweet air of heaven, and watched by its kindly constellations—that hour brought to the unhappy prisoners of the rock a peculiar sense of desolation and fear, for it was a token that they were, for the time at least, forgotten; that those whom they knew and loved slumbered, and thought not of them. They laid themselves down on their beds of leaves, but the horrible thirst, which consumed them like an inward fire, grew fiercer with the endeavour to court repose; and the blood that crept slowly through their veins seemed to have become a current of liquid flame. Sleep came not to their eyes, or came attended with dreams of running waters, which they were not permitted to taste; of tempests and earthquakes, and breathless confinement among the clods of earth and various shapes of strange peril, while their friends seemed to stand aloof, and to look coldly and unconcernedly on, without showing even a desire to render them assistance.

CHAPTER VI.

My brother's soul was of the mould
Which in a palace had grown cold,
Had his free breathing been denied
The range of the steep mountain side.
~ *Prisoners of Chillon.*

Shall Nature, swerving from her earliest dictate,
Self-preservation, fall by her own act?
Forbid it Heaven! let not, upon disgust,
The shameless hand be foully crimsoned o'er,
With blood of its own lord.
~ Blair's "Grave"

On the third day the cavern presented a more gloomy spectacle than it had done at any time since the fall of the rock took place. It was now about eleven o'clock in the morning, and the shrill singing of the wind about the cliffs, and through the crevice, which now admitted a dimmer light than on the day previous, announced the approach of a storm from the south. The hope of relief from without was growing fainter and fainter as the time passed on; and the sufferings of the prisoners became more poignant. The approach of the storm, too, could only be regarded as an additional misfortune, since it would probably prevent or obstruct for that day the search which was making for them. They were all three in the outer and larger apartment of the cave. Emily was at a considerable distance from the entrance reclining on a kind of seat formed of large loose stones, and overspread with a covering of withered leaves. There was enough of light to show that she was exceedingly pale; that her eyes were closed, and that the breath came thick and pantingly through her parted lips, which alone of all her features retained the colour of life. Faint with watching, with want of sustenance, and with anxiety, she had lain herself down on this rude couch, which the care of her companions had provided for her, and had sunk into a temporary slumber. The priest stood close to the mouth of the cave leaning against the wall, with his arms folded, himself scarcely changed in appearance, except that his cheek seemed somewhat more emaciated, and his eyes were lighted up with a kind of solemn and preternatural brightness. Le Maire, with a spot of fiery red on each cheek,— his hair staring wildly in every direction, and his eyes bloodshot, was pacing the cavern floor to and fro, carrying his rifle, occasionally stopping to examine the priming, or to peck the flint; and sometimes standing still for a moment, as if lost in thought. At length he approached the priest, and said to him, in a hollow voice,

"Have you never heard of seamen on a wreck, destitute of provisions, casting lots to see which of their number should die, that the rest might live?"

"I have so."

"Were they right in so doing?"

"I cannot say that they were not. It is a horrid alternative in which they were placed. It might be lawful—it might be expedient, that one should perish for the salvation of the rest."

"Have you never seen an insect or an animal writhing with torture, and have you not shortened its sufferings by putting an end to its life?"

"I have—but what mean these questions?"

"I will tell you. Here is my rifle." As he spoke, Le Maire placed the piece in the hands of Father Ambrose, who took it mechanically. "I ask you to do for me what you would do for the meanest worm. You understand me?"

"Are you mad?" demanded the priest, regarding him with a look in which the expression of unaffected astonishment was mingled with that of solemn reproof.

"Mad! indeed I am mad, if you will have it so— you will feel less scruple at putting an end to the existence of a madman. I cannot linger in this horrid place, neglected and forgotten by those who should have come to deliver me, suffering the slow approaches of death—the pain—the fire in the veins—and, worst of all, this fire in the brain," said Le Maire, striking his forehead. "They think,—if they think of me at all,— that I am dying by slow tortures; I will disappoint them. Listen, father," continued he; "would it not be better for you and Emily that I were dead?—is there no way I—look at my veins, they are full yet, and the muscles have not shrunk away from my limbs; would you not both live the longer, if I were to die?"

The priest recoiled at the horrid idea presented to his mind. "We are not cannibals," said he, "thanks be to Divine Providence." An instant's reflection, however, convinced Father Ambrose that the style of rebuke which he had adopted was not proper for the occasion. The unwonted fierceness and wildness of Le Maire's manner, and the strange proposal he had made, denoted that alienation of mind which is no uncommon effect of long abstinence from food. He thought it better, therefore, to attempt by mild and soothing language to divert him from his horrid design.

"My good friend," said he, "you forget what grounds of hope yet remain to us; indeed, the probability of our escape is scarcely less to-day than it was yesterday. The letter sent out of the cave may be found, and if so, it will most certainly effect our deliverance; or the fall of the rock may be discovered by some one passing this way, and he may understand that it is possible we are confined here. While our existence is prolonged there is no occasion for despair. You should endeavour, my son, to compose yourself, and to rely on the goodness of that Power who has never forsaken you."

"Compose myself!" answered Le Maire, who had listened impatiently to this exhortation; "compose myself! Do you not know that there are those here who will not suffer me to be tranquil for a moment? Last night I was twice awakened, just as I had fallen asleep, by a voice pronouncing my name, as audibly as I heard your own just now; and the second time, I looked to where the skeleton lies, and the foul thing had half-raised itself from the rock, and was beckoning me to come and place myself by its side. Can you wonder if I slept no more after that?"

"My son, these are but the dreams of a fever."

"And then, whenever I go by myself, I hear low voices and titterings of laughter from the recesses of the rocks. They mock me, that I, a free hunter, a denizen of the woods and prairies, a man whose liberty was never restrained for a moment, should be entrapped in this manner, and made to die like a buffalo in a pit, or like a criminal in the dungeons of the old world,—that I should consume with thirst in a land bright with innumerable rivers and springs,—that I should wither away with famine, while the woods are full of game and the prairies covered with buffaloes. I could face famine if I had my liberty. I could meet death without shrinking in the sight of the sun and the earth, and in the fresh open air. I should strive to reach

277

some habitation of my fellow-creatures; I should be sustained by hope; I should travel on till I sank down with weakness and fatigue, and died on the spot. But famine made more frightful by imprisonment and inactivity, and these dreams, as you call them, that dog me asleep and awake, they are more than I can bear.— Hark!" he exclaimed, after a short pause, and throwing quick and wild glances around him; "do you hear them yonder—do you hear how they mock me!—you will not, then, do what I ask?—give me the rifle."

"No," said the priest, who instantly comprehended his purpose: "I must keep the piece till you are more composed."'

Le Maire seemed not to hear the answer, but laying his grasp on the rifle, was about to pluck it from the old man's hands. Father Ambrose saw that the attempt to retain possession of it against his superior strength, would be vain; he therefore slipped down his right hand to the lock, and cocking it, touched the trigger, and discharged it in an instant. The report awoke Emily, who came trembling and breathless to the spot.

"What is the matter?" she asked.

"There is no harm done, my child," answered the priest, assuming an aspect of the most perfect composure. "I discharged the rifle, but it was not aimed at any thing, and I beg pardon for interrupting your repose at a time when you so much need it. Suffer me to conduct you back to the place you have left. Le Maire, will you assist!"

Supported by Le Maire on one side, and by the priest on the other, Emily, scarcely able to walk from weakness, was led back to her place of repose. Returning with Le Maire, Father Ambrose entreated him to consider how much his niece stood in need of his assistance and protection. He bade him recollect that his mad haste to quit the world before called by his Maker would leave her, should she ever be released from the cavern, alone and defenceless, or at least with only an old man for her friend, who was himself hourly expecting the summons of death. He exhorted him to reflect how much, even now, in her present condition of weakness and peril, she stood in need of his aid, and conjured him not to be guilty of a pusillanimous and cowardly desertion of one so lovely, so innocent, and so dependent upon him.

Le Maire felt the force of this appeal. A look of human pity passed across the wild expression of his countenance. He put the rifle into the hands of Father Ambrose. "You are right," said he; "I am a fool, and I have been, I suspect, very near becoming a madman. You will keep this until you are entirely willing to trust me with it. I will endeavour to combat these fancies a little longer."

CHAPTER VII.

A burst of rain
Swept from the black horizon, broad descends
In one continuous flood. Still overhead
The mingling tempest weaves its gloom, and still
The deluge deepens.—*Thomson.*

In the mean time the light from the aperture grew dimmer and dimmer, and the eyes of the prisoners, though accustomed to the twilight of the cavern, became at length unable to distinguish objects at a few paces from the entrance. The priest and Le Maire had placed themselves by the couch of Emily, but rather, as it seemed, from that instinct of our race which leads us to seek each other's presence, than for any purpose of conversation, for each of the party preserved a gloomy silence. The topics of speculation on their condition had been discussed to weariness, and no others had now any interest for their minds. It was no unwelcome interruption to that melancholy silence, when they heard the sound of a mighty rain pouring down upon the leafy summits of the woods, and beating against the naked walls and shelves of the precipice. The roar grew more and more distinct, and at length it seemed that they could distinguish a sou

278

of shuddering of the earth above them, as if a mighty host was marching heavily over it. The sense of suffering was for a moment suspended in a feeling of awe and curiosity.

"That, likewise, is the rain," said Father Ambrose, after listening for a moment. "The clouds must pour down a perfect cataract, when the weight of its fall is thus felt in the heart of the rock."

"Do you hear that noise of running water?" asked Emily, whose quick ear had distinguished the rush of the stream formed by the collected rains over the rocks without at the mouth of the cave.

"Would that its channel were through this cavern," exclaimed Le Maire, starting up. "Ah! here we have it—we have it!—listen to the dropping of water from the roof near the entrance. And here at the aperture!" He sprang thither in an instant. A little stream detached from the main current, which descended over rocks that closed the mouth of the cave, fell in a thread of silver amid the faint light that streamed through the opening; he knelt for a moment, received it between his burning lips, and then hastily returning, bore Emily to the spot. She held out her hollowed palm, white, thin, and semi-transparent, like a pearly shell, used for dipping up the waters from one of those sweet fountains that rise by the very edge of the sea— and as fast as it filled with the cool, bright element, imbibed it with an eagerness and delight inexpressible. The priest followed her example; Le Maire also drank from the little stream as it fell, bathed in it his feverish brow, and suffered it to fall upon his sinewy neck.

"It has given me a new hold on life," said Le Maire, his chest distending with several full and long breathings. "It has not only quenched that hellish thirst, but it has made my head less light, and my heart lighter. I will never speak ill of this element again—the choicest grapes of France never distilled any thing so delicious, so grateful, so life-giving. Take notice, Father Ambrose, I retract all I have ever said against water and water-drinkers. I am a sincere penitent, and shall demand absolution."

Father Ambrose had begun gently to reprove Le Maire for his unseasonable levity, when Emily cried out—"The rock moves!—the rock moves! Come back—come further into the cavern!" Looking up to the vast mass that closed the entrance, he saw plainly that it was in motion, and he had just time to draw Le Maire from the spot where he had stooped down to take another draught of the stream, when a large block, which had been wedged in overhead, gave way, and fell in the very place where he left the prints of his feet. Had he remained there another instant, it must have crushed him to atoms. The prisoners, retreating within the cavern far enough to avoid the danger, but not too far for observation, stood watching the event with mingled apprehension and hope. The floor of the cave just at the edge, on which rested the fallen rock, yawned at the fissures, where the earth with which they were filled had become saturated and swelled with water, and unable any longer to support the immense weight, settled away, at first slowly, under it, and finally, along with its incumbent load, fell suddenly and with a tremendous crash, to the base of the precipice, letting the light of day and the air of heaven into the cavern. The thunder of that disruption was succeeded by the fall of a few large fragments of rock on the right and left, after which the priest and his companions heard only the fall of the rain and the heavy sighing of the wind in the forest.

Father Ambrose and Emily knelt involuntarily in thanksgiving at their unexpected deliverance. Le Maire, although unused to the devotional mood, observing their attitude, had bent his knee to imitate it, when a glance at the outer world now laid open to his sight, made him start again to his feet with an exclamation of delight. The other two arose, also, and turned to the broad opening which now looked out from the cave over the forest. On one side of this opening rushed the torrent whose friendly waters had undermined the rock at the entrance, and now dashed themselves against its shivered fragments below. It is not for me to attempt to describe how beautiful appeared to their eyes that world which they feared never again to see, or how grateful to their senses was that fresh and fragrant air of the forests which they thought never to breathe again. The light, although the sky was thick with clouds and rain, was almost too intense for their vision, and they shaded their brows with their hands as they looked forth upon that scene of woods and meadows and waters, fairer to their view than it had ever appeared in the most glorious sunshine.

"That world is ours again," said Le Maire, with a tone of exultation. "We are released at last, and now, let us see in what manner we can descend."

279

As he spoke, he approached the verge of the rock from which the severed mass had lately fallen, and saw to his dismay that the terrace which had served as a path to the cavern, was carried away for a considerable distance to the right and left of where they stood, leaving the face of the precipice smooth and sheer from top to bottom. No footing appeared, no projection by which the boldest and the most agile could scale or descend it. Le Maire threw himself sullenly on the ground.

"We must pass another night in this dungeon," said he, "and perhaps starve to death after all. It is clear enough that we shall have to remain here until somebody comes to take us down, and the devil himself would not be caught abroad in the woods in the midst of such a storm as this."

The priest and Emily came up at this moment:—

"This is a sad disappointment," said the former, "but we have this advantage, that we can now make ourselves both seen and heard. Let us try the effect of our voices. It is not impossible that there may be some person within hearing."

Accordingly they shouted together, and though nothing answered but the echo of the forest, yet there was even in that reply of the inanimate creation something cheering and hope-inspiring, to those who for nearly three days had perceived that all their cries for succour were smothered in the depths of the earth. Again they raised their voices, and listened for an answering shout,—a third time, and they were answered. The halloo of a full-toned, manly voice arose from the woods below.

"Thank heaven, we are heard at last," said Emily.

"Let us see if the cry was in answer to ours," said the priest, and again they called, and again a shout was returned from the woods. "We are heard—that is certain," continued he, "and the voice is nearer than at first,—we shall be released."

At length the sound of quick footsteps on the crackling boughs was heard in the forest, and a young man of graceful proportions, dressed, like Le Maire, in a hunting-cap and frock, emerged into the open space at the foot of the precipice. As he saw the party standing in the cavity of the rock, he clapped his hands with an exclamation of surprise and delight. "Thank heaven, they are discovered at last! Are you all safe—all well?"

"All safe," answered Le Maire, "but hungry as wolves, and in a confounded hurry to get out of this horrid den."

The young man regarded the precipice attentively for a moment, and then called out, "Have patience a moment, and I will bring you the means of deliverance." He then disappeared in the forest.

Emily's waking dream was, in fact, not wholly unfulfilled. That young man was Henry Danville. she knew him by his air and figure as soon as he emerged from the forest, and before she heard his voice. He had been engaged, with many others belonging to the settlement, in the pursuit of their lost curate and his companions, from the morning after their absence, and fortunately happened to be at no great distance when the disruption of the rock took place. Struck with astonishment at the tremendous concussion, he was hastening to discover the cause, when he heard the shout to which he answered.

It was not long before voices and steps were again heard in the wood, and a crowd of the good villagers soon appeared advancing through the trees, one bearing a basket of provisions, some dragging ladders, some carrying ropes and other appliances for getting down their friends from their perilous elevation. Several of the ladders being spliced together, and secured by strong cords, were made to reach from the broken rocks below to the mouth of the cavern, and Henry ascended.

My readers will have no difficulty in imagining the conclusion. The emotions of the lovers meeting under such circumstances are of course not to be described, and the dialogue that took place on that occasion would not, I fear, bear to be repeated. The joy expressed by the villagers at recovering the worthy pastor brought tears into the good man's eyes; and words are inadequate to do justice to the delight of Le Maire at seeing his old companions and their basket of provisions. My readers may also, if they please, imagine another little incident, without which some of them might think the narrative imperfect, namely, a certain marriage ceremony, which actually took place before the next Christmas, and at which the venerable Father Ambrose officiated. Le Maire, when I last saw him, was living with one of Emily's children, a hale old man of eighty, with a few gray hairs scattered among his raven locks, full of stories of his youthful adventures, among which he reckoned that of his imprisonment in the cave a decidedly the best. He had, however, no disposition to become the hero of another tale of the kind, since he never ventured into another cave, or under another rock, as long as he lived; and was wont to accompany his narrative with a friendly admonition to his youthful and inexperienced hearers, against thoughtlessly indulging in so dangerous a practice.

The Library of Early American Literature

Currently Available Titles

* **BENJAMIN FRANKLIN**: Selected Writings

* **ROBERT ROGERS**: Collected Works

* **ETHAN ALLEN**: "Narrative" and *Reason, the Only Oracle*

* **MERCY OTIS WARREN**: Selected Works: Plays and Poetry

* **PHILLIS WHEATLEY**: Complete Poetical Works, *Plus* extant Poetry and Prose of Jupiter Hammon

* **DAVID HUMPHREYS**: Collected Works

* **TIMOTHY DWIGHT**: Selected Works

* **JOEL BARLOW**: Collected Works

* **PHILIP FRENEAU**: Collected Poems

* **HUGH HENRY BRACKENRIDGE**: *Modern Chivalry* abridged

* **ROYALL TYLER**: Selected Works

* **CHARLES BROCKDEN BROWN & WM. DUNLAP**: *Life of Charles Brockden Brown*

* **WASHINGTON IRVING & JAS. KIRKE PAULDING**: *Salmagundi*, First AND Second Series

* **SAMUEL WOODWORTH**: Complete Poetical Works

* **DAVID PORTER**: *Journal of a Cruise Made to the Pacific Ocean* (1822 ed.)

* **WILLIAM CULLEN BRYANT**: Complete Poetical Works

* **JAMES FENIMORE COOPER**: *History of the Navy of the United States* (1847 ed.)

* **JAMES KIRKE PAULDING**: Five Historical Novels

* **WILLIAM GILMORE SIMMS**: "Atalantis: A Story of the Sea;" *Southern Passages and Pictures*

* **COTTON MATHER**: *Magnalia Christi Americana* (1702), in two volumes

* **FEDERALIST LITERATI**: Alsop, Dennie, J. B. Linn, Dunlap, and E. H. Smith.

.

Made in the USA
Las Vegas, NV
06 December 2024

13491002R10164